M.B. Dallocchio

The Desert Warrior

Latte Books | Las Vegas

Latte Books
848 N. Rainbow Blvd, #2268
Las Vegas, NV 89107

The Desert Warrior is a work of nonfiction. Nonetheless, some of the names and personal characteristics of the individuals involved have been changed in order to disguise their identities. Any resulting association or resemblance to persons living or dead is entirely coincidental and unintentional.

For information regarding discounts or bulk purchases, please contact sales: (702) 879-5025 or business@lattebooks.com

Manufactured in the United States of America

1 2 3 4 5 6 7 8 9 10

Library of Congress Catalog Card Number: 2017954119

ISBN-13: 978-0-692-94579-7
ISBN-10: 0-692-94579-2

On "The Desert Warrior"

"Dallocchio spoke eloquently of her combat experiences in Iraq at an event I sponsored in San Francisco in 2013. Now she has written a gripping personal account of her challenges not only as a service member and veteran but also as an individual seeking truth in a bigoted world of deceit and abuse.

First, this warrior is a woman, multiracial, who as a member of Team Lioness, searched for bombs and weapons in housing areas during the early days of the Iraq War. I repeat, she was a woman in a combat zone, subjected to harassment and ridicule. When she refused to go along with military corruption endemic in the U.S. military in a foreign land, she suffered hostilities from her superiors.

The unfairness in her life, including childhood abuse, leads to thoughts of suicide, but she finds the strength to survive. She captivates the reader by relating dreams of empowerment presented to her by the Desert Warrior, a mystical figure from her Chamorro background. Finally, she completes this complex journey of finding "home" in a way that is an uplifting lesson for women of today facing inequalities pervasive in our society.

She fortunately rejected a publisher's suggestion that she turn her book into a fictional account—the courage it took to write her story shouldn't be manipulated. She is the real deal."

- Congressional Rep. Jackie Speier, D-CA

On "The Desert Warrior"

"The Desert Warrior" could belong to the genre of Hunter S. Thompson's "Fear and Loathing in Las Vegas," Jack Kerouac's "On the Road," and Ken Kesey's "One Flew Over the Cuckoo's Nest."

Any reader familiar with "The Odyssey," or the opus "Odysseus in America," will recall that the seer who told Odysseus how to get home was Tiresias, the blind, transgendered prophet. Tiresias told Odysseus he had to get the "west wind" to blow him home. In "The Desert Warrior," a vision appears calling the author west into the desert of the US Southwest. None of this is coincidence.

It's definitely a psychedelic "road" book. Dallocchio's visions in the book speak to a Native Chamorro (Pacific Islander) tradition of dream interpretation and have mythic resonance. The author combines two great literary traditions, one ancient, the other post-modern, to create an authentically unique 21st century archetypal narrative of a soldier's homecoming.

What Dallocchio appears to be saying about her return home, to a redefinition of home, is that she's making an odyssey from the profane space of war and her experience of combat to a sacred space called "home." "The Desert Warrior" journey works on three levels: one - the physical movement around the world and across the country; two - the inner journey; and three - the mythic journey which is universal.

"The Desert Warrior" is an important statement about the "new" or 21st century veteran and the experience of homecoming to a changing America.

- Lieutenant Colonel Michael Zacchea, USMC (Ret), author of "The Ragged Edge"

On "The Desert Warrior"

No one comes home unscathed and one's old self is no longer hanging in the closet. Dallocchio captures the atrocities that comprise the combat theater of operations and the revolting experience of reintegration at the hands of a deaf and blind society so acutely attuned to looking the other way….humans despicable inhumanity to one another. Her gift for chronicling the egregious nature of toxic leadership run amok and the pilfering of souls has been woven into a masterpiece of truth-telling.

I know. I walked through this valley of death with her. She has not missed a single beat of the shattering realities and monstrous acts of those sufficiently contemptible to be doing hard time at Leavenworth. Blessed are those charged with pulling the feathers from the ostriches that define the 99.5 percent of the American populace who have never and will never wear the uniform.

- Colonel Kathy Platoni, US Army (Ret), Psy.D., DAIPM, FAIS

The Desert Warrior is a narrative deployment - one woman's journey through terrorism and bigotry in Iraq and at home. Safe behind the armor of Dallocchio's brilliant, fierce, and often funny voice, the reader views war through a female lens. With the balls and brilliance of the best of gonzo journalism, this combat warrior writer guides us through the frightening, friendly fire of being at war at home and abroad.

- Patricia Lee Stotter, Two-time Emmy Award-winning composer, filmmaker, and writer

CONTENTS | PART I

CONTENTS | PART II

PART I

1 QUIXOTE IN RAMADI

To stay alive, you have to keep moving. Running, relocating, driving, doing everything in your power to stay in motion and make it to safety. This is war, traveling to places you've never been, being the odd person out, sensing danger, constantly anticipating the best and worst.

Equipped with just pure luck in the midst of combat, you dodge enemy fire, ambushes, and all related attempts to stop your pulse. Your drill sergeant's voice screaming through your head, "Stay alert, stay alive! Keep running!"

"Home." This was my mantra, my four-letter savior. At age 23, I was on the streets of Ramadi, Iraq. It was 2004 and those words blasting through my head as loud as the explosions all around me. The screaming in my psyche and from those suffering around me kept me moving. The scent of papyrus, ancient dust, burning trash, carbon residue, charred insurgents' flesh, and hints of eucalyptus engulfed my senses as the whirring bullets and mortar rounds thrust me from checkpoint to checkpoint. Running through the arid desert metropolis with 80 pounds of gear and equipment, sweat poured down as I ran the fastest I've ever run in my life.

GO! GO! GO!

A moving target is harder to kill, and I didn't stop running, maneuvering, until I reached home base, where I could breathe between death-defying sprints. I just need to make it home alive, and this will all be over, I told myself. Home. I kept running, past housing compounds and multi-level apartment buildings and businesses, people standing on rooftops with cell phones staring at me as they spoke quietly and swiftly, alerting others of U.S. military personnel running down the street, an explosion goes off.

The feeling of madness that roars and twists through the soul, a psychological tornado, destroying everything in its path and when death passes you by, the sweet honey of surviving against all odds transmutes the adrenaline rush into addiction. Anything you ever felt before never feels quite like the ecstasy of facing death itself and surviving. And nothing is as horrible as living with the guilt of seeing those who couldn't escape – and there's nothing you can do about it. I live another day smiling at death with no time or space to mourn my friends or the complete unraveling of an ancient civilization.

A woman in combat? Yes. Since when? Since Native American warrior Buffalo Calf Road Woman knocked that prick General George Custer off of his horse. Since Pantea Arteshbod propelled herself to become one of the greatest Persian commanders during the reign of Cyrus the Great. Since Hua Mulan disguised herself as a male to engage in combat and became one of China's most respected heroines.

For a woman, from the time we're born, life is a fight. But in the short history of the U.S. and among its weird puritanical hypocrisies, the concept of a woman in combat seems incomprehensible. Yes, women like me were sent into firefights in Ramadi before it became a foaming-at-the-mouth political talking point for pundits. And, no, I wasn't baking cookies to comfort the brave men. I was a sergeant on Team Lioness, an all-female combat team attached to Marine infantry units performing checkpoint operations, personnel searches for weapons and explosives, and house raids. I was out getting shot at and running in the middle of Ramadi nearly a decade before the DOD policy ban on women in combat was lifted in 2013.

Working 50-60 hours a week back home, both in Army and civilian positions while attending college full-time, Iraq was a welcome break from an over-worked life. Six months after Bush's invasion of Iraq in 2003, shortly after my 22nd birthday, I got my orders to deploy. I wrote my will, leaving everything to my parents. Updated my records and shots, and was ready to meet my new unit in Indiana. Out of close to 500 people in my field hospital unit in Florida – we specialized in medical support in South and Central America – I was one of thirteen set to deploy, and of that thirteen, I was the only one sent to Iraq. The rest were

ER medics sent to Afghanistan.

I flew to Indianapolis to meet the people I'd travel, work, and live (or die) with in Iraq. Everything was moving so fast, I didn't have the time to process this life-changing morsel that was uprooting my life and propelling me into the most dangerous place in the world in the middle of a violent urban war.

"Who's the raghead?" said a staff sergeant as I entered the building of my new unit.

"Excuse me?" I said, glaring at the self-righteous white male as he regarded me with disdain, a hatred deeply embedded into the psyche of Indiana, a safe space for the Ku Klux Klan. He huffed and turned the other way, shaking his head. "That's what I thought, dick-face."

At Fort Benning, Georgia prior to our 26-hour flight to the Middle East, the microaggression circus continued.

Any time I spoke up, the command leadership pushed back at me: "You Chinese/Mexican/Indian bitch. Shut the hell up and stay in your lane." I didn't expect this group of right-wing, evangelical Christian, xenophobic bigots to understand I was an animist biracial Chamorro-Irish woman, and I sure as hell didn't dare to disclose sexuality in the age of Don't Ask Don't Tell (DADT) policy. But I hadn't anticipated how psychotic they'd be. This was a mental health unit that would make Nurse Ratched a better alternative. In this predominantly female command peppered with a few enabling male chauvinists pulling the strings, my non-submissiveness as a woman of color was convenient for target practice. If you didn't submit as a Legionnaire of the Patriarchy, you were SOL – shit outta luck.

Amid weapons and urban warfare training exercises out in the woods in the Deep South, I told myself I was going to suck it up for a year and get the hell away from this mobile asylum of sociopaths. As my parents and my fiancé, Yves, were falling apart over the phone, understandably emotional over my departure toward Iraq, I took every ounce of worry over my new unit's aggression toward minorities, and my concern over possibly coming home in a casket, and tucked it away into a ruck sack in my psyche.

The invisible pack I carried on my shoulders and back had always existed, it was just in Army colors. In my family, I had to be strong, independent, and adaptive while swallowing my torment and sadness. There was rarely a moment where I could simply unpack my bag and rest, and I accepted this as the hand I had been dealt in life. I could watch others cry, fall apart, and break down, but I was never exactly afforded such a luxury. So, I put my energy into helping others the best ways I knew how, sharing my insider secrets for keeping it together when your world comes crashing down. More importantly, I couldn't afford to fall apart because I had soldiers to take care of and a mission in Ramadi, Iraq ahead of me. I packed my concerns, my fears over what I saw ahead of us in Iraq, my love of life and everyone who mattered to me, in travel journals in my cargo pocket in and into my psychological pack that had yet to take on the weight of Iraq.

Aside from this laughable mental health detachment I was assigned to gnawing at my back, one of the three people coming with me to Ramadi, the most dangerous city in Iraq in 2004, was Captain Jack. If dealing with blaring unit corruption wasn't enough to make me fear for my career and well-being, Captain Jack spiced things up through his own brand of hyper-aggressive bigotry toward me in every intersectional way. He had a penchant for belittling every minority group between black and white on the skin color spectrum. Latino, Asian, Middle Eastern, Native American, Pacific Islander – you are all shit to this Captain and he let me know it daily.

"Fucking feminist!" He would whine after I would confront him over his persistent insults. He wouldn't say it directly to my face just then. He would say it to other officers who appeared embarrassed but backed away as though to say, "I don't want to be involved."

As we flew over Europe into the Middle East, the first lights we saw were the sunrise and the oil fields on fire below. Upon arrival in Kuwait, we departed for the ammunition depot to pick up our assigned amount of bullets, 210 rounds for each soldier. While our commander, a subservient WASP female, and the Chaplain, who routinely made us pray bizarre Evangelical requests for Jesus in front of our formation, huddled in fear inside of our bus with other members of our leadership as I was sent out to retrieve our assigned ammunition to carry with us into Iraq. We weren't even in a war zone yet and these big talkers were already shitting their pants.

Most of the unit was heading toward larger, safer bases such as Balad Air Base and the Green Zone in Baghdad, so I didn't mind being the labeled cannon fodder heading to Ramadi, the hotbed of the insurgency and capital of US military deaths, in an accepted exile far from the Indiana Klan. Getting shot at by insurgents sounded safer than staying near these people.

"We're now entering Indian Country!" said the First Sergeant, beaming with pride in the desert sands of Kuwait. "Operation Iraqi Freedom" in his eyes was merely a euphemism to slaughter "savages" – AKA brown people.

"Question, First Sergeant," I asked with a mischievous grin, "if we're heading into Indian Country and fighting savages, which side am I fighting on again?"

First Sergeant huffed and grimaced as he turned away from me as I could barely make out his, "sensitive minority" comment that he didn't have the stones to say toe-to-toe, I with my M16A2 rifle and he with his tiny pistol.

Chuckling to myself as they cowered in fear, I was thinking how the Indiana bigots talked down to anyone different from them in race, religious beliefs – or lack thereof – sexual preference, you name it. These self-proclaimed patriots were the most petrified. I laughed as they scurried toward the Emerald City of the Green Zone in Baghdad as us untouchables slept in Bedouin tents out in the middle of nowhere in Kuwait and received additional training from Special Forces for another week before we landed in our respective fragile, war-torn Iraqi cities in 2004.

Being far away from home was nothing new. As a military brat who moved every 2-3 years of my life since birth in New York City and enlisting in Oakland, California, working nonstop for a meager salary was actually a nice change from being an anchor in my own family back home that was rife with skeletons in the closet. Team Lioness, being the mental health supervisor for Ramadi, performing medic duties, and taking care of other people came naturally.

Team Lioness was comprised of 16-hour shifts and created by Army and USMC officers to handle Iraqi women and children in the city. It was baptism by fire, and I felt like there was a wall between me and what was happening. We were picked up in the moonlight at 4am, the shift started, and we returned close to midnight. Then, we woke up at 3:30 to do it again. Wherever the Marines needed you, whether for a house raid or to pat down Iraqi families at checkpoints, as a Lioness, you went – no questions asked.

Many of the Marines around us were hilarious and often shied away from discussing or contemplating politics or our motive for being there. These were not the fame-hungry types we so often see in popular film parroting conservative drivel. We were all aware of what was happening and worked in the cesspool daily. Iraqis were scared of us, mad at us, disappointed in us as the Saudis we were fighting were destroying their homeland – and we brought them there.

The waves of children crying, people who were frightened of me was not glamourous in the slightest – it was awful. I wasn't scared of searching people for bombs or other dangerous contraptions, I just didn't like feeling like the Empire. I didn't like being part of anyone's trauma. While I had no issue with raising my rifle to a jihadist, I certainly didn't sign up for terrorizing innocent people. How would I feel to have my own children witness the ongoing violence and carnage in Ramadi? To say it merely "bothered" me would be a great disservice to properly explaining the origins of my combat PTSD.

Before going into Iraq, my proud Chamorro mother, indigenous to the Mariana Islands in Oceania, pulled me aside and reminded me of our past. "You're going into someone else's country, have respect," she said.

No one else was saying this at the time. I understood as a Chamorro since our land has been occupied since the 1500s. We've never really had our own country since and now it's annexed by the United States. My mother and I were very aware that we're "occupied" and have little control of our fate as a people. I was going as the occupier this time, much like Spain, Germany, Japan, and now the US have occupied our land. I was well-aware of my newfound positionality here and what colonialism does to people for generations on end.

In effort to try and be respectful of the country we invaded – there's a contradiction – I attempted to learn basic Arabic. "Teach Yourself Arabic" was a book on Modern Standard Arabic (MSA), which was not Iraqi Arabic dialect. Iraqi Arabic is unique with a ton of colloquialisms you won't find in language instruction books. I traded language lessons with Iraqi interpreters for snacks or sketched their portraits in between missions in Iraq to at least try to communicate. My lifelong passion for art and languages came in handy in between firefights.

"Don't be afraid, Sweetheart. Do you want candy?" I felt like the Gestapo with sweets to temporarily numb the pain.

Ramadi was roughly the size of Oakland and was cut in half by the Euphrates River. You hear bullets, calls to prayer, and insurgents using the mosque for coordinates to strike. Mortars, rocket-propelled grenades, and firefights danced in unison to form a maddening orchestra that served as the soundtrack to my life and everyone else who had to endure in that forsaken city.

On base, you weren't safe – indirect fire was constant and the camp was just protected by shitty concertina wire and a tank at the front gate. Mortars came in and our artillery went blasting back. Missiles coming and going daily made daily living feel like an endless game of *Battleship.* You got used living or working in buildings shaking from explosions, you got used to dealing with your minor injuries or concussions because seeing a doctor could mean you would be leaving your comrades behind – and no one would dare abandon their brothers and sisters unless death or maiming was involved. All indirect fire can kill you, sever limbs, or take off your head – and you stayed and dealt with it until you physically couldn't.

In the city or on the camp, there was nowhere to rest. You were open, awake. On one side, you had the city of Ramadi and had to be wary of sniper fire from apartments or the water tower before us. On the other side was the wide-open desert. Somehow, I loved it.

Camp Ar Ramadi often felt like a bingo card for bombs, but lying in those quiet moments on the roof of our compound in Ramadi were surreal. Whether under soothing winds on a sun-scorched day or under an indigo night blanket of shooting stars over the desert, if you sat and listened to the quiet moments between the chaos, you could hear the universe speak. The universe said, "This, too, will pass, if you allow it." Those miniscule moments of desert sky clarity were my sanity.

Captain Jack continued to harass and threaten me like an abusive father, "If you want to die so bad, I'll shoot you myself!"

This was not someone who is trying to motivate or lead. He and another male hid in their rooms on the camp while we worked in Team Lioness. When we returned, they chastised us for being women, told us we didn't belong, that we weren't good enough, and that they hoped we died or was made an example through violent sexual assault.

If I wasn't catching heat from Saudi insurgents who wanted me dead, I was catching heat from racist WASP Americans from the Midwest wearing the same uniform, who also wanted me dead. This deployment started out with a laugh at all the John Wayne types running scared into the Green Zone, but now they were at the helm with money and power. Marines and soldiers alike learned what kind of people drifted in from the unit, and often offered to take Jack out to the desert and disappear him. While I had declined, I was conflicted. If anyone was going to whack Captain Jack, I call dibs.

Our Ramadi comrades didn't give us flack, yet were predominantly infantry and male. Mental health for Anbar was mostly the four of us, but considering the cowardly lions were too afraid to leave camp, it was Jones and I, two female soldiers who provided mental health crisis response throughout Anbar Province while Navy assets in Blue Diamond and Al Taqqadum resisted leaving their camps as well. As women, we didn't have many days off. The men around us sure did, but you wouldn't catch them telling that to spouses and family back home. I was dealing with direct combat, listening to other people suffering from PSTD or physical injuries. In mental health, self-care is emphasized but there wasn't a lot of time for it. A solar-charged iPod and a travel journal was where I lost myself in the later hours before bed. More memories packed, tucked away in that ruck sack.

In movies, war only looks romantic. "Tell my gal I love her…" close-up shot, and fade out. It doesn't work as beautifully and neat in real life. Flying chunks of human flesh and screaming orphans really put that Hollywood take into perspective and there is nothing clean or sterile about any of it. When people die, it's fucking horrible. People are at their most vulnerable and desperate points and seeing the helplessness in someone bleeding to death in your arms opens your eyes to the complete, pointless insanity of war. It starts to feel like you're watching an animal die, but you realize you're an animal too and that this is the antithesis of our existence.

Whether it's an Iraqi widow mourning her dead loved ones standing helplessly in the rubble of her former home or a dying soldier in an Iraqi city street asking, "Why, God? Why is this happening? Where are you?" I can't help but wonder the same. You realize that there is no justice, no karmic retribution swift enough, and that happy endings are a terrible, terrible lie. We are all subject to the same blind boot stomp and our luck is merely where we happen to be standing when death inevitably comes roaring down upon us.

I'm sorry that I have to say it like this, but you deserve to know war for what it really is and not the sanitized fantasy we often see in military memoirs, biopics, and infotainment news. Women and men were both used in combat, but women didn't get the training, awards, accolades, documentation, or credit. Team Lioness was a project done on the down-low not to make a political statement, but to maintain order and security. When women and children freaked out, men followed suit. Our job was to be the intermediary, to ensure no weapons, explosives, or surprises. Iraqi women bolted toward Team Lioness soldiers about hidden weapons or the misdeeds of their husbands. At least among Iraqis, and not Saudi insurgents, I was treated as far less of an enemy than my unit headquarters in Baghdad.

Team Lioness started in Ramadi because it was such a clusterfuck of a city. Insurgents came in through Syria and on through Hit, Haditha, and to train in Ramadi before moving onto Fallujah then Baghdad. Insurgents invaded the main roads, the arteries of a modern Mesopotamia, spreading throughout Iraq like body lice.

On a week-long journey to Baghdad for additional suicide prevention training I discovered how the majority of my crazed Indiana unit lived. The Green Zone in Baghdad was where journalists, State Department officials, and other Defense darlings lived along with our leadership that left the rest of us out in other cities. The Green Zone was a heavily fortified area with multiple checkpoints and was not as heavily attacked as areas in Anbar Province. The reason why Ramadi wasn't as widely covered, even if it was the heaviest casualty area, is because journalists just didn't show up and relied on CENTCOM for carefully crafted reports. They would present the story as though it came from the front lines when they were really reporting from a decadent dining facility rooftop that served steak and lobster. No, it was all in the Green Zone, acting as though they were in the thick of combat. They weren't. Americans and other viewers abroad didn't know any better, and that's how Department of Defense and corporate media preferred it. War is highly profitable and if you knew better, it would simply be bad for ratings.

"They're using the money meant for our radios, night vision, and actual mission-essential gear for TVs and XBox and shit! AND they're already mailing some of this shit home for themselves!" Jones whispered to me with a righteous anger during our Baghdad visit as we caught a glimpse of the charmed life most of our mental health unit counterparts were enjoying while we were stationed in the seventh circle of Middle Eastern hell in Anbar Province.

Money laundering with federal funds, which our power-hungry command conducted while placing soldiers of their choosing under a magnifying glass in the sun, is a felony. After taking photos of DOD-funded escapades witnessed in Baghdad while scribbling notes in my travel journal, I brought this to the attention of an officer in the unit who shrugged it off and told me to let it go. Easy for her to say, and easier for her to let other people risk death or injury while she was enjoying salsa lessons with State Department employees inside Saddam's palace. All those Army regulations that were rammed down our throats since I was 17 were now obsolete when my unit was handed spending money and unchecked power to abuse soldiers in their care – both mental health personnel and actual patients.

While the norm in the Green Zone was drunken parties, philandering, laundering money and abusing everyone in their midst, my norm in Ramadi was a polar opposite. Throughout my time in Iraq, I could be sitting next to someone chatting about music one minute and then watching them die or get severely injured the next. However, no matter how many children or adults I watched die as I tightened tourniquets or provided last minute CPR, my norm never felt acceptable.

When you hold someone as they die, your sense of invincibility diminishes with each gasp for air and a darkness sets in that could only be described as an inescapable despair. You realize that the bloodied corpse beneath you could be anyone you love, that it could be you.

When I was able to access the internet, I would read what I could about the war going on around me but found that Ramadi, and Anbar Province in general, was scarcely covered.

"I can't believe this shit. This is what mainstream media is feeding the masses back in the US?" I said incredulously.

"Better believe it, Sergeant. You won't find any journalist looking to keep their job pulling any maverick moves such as telling objective truths," said a Captain on his way out of the particle board-lined shack that was our makeshift internet hub.

"If people knew what was really going on here, they wouldn't be okay with it," I said.

"They won't find out, and you can be sure that they will remain blissfully ignorant while we take the heat for everyone else's chicken fried choices," the Captain muttered.

As the door shut behind the Captain and artillery fire blasted outside, I stared into the dimly lit space before me where all of us walked back out into war-torn reality. That dimly lit space was my purgatory, a realm in which I dreaded something I could not yet name. It wasn't the Mujahedeen outside, openly and unabashedly cruel patriarchs of Wahhabism, nor the cruel Evangelical patriarchs of my command. No, it was the desert of information that was back home that worried me most. If simple facts were being withheld, hung out to dry, and distorted here in the middle of "Operation Iraqi Freedom," I was concerned that the violent, desperate reality I lived in Anbar Province was the future of the world. A misguided planet hurtling toward a brick wall while everyone was arguing over who was riding shotgun.

"What kind of nerve do these people have? How do people in the Green Zone feel gaining weight in Iraq while our food supply trucks are being blown up!" I ranted as Jones listened throughout half of the year-long deployment until she was medically evacuated herself.

In my own desert of loneliness, I flew in a Blackhawk helicopter over Lake Habbaniyah, my favorite memory. Flying over the desert and Iraq look damned gorgeous from above. The golden sands and the turquoise blue lake below transported me to another place in time. It's so beautiful, I thought to myself. On the ground, it was a nightmare, but flying above it made me see a bigger picture of how my life has changed in this seemingly open, ethereal desert. On the ground, the smell of dead bodies, expended 50 caliber rounds contrasted the scent of lamb on a spit, warm Iraqi bread fresh from a charcoal oven, and tea in clear glass teacups.

As my comrade makes it back to the US, Army Divisions switches places, Captain Jack was sent to pizza and burger-laden Balad Air Base, and Lieutenant Colonel (LTC) Platoni arrived to take his spot.

"Commander says they only sent people to places like Ramadi and Baquba because they're prepared to tell your family that you're dead. Everyone in the Green Zone, Camp Victory, or Balad is safe for a reason. Their personal reason," a fellow sergeant confided in me from the Green Zone. He sounded defeated in explaining how LTC Platoni was being punished for speaking out against malpractice and corruption in our unit in addition to facing harassment over her Jewish-Italian heritage.

Imagine your own leadership in a war zone is actively vocalizing that they want you to die. They enjoyed the power trip like a terrible cosmic gag. In this mental health unit, being in a city on fire felt safer than being with the Klan-oriented folks of the Green Zone. The deployment felt like an experiment to drive people insane and LTC Platoni thought the same. She was worried, and her own psychological ruck sack was getting heavier with each new random threat from our Phyllis Schlafly-esque command structure. We combined our documents and turned a hefty packet into the Judge Advocate General in Ramadi.

Ramadi's small legal team of Army attorneys informed us that we had a bona fide case to legally relieve the command in the Green Zone due to rampant fraud, waste, and abuse. To our misfortune, the Baghdad Inspector General (IG), the highest legal authority in Iraq, stopped it. We later learned he was a close friend of our commander. When they sent LTC Platoni home for R&R (a two-week break for people deployed for a year or longer), I was immediately notified by unit leadership that I would stand trial for mutiny. I was accused of conspiring to illegally overthrow my commander. While I spoke out, I had followed proper military procedure, and this was pure retaliation.

Upon learning of my upcoming trial, I confided in my fellow compound Marines as I packed my belongings. While smoking my last cigar on the roof overlooking the smoke coming from a nearby explosion, my life was passing before my eyes from the edge of the Euphrates River. My dear Marine buddy, Joel, passed me a C-4 explosives satchel. I opened it and to my surprise I uncovered full-metal jacket hollow points, designed for maximum bodily damage.

"This is around 500 rounds, dude," I said, slightly taken aback in contemplating my upcoming fate. It was just me, an anachronistic knight errant rattling my sabre at U.S. Army windmills. The madness, absurdities, and corruption tore through my soul and exploded at last.

"Don't let them take you alive to Leavenworth. If your life is over, sister, go out with a fucking bang," Joel told me with a glimmer in his eyes.

My plan, now that my life was allegedly over? I was going to land in Baghdad and kill every racist piece of shit in that miserable fucking unit.

2 FALLING INTO FALLUJAH

Adversity has the remarkable ability of introducing the real you to yourself. In surviving multiple forms of trauma as a child, I had held the belief that I would never become the monsters around me. However, in the Army and facing either abusive criminal bigots wearing the same uniform or Saudi jihadists, it's hard not to turn into a bloodthirsty beast yourself. We all have to be vigilant that when we're fighting monsters that somewhere along the line we don't transform into one ourselves.

To stand alone when everyone around you appears to have their weapons pointing in your direction is a great life lesson on having allies. In an unexpected twist of fate on the flight to Baghdad to stand trial for Mutiny, we made an emergency landing in Fallujah where my Uncle Mike, who was part of a Navy construction team from Hawaii, was stationed. Over the week that I was stranded in Fallujah, I turned 24 while Uncle Mike talked sense into me.

"The pen is mightier than the sword. Put all your documentation on your commander's desk and let her and her cronies know that if she takes you down for Mutiny, they are all going down with you too," he said.

In that time, I typed out a statement, 39-pages single-spaced. Upon meeting my commander in Baghdad, I put the report on her desk, and said, "I know where every media outlet is sleeping here tonight, whether it's the Al Rasheed or Hotel Palestine. If you take me down, I will take all of you mother fuckers with me."

The charge of Mutiny used to be death by firing squad. Leavenworth is the worst possible prison sentence and after, your life is over. But I thankfully gave Uncle Mike's advice a shot.

In Ibn Sina hospital, I stood in a Kangaroo court trial among officers from my unit and lazy officers from Fort Campbell who would all go home and tell everyone hero stories over buffalo wings. They pulled me apart for hours, stripping me of my medals, to include a combat action badge that was awarded to me by a Marine Corps EOD Master Sergeant. Mutiny was reduced to an Article 15 charge, and I was slapped on the wrist for disrespecting an officer. Taking photos and keeping a journal for both evidence and artistic release, in the end, saved my hide. My psychological ruck sack had become noticeably heavy.

Young soldiers and Marines 19, 20 years old, people in military less than a year were launched right into this brutal war. Nothing can really prepare you. As a pre-9/11 enlistee from a military family, I understood the military as a job, not as some wild-eyed glory hunter feigning it's all about the red-white-and-blue, mom, baseball and apple pie. There's always a backstory for every enlistment and those true stories are often not so splendid.

Most of the people I knew joined the military because they couldn't afford an education or healthcare. Mobility in their respective cities or towns was limited with just a high school education. Most enlistees I knew were poor, but they were often too embarrassed to admit it and were some of the most optimistic, quixotic people I've ever met. Like a bunch of temporarily embarrassed billionaires, it was only a matter of time before they bought that luxury car, or that over-priced purse, or that dream vacation. But none of those things would ever happen unless they took out an obscene line of credit and were in debt for the rest of their lives. If they were able to get college loans – if their parents had good credit, but if your ass was poor, that was highly doubtful – you'd be in another form of debt for the rest of your life through student loans.

The military was a job with healthcare and educational benefits and when you're poor, it's one of the few options you have to escape impoverished, economically devastated neighborhoods, abusive families or partners, drugs, and whatever ailments one can face when strapped to the lowest rungs of the American socioeconomic ladder. Before I enlisted in high school, I did tarot card and palm readings or portrait sketches, selling goods and services to classmates for $10-$20 a pop so I could avoid eating gruel in our high school cafeteria. Since the military entrance exam, known as the ASVAB, was mandatory in poor East Bay schools in Northern California, recruiting people like me made sense. The Armed Forces recruiters knew quite well they were in a target-rich environment to make their quotas off the children of disenfranchised Bay Area families.

I wasn't afraid of military service, even as a teenager in high school. Having grown up experiencing assault as a child, moving constantly, and seeing mental health issues on both sides of my family, life alone was reason enough to seek out mental health as a profession. This much knowledge acquired early on in life suggested to me that I had some sort of responsibility to put my hard-learned life lessons to use and help others get out of their personal hell too.

"You can always get a student loan to pay for UC Berkeley or University of San Francisco. Don't give up!" my AP English high school teacher assured me. But it was too late, and she was wrong. I was only offered a $2,000 Stafford Loan for federal financial aid for college and neither universities, $14,000 to $8,000 respectively per academic year, would be sufficiently covered no matter how much I drew or read tarot for money. My dream of becoming a clinical psychologist was encouraged and nurtured by the Army recruiter, suggesting a path starting with becoming a medic and mental health specialist, then onto Officer Candidate School (OCS) – but OCS didn't happen. I ended up in Iraq as a Lioness and sergeant, wrestling people to the ground to make sure they weren't armed with a bomb vest, tying tourniquets on bleeding limbs, and providing trauma counseling for a year-long deployment.

"You've picked the wrong branch, soldier!" Marines in Ramadi used to say, referring to lengthy Army deployments. Marines and Navy personnel deployed for 6 months, the Air Force typically 1-3 months, and the Army was a year or more at a time. But it wasn't the deployment length or even the violence that was killing me, it was a small group of corrupt soldiers in Baghdad.

Thrown into West Baghdad after the charges were dropped out of fear of media exposure, I spent my last few weeks in Iraq sleeping alone in a large Army tent. This was part of their punishment, to keep on trying to break me. Sand floors and cots cradled me until we left the country as I was advised by my new officer to take my time alone to think about the future.

"You've been through too much, and let's face it, you're lucky to be alive. Go apply for scholarships to finish college, do anything. Just try to take your mind off of the past year. Look forward to going home in the last few weeks left," the kind officer in West Baghdad advised.

Dead people don't have to feel pain, guilt, regret. Dead people are the lucky ones. People shared their religious explanations and God's plan existing in spite of so much irreversible carnage, but after Iraq I seriously doubted God even existed. Losing my religion on walks through tent city outside of Baghdad International Airport, a soldier named Eugenio repeatedly bumps into me. We met in during my trips to the Green Zone where he followed me around like a lovesick adolescent. Love was far from my psyche. He would find me alone in tent city under scorching sun or enchanting desert moon and sit next to me as I aired my grievances over the war, but I'm not sure he's actually listening. I need to get back on the road.

Haunted by Ramadi and the corruption in Baghdad's Green Zone, I would to jump in a Humvee alone and go to bazaars outside of my camp and talked to Iraqis, who held conversations with me over gyros with mango chutney while Amr Diab and Nancy Ajram crooned over Arab pop channels. In exile, I felt more comfortable in confiding in others who were allegedly my enemy, and found more compassion in strangers who saw me as the invader than my own unit.

"You'll come back to Iraq one day. I know it. Promise me you won't forget us," one of the female Iraqi interpreters said before my departure back to the US.

"I promise I won't forget you," I said, feeling helpless to help change her situation let alone mine. I couldn't forget her or anyone else impacted, maimed, or killed by this war. Not even if I tried.

One with a conscience can't help but feeling complicit in the unraveling of their country and how it was such a huge disservice to them. Our leaders made this terrible decision that demolished Iraq and it was such a disservice to our own military as well. Here, this was no video game or a news segment.

I thought about my so-called trial in Baghdad every night.

This unit mistreated Iraqis, using them as servants as though it were British Imperial India – and we called it Operation Iraqi Freedom. I felt like a patient in an inpatient psych ward standing trial. I always wondered how Chamorros must have felt when Inquisition-era Spanish troops arrived to the Marianas in the 16th Century, and what they told them in the beginning of a systematic ethnic cleansing:

You're not a human being, I'm better than you because I'm white and close to God who is also white. You're nothing but a godless fucking Indian. You are subhuman, worthless, and I can do what I want to you because this holy book gives sanctifies my manifest destiny fantasies without any sense of accountability.

Centuries later, I'm hearing the same thing. These people are conquistadors, a bunch of empty-vessel Columbus-folk with no moral compass yet throwing the Bible in my face. This is why the world is in a terrible state and in perpetual strife. These people just take and take, claiming it's their divine right to rape, torture, pillage, and burn. I wanted to die that night.

Stripped of a Combat Action Badge earned in Ramadi and related medals, I took off one of my boots and loaded my rifle. Before I could lodge my big toe in the trigger well with the M16A2 barrel in my mouth, LTC Platoni walked in, pulling me off my weapon and into her arms where we cried together for hours.

Being Chamorro is being part of a race where people think you died a long time ago or don't know you exist. I lived life as an invisible, unaccounted for woman, and I dealt with it. However, Iraq put everything into the worst perspective at the absolute worst possible time in my life.

Being a female combat veteran means that the general American public also doesn't know I exist, that I actually engaged in direct combat, and thinks I was just a cute nurse in a secure hospital with a tray of blueberry muffins singing Yankee Doodle Dandy with a tight miniskirt like a WWII pinup girl waiting with my mouth open for the men to come home. No one knows what I did. I didn't get the accolades or special training Special Forces gets but I still did the same work but without the credit. I got nothing. It was like my whole deployment never happened. I was nothing more than a ghost.

As I left the vast desert sands of Iraq, I found myself longing for dead or evacuated friends, regretting that I wasn't in that vehicle when those five Marines I worked with on Lioness died, that female soldier I held as she passed in my arms, or any other newfound friend-turned-corpse for that matter. Perhaps I could have done more to ease the pain of everyone else around me. I felt alone, and my Don Quixote-esque optimism of feeling I could make a difference vanished, an oasis in the desert. The airplane lifted above the chaos and war below me. I felt guilt in being able to leave while millions of people here have no way out and must endure the war for as long as it may last. A part of my spirit was pulling away from the fibers of my sanity. I left a piece of my soul that will always rightfully belong in the desert.

3 HOMECOMING BLUES

Under the city lights of Ramadi, I run alone through a desolate metropolis and yearn for home. As I sprint through various homes, compounds, and alleys, I can't find my way. I'm lost. I notice strange people behind me, closing in on me. There's a corpse ahead of me. It's tossed aside near a bullet-riddled storefront. I'm alone and in deep trouble. As I make my way past the body setting into rigor mortis, an explosion stemming from the rigged corpse hurls me into the air, high into the desert sky. The blast waves rattle my skeleton and pierce my ears with an aching metallic ping as I let out a blood-curdling scream—a scream that wakes me up to the present.

Lying in a pool of sweat and breathless, as if I had been running all night, my mother knocks on the door.

"Is everything okay?"

"Yeah, I'm fine. Just a nightmare," I say, wiping the sweat off my face.

She lingers for a few seconds in the hallway, sighs, and hesitantly walks toward her room on the other side of the house. I am mortified.

Everything in my being wanted nothing more than to fling the doors open, look my mother in the face during mania, and tell her, "I've come home, but after escaping death, watching friends die, facing persecution and false charges for a crime I didn't commit, I'm not okay. I saw my unit commit felonious theft of government funds, a colonization of Iraqis, and the perpetrators are free and face no prosecution. I'm not okay. I saw innocent people die – soldiers, Marines, Iraqis, and worst of all, children – I'm not okay. I'm not sure if I'm ever going to be okay again. Most of my money and all my belongings are gone. Now, my sanity is well on its way too. My ex-fiancé I broke up with in Iraq wants me dead. I know I'm back physically, but my mind is still a shipwreck in the desert. With you, with everyone around me, I'm alone. I'm painfully alone in a way I can't quite verbalize yet and I don't know why I don't feel anything anymore. Please, please, please help me!"

There's no point. I could unleash a litany of my inner demons but would I be understood? Who here in the middle of Jacksonville, Florida would understand what's quickly deteriorating my inner peace or what I'm going through as a combat veteran who got an extra round of torture by people who shared the same uniform simply for being a woman of color?

As much as I desired to hug my mother and tell her everything to reconnect my soul from one broken world to the next, I'm reluctant. Instead of swallowing my pride, I died a little on the inside as I kept my secrets tightly held to my chest and the door firmly closed. Not a tear permitted to fall. In this world of watching war and violence on HDTV, people like me were outliers, oddities who sounded absolutely insane in detailing disturbing dispatches from a desert Wonderland.

In the early morning hours, lying in a guestroom bed in my parents' house, I hear nothing. No explosions, no whirring generators, no bullets, no screaming. Nothing. It is confusing and terrifying. All I hear is the sound of passing cars and the heater kicking on every so often. I stare around me at the bookshelves in the room and feel for my arms and legs to make sure they are still there – an old habit from the field.

I wasn't always like this…this hypervigilant mess soaked to the bone with perspiration and terror. Once upon a time, long before Iraq, I was a relentless optimist. Even after surviving childhood trauma, moving through eight schools as a military brat, and joining the Army at 17, I was still a wild-eyed romantic. I was once deeply in love with being alive and was assured that no one was stealing my peace.

Having seen the worst in people when I was young, I aspired to not be like the merciless, soul-extracting vampires from my early years. From a teenage girl who would wax poetic about A Natural History of the Senses to devouring world music, literature, and art, I joined the Army as a kid with no means to access a higher education and an extensive family military history. At age

23, I was engaged to be married and had mapped out my life as I entered into a long journey into the night through Iraq. At 24, now a war veteran at home in my last few months of Army enlistment, I don't see that optimistic, curious young woman in the mirror anymore. An enduring apathy has drenched my senses and poisoned my blood, leaving me denied of any real feeling other than paranoia and rage. In the mirror, as a recently returned combat veteran, I can only see a monster.

Just a few weeks prior, I had flown home from Iraq to Fort Benning, Georgia, where I out-processed from active duty, then my parents' house. No longer engaged, emotionally amputated from Iraq, and unsure of any real concept of home. While completely aware I'm not in the middle of a street in Ramadi linking arms with the Grim Reaper, I ache in frustration that I don't feel I belong here anymore. My parents' guest bedroom, Florida, the United States, the damn planet – you name it. No one around me knows what happened to me; and if I dared hint at a few small details from my deployment I felt instant judgment.

"Did you kill anyone?"

This question tore through my skin and shattered my insides, filling me with fury as the questioner anticipates an answer with either disdain or excitement in their eyes. As both an Army medic and a mental health sergeant, I knew that these vivid nightmares were just the beginning. My former invincible self didn't think this would be happening to me.

My goal was to make it home when I was running for my life in Ramadi. Now, I struggle to find a home, as no place I've been so far, not even my parents' home, feels safe. I didn't even know what home or a safe place was supposed to look like anymore, but it sure wasn't here. My vision of home while rocketing down streets in combat boots in Ramadi was beyond a barrier that shielded me from bullets, explosions, and shrapnel.

Home, to me, is simply a place I could feel safe, unjudged, understood. Anytime I remotely reached out, gave anyone a bread crumb of Iraq, I didn't get the feeling that anyone really wanted to listen to what was truly gnawing at my psyche. I got the feeling any eager inquirers expected a Hollywood breakdown of blood, guts, and glory with a smile and a salute; not a complex story of my devolution as a human being. Real war stories are never, ever glamorous.

The first few months of being back, I fiercely shielded myself from reality in between my impromptu road trips. To calm my nerves, to escape those feelings of impending doom that crawled up my spine, I would jump into my car and just drive. Zooming up and down Highway 95, racing up through Georgia, then down to St. Augustine or Destin or St. Petersburg on sunshine-kissed roads, I simply existed. I was no longer adrift in chaos in that dreamlike desert. Just orange trees, clean streets, swamps, deep-fried Twinkies, strip malls, and stucco-sided houses. None of it made any sense.

On the road, I catalogue my nightmares overwhelming my senses. Insomnia haunts me. During the day, I stare through my windshield and just drive. I'm in control on the road, but at night my paranoia picks up the pace. Wheels turn in my head, grinding gears against the last few gentle strands of tranquility I have left. When not behind the steering wheel of my car, my angst propels me to sit across the front door of the house, staring for hours in the dead silence of night; watching as though bloodthirsty insurgents were creeping around outside.

Around 8 am one morning, a knock came at the door. Quickly, I sprang to my feet with a knife in my hand. I peered through a small opening in the curtain in the window next to the front door. No one. I checked the windows in the dining room, and as my dad appeared, he asked who it was. As I opened the door with a sense of eagerness to maim whoever was attempting to disturb us, still, there was no one. I looked down and spotted a vase filled with roses on the welcome mat with a note.

"Well, bring it inside," my father said.

"No, I need to check it first. Stand back," I bark, as I look around the vase for wires or any oddities. I peered at this floral arrangement like a potential improvised explosive device (IED). Feeling the adrenaline rushing through me, I did, in fact, have an added reason to be paranoid aside from just returning from Iraq. I had lost almost everything I'd had before my return to the United States due to a relationship that turned sour mid-deployment. These flowers, with a note saying I love you, were sent by my ex-fiancé.

Prior to deploying, I was engaged, living with my fiancé,

working close to 60 hours a week while attending college, and serving as the neuropsychiatric ward non-commissioned officer-in-charge for a combat support hospital in Florida. About midway through my deployment in Iraq, we broke up. He didn't take it well. This now former fiancé ended up stealing over $20,000 of my money made in Iraq (out of $30,000 total) from our shared bank account. We were supposed to get married after I returned, so I entrusted him to make my last few credit card payments while I was overseas. There were no blaring red flags in our relationship until I got my orders for Iraq.

"Women shouldn't be in the Army, and definitely shouldn't be in combat," Yves complained.

Funny, he never expressed any contempt over my military service before I was getting ready to deploy. I brushed off his hurtful, misogynist comments and attributed it to immature coping mechanisms. He was scared. He had to be, right? When I was in Iraq, he accused me of cheating on him, only for me to discover his partying and club-hopping was getting out of control while I was getting shot at. As you can imagine, that felt quite unfair. The accusations of infidelity were sharply aimed at me, and I quickly discovered that he was merely projecting. During my R&R, we reunited in his native France and I gave it one last shot to figure out if we were better off together or apart. Before departing from Charles de Gaulle airport in Paris in the middle of 2005, I knew with 100% certainty that we were finished. After spending time with him in this break from combat chaos, I realized that the relationship had been woefully one-sided. He was enjoying the extra money from my unspent pay overseas and had no interest in remotely asking how I was coping physically or mentally in combat. When I broke it off, he threatened to kill me.

An attorney in Jacksonville told me that the cost to go after him, and win, would probably cost me close to the amount I lost in the first place, so it wouldn't be worth my time. Law enforcement alluded to the same, that it was a futile pursuit and to simply be careful in sharing accounts and my belongings next time. I looked at the flowers in disgust, threw them onto my parents' lawn, and chucked the vase in the trash. Years of my life, wasted, gone, and further damaged by some selfish bastard who thought a floral arrangement would mend the wounds.

Nightmares of the unit I was with in Iraq plagued me, and I had a hard time talking to anyone about the experience. It was so personal; I couldn't share it with just anyone. After surviving mental hell in Iraq and getting ripped off by my asshole ex, I was squeamish about sharing my phone number, let alone how my inner demons tortured me. So, I asked both of my parents one night if I could talk to them about it. Perhaps getting some of the most severe traumatic memories off of my chest would help quash the insomnia. It was worth a shot.

"I need to tell someone what happened over there. I'll brew a pot of coffee, and just give me a few hours to tell you everything, every painful detail that I can get out of my head. After that, I'll never speak of any of it again." I implored my parents, manic and bleary-eyed.

Neither of my parents, as happy as they seemed to have me back from deployment, accepted. They didn't want to know what happened, claiming it would hurt too much to know. I have to admit, I was a bit angry at the response, but I rescinded the offer and told them to forget I had asked.

They were great at sending me care packages large enough to feed me and some of the other soldiers and Marines I lived with in the compound in Ramadi when our food supply trucks were blown up. They exhibited love through their talents of cooking amazing food and fussing over whether or not I ate yet, but handling real-world problems was not their forte. I felt that psychological ruck sack again, weighing me down more than ever and not having the space to just unpack both bewildered me and pushed my pain deeper into a dark corner.

My mother could go on ad nauseam about my eating, "Have you eaten yet today? Why not? Are you sick? Don't get too skinny or your ass will disappear." If I came to my parents about a serious problem, I was typically asked what I'd like to eat. Estufao, savory Chamorro stew, to choke back the bloody guerrilla warfare? Thanks.

There are people who come home from war and want to talk about the pain, but no one wants to listen; there are others who want to keep silent and repress the memories, and all their family and friends want is to talk about it. I call this the war veteran reintegration paradox.

Examining my few options for venting my post-war angst after my parents rejected my plea, I jumped angrily into my car and started driving. Driving was one of the only outlets I had left in my life. Everything else seemed to be chaotic outside the confines of my car, my bubble. I ate what I wanted to, gorged on fast food, and reveled in ridiculous trivial bits of everyday American life—not because I greatly missed any of it, but because I could.

My drives in Florida provided a sense of freedom to do what I wanted without dealing with roadside bombs or someone actively and attentively attempting to kill me in Iraq. Driving down dangerous roads, conducting missions with Marine infantry units throughout the city of Ramadi, and providing emergency medical and mental health care was part of my daily life in Iraq. Driving in Iraq was the only thing that made me feel like I was in control of something (even if it was a shitty, partially-armored HUMVEE) while I was surrounded by what looked like the apocalypse. Whether driving in Ramadi or Jacksonville, I could convince myself everything was going be okay. It was when I wasn't behind the wheel that I felt vulnerable, exposed, unprotected. When I felt the void, that terrible nothingness that cloaked my senses and reminded me of my worst moments in Iraq, I could jump in my car to greet the road in a windy, speed-filled embrace with a smile on my face, convincing myself that I could escape the past.

This honeymoon sublimation phase didn't last very long.
It was about three months since I had returned from Ramadi, and less than two months since I'd started a full college course load to keep my mind off all that I had endured the previous year. I re-enrolled for spring semester 2006 at the University of North Florida in Jacksonville, where I started studying psychology and working full-time well before I deployed. Upon arrival back to Florida in late 2005, I switched my major to political science and international relations.

Unfortunately, studying and the corresponding coffee binges weren't distraction enough from the images spinning in my head. A montage of carnage was constantly on display in my mind's eye while 19-year-olds yammered on about their opinion on the war—even though most of them had never left the United States or the comfort of their parents' pockets, with the exception of perhaps

Mazatlán for spring break.

At the age of 24 and as an Army sergeant now sitting in a sterile university classroom, I was looking back on my year in Ramadi, in which I endured some of the bloodiest counter-insurgency battles of the war. While sitting in a college philosophy class listening to the professor drone on about dead white guys, I could see people dying around me in my mind.

There wasn't any proper venue in which I felt I could bring this up, and I had no intention of doing so anytime soon.

The classroom environment hadn't changed, but I had. Like so many other veterans re-entering to academia, I chose to blend in and not draw attention to my veteran status. If I was going to talk about the war, I preferred to discuss it with people who had been on the battlefield and had similar experiences. However, I knew no one personally in my city who was in Iraq, let alone anyone who deployed with me. Alone, yet unafraid by this, I kept quiet and moved about the campus undetected.

Up to this point, I seemed to superficially fit in with my classmates. Other than being a few years older than the average undergrad, there was really no way to distinguish me from any other college student by appearance alone.

One morning, as the philosophy professor opened the floor for discussion, other students began sharing diverse views of war throughout history. How they got onto that topic, I had no clue. You could find me typically sitting quietly in the back, minding my own business until class ended—but not this time. A female student spoke up; she was only 19 but, of course, knew what she needed to know about Iraq from news sources online. She said that everything American soldiers were doing in Iraq was wrong, and they all deserved to die.

"Excuse me?" I interrupted, "I was in Iraq for a year and, based on your generalized viewpoint, I should be dead?"

"Well, we didn't belong in Iraq in the first place," another student said.

I told the student that I agreed with her that the United States shouldn't have gone into Iraq, but now that the American troops were there, they couldn't just pick up and leave. That would be a disservice to the Iraqis.

The power vacuum the 2003 invasion created gave me the

uneasy feeling about Iraq's future, and all that people like me had done was in vain.

"We have to fix it. We have to make things right before we leave, and we have the ability to do so," I said, attempting to maintain composure.

Usually, when I spoke up in the classroom, I stayed in student mode, articulating my thoughts and opinions without profanity. But, I couldn't maintain that reaction for long after hearing something so callous and flippant that went against the core of my being. That's when I reverted to my role as sergeant, and the person I was talking to became a subordinate.

The 19-year-old continued to mutter negative stereotypes about veterans "killing babies" and so on. In an instant, I felt my entire year on the battlefield was being invalidated and violated by this student and by those who remained silent in their seats. At 17, I joined the Army. I had already served in the military for over seven years by this time and had worked for everything I had. Now, a 19-year-old living off of her mom and dad was telling me how life worked.

"You don't know what the fuck you're talking about," I said, glaring steely-eyed at her, a war-made realist with no tolerance for frivolous attacks.

"At least I've been there. Where have you been outside of the U.S.? Say what you've just said one more time. Please," I asked, knowing quite well that I was now baiting her into a fight that she unknowingly sparked.

She repeated what she said verbatim, quite brazenly—all of us deserved to die for being in Iraq. I sat there and felt my honeymoon phase turn off, and like a light switch, I was turned on to fight mode.

"Really? Why don't you come over here and kill me then?"

The 19-year-old girl exclaimed, now visibly nervous after meeting the expression her statement caused. Her eyes were wide and her voice quaked as she replied, "I don't have to sit here and listen to you."

"Neither do I, so you can do us all a favor a keep your ignorant mouth shut. What the hell have you handled in your life without relying on mommy and daddy to foot the bill, you spoiled imperial brat?!"

She looked at me in astonishment for a moment, then quickly turned around in her seat.

"You openly disrespect me, tear my life apart in a sentence, and you know absolutely nothing about life or suffering. I invite you to prove me wrong on that. Months ago, I was helping a young woman your age who got her legs blown off by a roadside bomb, and you're telling me that she deserved to die a slow, painful death. Fuck. You. Put your money where your mouth is and come over here and kill me yourself if you think I deserve to die."

She remained facing forward—just a few seats ahead of me and to my left. I had been gripping the sides of the desk with wrathful arms and hands but with an expressionless face, a calm, murderous affect that would be more fitting of a serial killer than a young undergrad. My facial muscles grew tense as I continue to stare at her with eyes that said, "I have no problem in taking your life in front of all your friends, just give me an excuse." I was longing to pick up the desk and smash it over her privileged head. I was dying for her to make the first move. It would be an excuse to act upon my desire and to return her gesture of disrespect with amplification. Please, get up.

The professor, as well as the other students, remained silent, seemingly in shock. After my outburst, there was no more blending in, no hiding that I'm a veteran.

Emotionally and mentally, I had little, if anything, in common with my classmates. We were oceans apart in life experience. The students had learned in a flash that despite my physical stature, I was more than capable of being overwhelmingly terrifying when angry.

Since returning from deployment, I've felt out of place, but I masked it and set it aside by simply paying attention to the things that most Americans take for granted. Food. Electricity. Clean running water. Toilets. Hell, toilet paper. Service on-demand. Wi-Fi. A safe place to sleep at night.

Driving down the road without your car being hit by an IED. Seeing clean streets not littered with corpses or the stench of rotting flesh. Still, it wasn't enough.

My first semester back at college was obviously a disaster. I couldn't concentrate, and my grades began to suffer. When students said they knew what was wrong with the war in Iraq and I tried to set the record straight, no one seemed to want to hear what I had to say, even though I had firsthand experience. I knew exactly what was going wrong but was preferably unheard, muted in my own community.

It was a day or so after that incident that I reached out to the regional VA office in Atlanta, Georgia.

"After coming back from Iraq, I don't feel okay. I just don't. I'm not interested in getting compensation or any money from you. I just need to get screened for mild traumatic brain injury and possibly PTSD. I tried to just enjoy being back, but the signs and symptoms are too persistent to ignore," I explained to the VA representative over the phone.

"That's all fine and well, ma'am, but how do I even know you were in the military, let alone Iraq? We're going to need a copy of your DD-214 to prove you were enlisted before we can do anything for you," she replied coldly, with a hint of mild irritation with my request.

Prove I was ever in the military, let alone Iraq? I needed to send her my discharge papers (DD-214), which was fine, but she continued to express disdain over the fact that I'm a woman who survived combat, and to her, this was impossible.

"Ma'am, women are not allowed in combat. There's just no way you could have any combat injuries. Women just aren't in combat, okay?" the woman said unapologetically.

"That may be the official policy, but that's not what's happening over there. I could send you photos and video if need be, but I don't have time to debate my life with you. I just want to talk to someone. Please," I replied.

She sighed in completely unwarranted frustration over the phone as though I was asking for something I didn't earn as a veteran: basic care from the VA.

"Send us your DD214, and then we can assist you," she snarled repeatedly.

"Ma'am, you pulled my records through my Social Security number, I don't think I can wait another month to get care. Isn't there someone or somewhere you could refer me?" I exclaimed, feeling my desperation was being viewed as vapid and meaningless.

She hung up.

The void is creeping in, the feeling of nothingness embracing me in a horrible cloak and ready to pull me into the abyss. The void, I feel, wants to take me to a dark place, and I feel that if I don't talk to someone, anyone soon, I could explode. As disgusted as I was by the first VA encounter over the phone, I mailed the DD214 and waited three weeks before making contact again with the regional VA office. I introduced myself, politely, and stated why I was calling. Iraq war veteran with multiple concussions, combat exposure, command persecution, prior homicidal and suicidal ideations. I relayed my information with the same dry tone as an internet provider assisting you with setting up a home router. Stay calm. Don't scare her. Maybe this time I can get help.

The voice of a different woman over the phone, who, like the one before her, began to question my military service and my experience in combat as a female.

"Look, I don't understand what you're saying to me. I don't have anything in here saying you were in the military or are even a combat veteran. I don't know what to tell you," she said.

"You do have records of me. I don't understand why I'm continually getting the run-around. I used to get GI Bill money from you. And you confirmed my name in your system using my Social Security number. I feel like I'm speaking Greek here and I don't know where else to go," I countered, now feeling my face heating up and a fist slowly forming in my other hand.

"Women are NOT in combat, ma'am! What you're saying just isn't true!" she scolded.

"Where do you get the gall to tell me the past year in Iraq was completely in my head? Do you realize what you're doing here? This treatment is why veterans commit suicide," I snapped back.

She hung up.

The alienation by not only my fellow Americans in a classroom, but also an institution that was designed and responsible for taking care of my health and mental health as a veteran felt exponentially worse. While I initially thought I needed the VA, this brusque treatment and rejection launched me into a state of desertion. They were leaving me behind, and I stood there in disbelief. First, my unit in Iraq, and now, the VA. I shouldn't have been surprised.

"What do I do now?" I asked myself, feeling exposed, raw, abandoned.

There was a crack in the universe. The person I was before Iraq and the person I see now were separated by a year of hell and were eons away from each other. There was no way to reconcile these two versions of myself. The former, an optimist, someone who believed in the greater good, that one person could make a difference. The latter, an experienced wild animal. A person who knew how easy it was to take someone's life, to destroy a city, a country. To look another person in the eyes and know I can end everything for them and retreat into nothingness. The person who believed that we're all animals on the inside.

As the homecoming blues set in, my anger, my sadness, the emptiness within stirred quietly. I couldn't sleep. I'd wake up five times a night with chronic pain throughout my body and had a skin reaction like hives that consistently appeared after a stressful event. I stopped going to class. I couldn't stand to look at anyone engaged in what felt like a conspiracy of silence. Every fiber of my being was slowly unraveling.

4 PARK YOUR WAR IN HARVARD YARD

With raw nerves and dreadful memories, my post-war insomnia was indulged with hours of research into details of the Iraq war that were missing from the mainstream media. I was addicted to information. From what I could tell, there were few outlets accurately reporting that the insurgency we faced in Iraq were not mostly Iraqi but Saudi. I had a mild interest in political science before I deployed, but my experiences on the battlefield in the middle of a desert amid an intense urban war obviously changed that. Politics were no longer just politics, it was my life.

With the encouragement of an officer I met in West Baghdad toward the last month of my deployment, I applied to the Harvard Public Policy and Leadership Conference (PPLC). Since my less-than-desirable return to UNF was now up in flames, I figured if my application went through, this would be a pleasant escape from the homecoming blues. Being one of 50 students around the United States to be invited to attend the PPLC, I was stunned to get news of my admission. The conference, which is hosted annually by the John F. Kennedy School of Government to create a diverse student body for their graduate programs, was a fairly big deal according to my professors, who were puzzled over my lack of enthusiasm. During a weekend in February 2006, I boarded a plane to Cambridge, Massachusetts. After the cab ride from Boston Logan to my hotel in Harvard Square, I wandered through the snowy perimeter of Harvard University thinking this may be a place where I could be heard. A forum in which others were awake, aware. A place where I could have a voice. My idealism was short-lived.

The first workshop I attended dealt with racial diversity. The professor was talking about diversity as if it were just a black and white issue, with meager references to Asian and Hispanic culture here and there. I thought he was limiting the discussion by only talking about a few groups, and while I waited toward the end in hopes of him covering indigenous groups, like Native Americans and Pacific Islanders, he didn't.

"Excuse me, I noticed that there were a few ethnic groups missing from the study. Is this study considered to be completed or is this an ongoing project?"

"No, this is not an ongoing project, and I just showed you all the data," the professor replied.

"I'm not trying to be difficult here, but I noticed that Native Americans and Pacific Islanders were excluded entirely. Is there a reason for that?" I asked.

It wasn't an attempt to be overly individualistic when I spoke up in class; I was just trying to make the point that there are other racial groups that he didn't cover, to include the aforementioned underrepresented groups.

"We didn't have time to cover Native Americans, and Pacific Islanders are in the same category as Asian," he gruffly responded.

Some people have described me as a walking experiment because no matter where I go, I stand out because of my ambiguous racial features. In this case, I simply wanted the professor to accept the premise that diversity is complicated, and it's unfair to put people in one of only four boxes when even the Census Bureau has caught on and recognized Asians and Pacific Islanders as two separate ethnic categories.

"You mean, without hesitation or reservation, that Asians and Pacific Islanders are in the same group? Totally indistinguishable genetically, geographically, or linguistically?" I asked.

"No, they are not," he argued, seeming to be surprised that I questioned his data.

"Do you not hear how racist that sounds? We need to talk about everyone and not just one or two groups. We need to include everyone if we're really promoting diversity, whether it's educational achievement or incarceration rates. Asians and Pacific Islanders are two different groups being lumped together erroneously. Even the Census Bureau recognizes these two groups as separate and distinct. Also, if you're not even discussing the indigenous people of the land on which you currently live, well, that's a problem. A colonialist problem," I said.

He then looked at me, sighed, rolled his eyes, and turned to answer the questions of other students. His cold dismissal of me as well as two indigenous groups of the U.S. insisted, "Who are you to question me, a Harvard professor?"

Needless to say, I didn't give a shit about his title, especially after witnessing him experiencing no qualms in blowing off an indigenous Pacific Islander in the middle of a diversity discussion.

After the lecture, I told the coordinator that the diversity workshop was not only a waste of time, but it also contained inaccurate, exclusive, imperialist rhetoric. It seemed far more ethnocentric to focus on one or two groups than anything promoting diversity and equality.

"You say it's about diversity, but it was solely about black and white issues with a spritz of Hispanic and Asian statistics. If you call that a diversity workshop, I want to go home. This seemed like a comprehensive program at first, and I was excited to come here; that's saying a hell of a lot for someone who just came back from being shot at in Iraq. But I don't think that I want any part of this anymore, Harvard or not," I said.

The coordinator apologized profusely, expressed her support and solidarity with me, and urged me to attend another workshop. The next workshop was also about diversity yet again, and the presenter was a former female U.S. ambassador to Yemen and Iraq, who spent a lot of time in the Green Zone with the Coalition Provisional Authority.

She made a comment that the United States military is more misogynistic than Arab men. A bit surprised by the stereotyped comment and egregious generalization, I took exception to this. I then raised my hand, and she turned her attention toward me.

"Ma'am, I was in the Army for eight years and in Iraq for one," I told the Ambassador. "As someone who's had an AK-47 pointed at my chest by an Iraqi soldier in Anbar Province, I can tell you there's some missing information in your analysis. I've had more passes made at me by Iraqi men than by American soldiers and Marines who I lived with. So, if you're going to make that stereotype, I'm here to tell you that I think you're wrong. Sexism is everywhere. Does it exist in the U.S. military? Absolutely. But, to insinuate that gender discrimination in the Middle East occurs any less is, well, insane." I got the feeling that Nawal El Saadawi herself could've strolled into this room and chimed in on patriarchy and internalized oppression, but no one or any inconvenient facts could make this ambassador's ego budge.

"Well, I was in the Green Zone," the lecturer said proudly.

"I was in Ramadi," I shot back. "Did you even leave the Green Zone?"

"No, I didn't," she said, sheepishly.

"Then, what the hell do you know about Iraq outside the imperial Emerald City? They had regularly scheduled yoga, Arabic classes, and patisseries where you were. You had porcelain toilets that were regularly cleaned by Iraqis. I, on the other hand, went to the bathroom in a plastic bag. Don't tell me you know the real Iraqis and the real American soldiers when you really don't. You hung out with other overpaid civil servants and contractors. And you're getting off on the fact that this audience doesn't know any better. Your whole argument's foundation is a sham," I said, irritated by her unchecked ignorance and opulent privilege.

The ambassador then said that she spoke with Special Forces soldiers, who are highly-trained to conduct specialized operations. So, she spoke with a few SF guys? Big deal. I had Special Forces guys baking peach cobbler for me in Ramadi. How they got the ingredients in a place like Ramadi is probably far more Top Secret than anything soldiers probably told her. That bit of information still didn't speak to her credibility. She dismissed my comments and kept speaking the same brand of rhetoric and simply continued telling the crowd a big fish tale that they gobbled up without question, nodding and staring on with admiration.

She was the face of the zombie apocalypse. After that, I kept raising my hand, but she wouldn't call on me. Finally, I got up and left in the middle of the speech. She had the power, platform, and privilege, and I didn't. I just wanted to go home, but I didn't know where that was anymore.

Later on in the evening was an event with a Q&A session that involved students from JFK School of Government as well as our PPLC group regarding public policy. I remember one student standing up to ask a question that quickly turned into what sounded like a shameless thesis or dissertation recitation. The intoxicating pretentiousness filled the air like opium smoke.

My skin is crawling. I find it hard to believe that this is the cream of the crop, the best of America's ivory tower, but, perhaps, this was it? Considering how poorly foreign policy has been handled by the United States, I'm quickly learning that there was a tragic disconnect between theory and application in even the best U.S. universities. Many of those politicians and high-ranking officials who squandered opportunities for advancement in Iraq were Ivy League alumni. Those wealthy sociopaths were screwing over military veterans and civilians at home and abroad through purposefully shoddy policy and strategy simply to turn a profit. Now, I was seeing their roots.

How history is taught, and perhaps how that combined with religion, contributes to a culture of blindly following the privileged while disinformation reigns, nudges at my sense of emptiness. That unexplainable malaise I felt while reading whitewashed news from that internet shack in Iraq now makes sense. The desert of information is perpetuated by people in this room. I wanted to run. The way you see someone run in a film when they encounter their first zombie. I never thought while watching those films that one of the infected ones would be a US diplomat.

On the chilly flight back, I felt less connected to my country than I was before the Harvard PPLC conference. I wondered if there was any place where I could feel comfortable to communicate what was a terrifying and psychologically devastating experience in Iraq. Instead of approaching the topic of war or diversity from a policy perspective, I was shut down for pointing out what I perceived as watered-down, pre-packaged disinformation for mass consumption.

When I returned home from the Ivy League self-love-fest drenched in manufacturing consent in Massachusetts, I was dying to sleep. I wanted nothing more than to close my eyes and forget the world for a few hours. It was futile, and my sleep patterns worsened. I was wide-awake throughout the night and stayed up for days, only crashing after 48-72 hours of insomnia for a short block of sleep. Then I'd repeat the cycle.

Only a few days had passed since my return from the conference, and in the middle of my rocky sleep schedule, I had what appeared to be a hallucination.

While wide awake around 3 am, I started walking down the hallway from the guestroom to the bathroom. But before turning into the bathroom, I glance out toward the dining room on my right. Whenever there's an open door, I was looking into other rooms as though I were still on patrol and scanning areas for security.

Instead of looking out and seeing the typically vacant and cold room, I see someone: one of the Marines I worked with in Ramadi who died from a roadside IED, still in desert camouflage while disfigured and covered in blood. He's sitting at the dining room table smiling at me with welcome home painted in blood on his face. I quickly jump to the other side of the wall in the hallway and take another look into the dining room. Holy shit. He's still there, smiling as though he's just stopping by for an in-town visit, waiting to have coffee with me.

With every tense muscle in my body, I asked, "Please don't visit me like this. I can't see you suffering like that anymore."

He's the picture of the Iraq I remember. Military personnel and civilians violently killed, undeservingly, while many of us made it home with not the faintest clue on how to live our lives after witnessing what looked like the end of the world. Slowly, I peer from inside the hallway into the dining room. He's gone.

Returning to bed, I tell myself to ignore the hallucination. The image of blood painting the words "welcome home" on the deceased Marine's face appeared in my dream upon closing my eyes. Nightmares I couldn't escape strangled me and waking moments during the day suffocated me.

After experiencing quite the jarring visual hallucination, I start painting to take my mind off the horrific images in my head. The dead Marine brought with him a parade of sadness and hopelessness I wish to forget. I turned back to painting, desperately trying to distract myself from horrific images in my head.

Art was an added prescription to complement my penchant for road trips. I was once passionate about art, but since coming back, I had no interest in it anymore. Having to force myself to paint, there was no passion in my work. Generic Bob Ross landscapes would be immediately discarded in the trash upon completion. There was nothing this amputated spirit could create with any meaning. Barely able to paint without hand tremors, I'm holding onto art for dear life.

Weeks had passed, and disturbed sleep patterns and wrath persisted. Art and short road trips up and down I-95 helped channel some of the anger into another outlet. To clear my head, I listened to stand-up comedy delivered by Ron White or Dave Chappelle, or watched Anthony Bourdain in the dark at 3am. Comedy or travel-related programs worked, temporarily, in helping to transport me to another place. As long as I was fixated on laughing or wanderlust, I wasn't thinking about dying.

Reaching out to different organizations over the course of the semester for a clue in what to do after facing VA rejection led me only to more dead ends with no apparent way out of my manifesting post-war traumatic symptoms. After numerous fruitless attempts to get a hold of well-known veteran service organizations to help or at least point me in the right direction regarding mental health or treatment for physiological ailments, I had no answers, no offers for assistance—just a lot of blank stares, unanswered emails, and rerouted calls that would end in an apathetic dismissal or a hang up.

Now, I'm in the middle of a desert—of a different kind—once again, without a radio, and no lifeline. I'm on my own. Having this happen in the initial part of my reintegration back into stateside life is a reality check that told me where I stood as a female combat veteran of color.

A stern, instinctive voice from my consciousness spoke up, and I distinctly heard the pressing suggestion: "Save yourself. No one is coming for you."

5 SAVANNAH, GEORGIA

In Portuguese, there is a peculiar, untranslatable word I adore: saudade. It's a type of melancholic nostalgia for something that will never happen again or didn't happen at all. In a sense, I felt I had a case of saudade in being home—the nostalgia for a peaceful sense of home I may never see again … or perhaps that home never existed at all? Since returning from Iraq, it's been difficult to focus on the present; each day is a struggle to not look too intensively on the past. What was said, done, or what could've been done to prevent unfortunate events, to make all the pain go away, or what could've prevented a situation that is now despairingly irreversible.

After a few months of experiencing a goddamn circus of a post-war reintegration, I began to grow closer to a Marine named Tony, with whom I kept contact after I returned from Iraq. He was still in Anbar Province as an intelligence analyst based in Al Taqqadum. My deployment was ending as his was beginning, and it all started from a Christmas card. It was a general "stay safe and happy holidays" greeting that I didn't think anything of until he kept the letters and e-mails coming.

In April 2006, we decided to meet halfway somewhere to see if our budding romance could make it stateside. He was stationed in Camp Lejeune, North Carolina, and I was still in North Florida, so we chose a city we had often passed yet never visited before: Savannah, Georgia.

We met at an Italian restaurant before the sun began to set in sultry Savannah. Tony emerged from his truck as a tall, thin, and dark-haired Marine with deadpan humor. Together, we strolled past charming, decaying cemeteries where corpses lie in Southern pride or segregated indignation.

Sauntering along Savannah's streets and pageant of her stranded ghosts amid Gothic Revival houses, we exchanged stories of our time in Iraq with laughter that thinly veiled our inner melancholy.

Southern charm, misappropriated nouveau-riche soul food, and tourist-saturated squares sheltered in an emerald cove like a jewel box for confederate ghosts confounded my senses. The old Savannah appeared to slowly peel back its cozy yet anachronistic antebellum garments to make way for a renaissance. The past dies a slow, painful death. I dreamt of my own rebirth, a shedding of old skin, but felt the stagnation in my own soul that I saw in the spirit of Savannah. Tony and I caroused around the embroidered lady-like southern city, went on a cheesy ghost tour, and closed the evening with frozen drinks on River Street. In between amorous gazes and Midnight in the Garden of Good and Evil references, we officially began dating.

"You don't know this yet, but I'm going to marry you," Tony said while gently holding my hand as we strolled past old colonial homes framed with Spanish moss and sleepy trees.

"Is that so?" I said, laughing in disbelief. He kissed me. My incredulity was muted.

The night after our first date in Savannah, I had a strange dream. I was alone in a desert at night when suddenly a mysterious man appeared. He started walking beside me and told me that this wasn't the time, and when the time was right, he would return. He was a bigger man than Tony, but I couldn't see his face. He held my hand and walked down a dark path with me to what seemed like an open road in the middle of this mysterious desert with orange streetlights. His deep, haunting voice comforted me. I believed him. He told me everything would be okay, even though what I was feeling was a vast emptiness and pain I could hardly verbalize. I thanked him, and he told me we would meet again when everything was right. I woke up puzzled.

After driving back down to Florida, I began wrapping up my next project: applying for the David L. Boren National Security Education Program (NSEP) scholarship to study abroad. While I was content with Tony, I still had an unshakeable urge to keep traveling. We were talking on the phone for an hour every night and taking turns in making eight-hour drives to see each other every weekend between Jacksonville, Florida and Jacksonville, North Carolina.

The road trips up and down Interstate 95 allowed me space to engage in road meditation. I would feng shui my thoughts and mental to-do list, blast my favorite music, and drink an assortment of caffeinated beverages as I flew down the tree-lined highway toward sweltering North Carolina.

These road trips, the sense of control on the highway for hours, kept me in my wartime comfort zone.

That travel bug was biting even harder, despite the budding romance. That bite left a nomadic itch that needed to be scratched. I needed a drastic change of scenery from the East Coast of the United States. My desire superseded any feelings I was developing with Tony, who was going to head back to Iraq for a few months immediately after my departure. He seemed to be understanding of my need for a bit more adventure, and since he was deploying, it was the perfect time to chart my course in another direction. His stint would be for six months in the Anbar Province, but I would be gone for a year to an unknown site in Europe.

Prior to finalizing my packet, one of my international relations professors, Nancy Soderberg, a former UN Ambassador under President Clinton, agreed to write a letter of recommendation on my behalf. She was open to hearing about my experience in Iraq, contrary to the experience with the U.S. Ambassador to Yemen during my Harvard visit. Both Professor Soderberg and my Russian history professor nudged me toward a Russian/Czech program in Prague, Czech Republic.

After discussing my next adventure with my professor, I went home to tell my mother about my plans. She seemed a bit worried but also somewhat relieved. She knew why I needed to leave again, that nothing seemed to fit since I've been back, but something else was on her mind.

"I didn't want to tell you while you were in Iraq, but I had a really hard time when you left," she said, with a somber affect.

"How so?" I asked, still slightly preoccupied with my own news.

"After you left, I started to have what my doctor later called panic attacks," she said.

"What do you mean by panic attacks?"

"I used to just feel afraid all the time. When dad left to work in the morning – Janice moved out and you were already in Iraq – I would lock myself in the bedroom. I would hardly go out to the kitchen, just staying in bed thinking that if I stepped outside, someone would knock at the door. I was thinking that I'd open the door to someone telling me you were dead. I thought if I stayed in the room until dad got home, that person wouldn't come."

I had no idea that this had gone on, and no one even hinted that she appeared to be headed toward a nervous breakdown. She continued to tell me that on occasion, a solicitor would knock on the door and she'd lose it.

She would stare out the window, waiting nervously for who was, really, just a sales or delivery person to walk away to confirm it was not someone in military uniform with bad news.

Sometimes the anxiety was too much, and her worst fears about what could happen to me in Iraq would overwhelm her. She would call everyone and anyone she knew to come to the house and visit, as she was afraid to be alone, too afraid to be by herself in the event of a death notice.

She ran outside one day knocking on doors in a panic, asking someone to help her. She was crying, telling a neighbor she was afraid, and that she didn't know what to do. That's when my father took her to her doctor and told him what was going on, and he insisted on ways she could manage her anxiety.

"You didn't seem all that interested in what I was going through in Iraq," I stated quite bluntly after months of not getting to vent myself, "I had no idea you actually were that worried."

"Of course! What do you think I am, an animal? I'm your mother!" She paused and appeared to be catching her breath as though she were slightly adjusting herself from a heart palpitation, "I just thought you'd always be there. And the thought of losing you, my youngest daughter, my last child, was making me insane." She spoke without any reservation over that last, painful word. Insane.

"I had no idea," I said, not knowing what else to do but listen and let her vent.

"Now you're here, but you don't know how bad it was to watch the news every night and read the names of other people's children," she started to choke back tears, and quite defiantly, she didn't dare let one fall, "having to see those dying people over there, children, families, funerals, people screaming, things blowing up, shooting in the streets, heads being chopped off and everything is falling apart. I thought to myself, my baby is over there. What the fuck am I going to do if I lose her?"

"That's the nicest thing anyone has ever said to me since I've been home," I said. In fact, I think it might have been the nicest thing, and the most candid thing, she's ever said to me. She could be, at times, overwhelmingly frank with her observations. While often lacking a filter, expressing her most vulnerable emotions was not her strong suit.

"I'm okay with you going to a place like Prague. I know you don't feel right being here. Maybe you'll feel better there. Maybe you just needed more time after Iraq to think about things before coming home. Don't get me wrong, we're happy to have you back, and Dad can now stop kissing your baby picture every night and crying," she said, chuckling over my dad's nostalgia as her chosen coping mechanism. Her response to this was merely an attempt to soften the blow of her own pain, which was far more disconcerting.

"I do feel like I came back home too soon or that something should have happened, perhaps some type of a buffer between combat in Iraq and fast food in Jacksonville," I said, actually feeling somewhat understood for the first time since being back. Not completely, but hey, this was a start.

"I prayed to Infant of Prague while you were gone. Maybe this is a sign for you to go there and get better?" she said, filled with what seemed to be a renewed sense of hope.

Much of my faith had been slaughtered well before my return, but having been raised Catholic, I understood what she was trying to say and do. She was trying to control an uncontrollable situation, trying to change an outcome that she thought would kill her too.

"Maybe," I responded.

Whether my news was of combat PTSD or winning a scholarship, these moments were never really mine. It was always about listening to someone else.

Everything in the broad spectrum of events was happening so fast, but I still felt like life was stagnant and happening in slow motion. My family was supportive of me going back overseas, and Tony was supportive of my decision. He often joked to his other Marine buddies that his girlfriend was a Russian spy secretly going back to the motherland. We hatched a plan to write each other and to call one another whenever we could: one of us in Iraq, the other in the Czech Republic or Russia.

After dinner one night at my family's home, Tony and I were about to watch "Flags of Our Fathers" with my father. My father had somewhat of a romantic view of war, and perhaps not listening to my story was a way to preserve not only his sanity but his fantasy of glorious battles that are not-so-charming in real life. Tony was lying on my lap as I sat up, and my father to our left was drinking a beer and telling us how this was supposed to be a great film.

The opening credits appeared and I began to focus. I wasn't a big fan of war movies anymore, especially after engaging in war in real life. You have to be in the right mood to watch movies like that after witnessing such grotesque actions firsthand. But this evening seemed perfectly fine, and I had Tony here with me, so I felt a sense of camaraderie. While he was a Marine, his time in Iraq was primarily spent on a base, not venturing outside the wire, or outside the confines of the encampment, and he was lucky to have not witnessed any carnage or engage in any direct combat. We had very different experiences but seemingly respected each other's service.

Suddenly, I felt tremors, but it wasn't me. Tony was shaking. I leaned forward as he was facing the screen and saw tears running down his face. Jesus, I didn't know what was happening. My former Army mental health sergeant habits kicked in, and I cleared my throat to get my father's attention, motioning with my left hand to cut the movie and that something was wrong. He gestured right back to me, pointing at Tony not being okay.

He saw that he was crying and made an excuse that he was tired and that we could watch the rest of the movie while he went to bed. My father handed me the remote and pretended not to see Tony in tears, nodded and whispered, "Good night."

After my father closed the door to my parents' bedroom, I looked back down at Tony.

"Hey, what's going on?" I asked, whispering while stroking

his hair.

"I don't know what's wrong with me," he said, sobbing into my lap.

"Was it the movie? Or is something else bothering you?"

"I don't know, maybe it's the movie. I just can't see any of that stuff right now, you know? I can't tell anyone about this. How could I? I know I can trust you and you're not going to judge me or laugh," he said.

"Of course, I'm not. There's nothing wrong with feeling overwhelmed or lost since coming back from Iraq. It's a normal response to an abnormal situation," there was part of my autopilot Army mental health spiel kicking back in. It was an involuntary reaction at this point. Listen to others and push your own feelings aside. It's remnant, perhaps, from a time when it was literally my job to take care of others, rather than be a burden myself.

"We've come back from what seemed like the apocalypse to a nation of detached zombie consumers who have only seen war through high-definition television. They don't know what happens on the ground. Everyone has an opinion and it's all so warped. Believe me, I know. It's all orchestrated bullshit. And I'm here for you like you're here for me. We're a team, okay?" I explained as I wiped the tears from his cheeks.

He looked up at me with his lips quivering and voice shaking, "I love you."

"I love you, too."

6 WASHINGTON, DC

Looking out of another airplane window, Washington DC-bound, I was mentally preparing to leave the United States again. Attempting to forecast my year abroad in Prague, I was feeling a return of that adrenaline rush I felt in Iraq. The rush I once felt for love and romance had peculiarly transferred into adoring unpredictable situations, possibly even danger, and the unknown. It felt strange when juxtaposed with everyday American life.

It was a cold hard reality of a country suffering happily from affluenza, complaining about Wi-Fi and Frappuccino flavors while millions around the world were starving, enduring war and violence, and were fighting with everything they had left to simply stay alive. Every part of my being was rejecting being back in the US like an antibody to a cancerous cell. I loved my country; I was just wondering where the hell it went or if it ever really existed as I had imagined.

Perhaps things were always this bad and it took Iraq to shake me out of my slumber. I didn't refuse to see the truth; it just didn't occur to me how warped reality in the US really was. There is an ocean of difference between seeing graphic depictions of violence overseas from the comfort of your own home and smelling the dead bodies firsthand. It's far too easy for anyone to cry war when it's not them having to look someone in the eyes and pull the trigger. It seems much easier to run through a barrage of bullets than it is to walk through the ruins of my post-war homecoming.

The video game-like detachment is far too overwhelming to digest.

My once passionate soul is now a pile of ashes. The concept

that people weren't so devious, that there was a sense of karmic justice; that a divine entity had mercy out there; Iraq changed all of that. My optimism is shot as I no longer believed that people got their just desserts; I believe that they go on to ruin more lives. Just look to Wall Street and any number of monolithic corporations. Look at any post-colonial environment or nation in which you see its vampiric effects continually feeding and feeding upon souls, flesh, and resources without satiety. I didn't believe in humankind anymore, and the life I was living felt like borrowed time.

Upon arriving in yellow-tinged Reagan International Airport in Washington DC, I hailed a cab to my hotel near Union Station. After dropping off my bags, I made a beeline to the White House. As a kid, my parents took my sister and I through much of the National Mall, snapping photos of monuments, memorials, and Arlington National Cemetery. What a strange picture that was of my parents pushing me in an umbrella stroller through a sea of dead service members' headstones – a place I'd return to as an adult to mourn my dead friends.

While seeing any variety of monuments or museums is an option, I just want to see the White House. I have so much anger bottled up inside of me at the privilege in Washington DC. The fact that draft-dodging, trust fund baby chicken hawks are clamoring to send people overseas to die weren't being prosecuted or even held remotely accountable for their actions enraged me. Seeing the White House is a way to see the roots of much of my pain in tangible form, to look at the abyss for what it is. Amid the stifling humidity, I walk toward the source. It's not like the heat we had in Iraq, scorching and dry. Washington DC has a late-spring, early summer heat that makes one feel as though they're trying to breathe in an aquarium – an aquarium of rich white fish.

By the time I had reach the south lawn of the White House, I'm drenched in sweat. Walking alone through a concrete jungle, I had time to process some of my frustration. I feel powerless to change my situation, but I know that I'm not ready to give up either. Here I stand outside the fence, an injured, angry veteran staring into the gaping maw of corporate interest over human lives, of money over principle, of sociopaths crippling the United States to pad their own financial accounts. I grip the black iron bars and look on in livid disenchantment.

The White House. Behold, a building of emptiness, a veneer for freedoms we don't really have anymore – if we ever did have much to begin with. I didn't linger. I just wanted to see where the true executioners live and dream that one day the US would wake up and see that the plutocracy is here and is strangling us with its sea monster-like tentacles every day.

In this field of buildings that barely stretch to grope the sky, elected officials sanction the rape and torture of our only planet, the one world we have. Corruption, rendition, the suffocation of whistleblowers, ground combat, air strikes, PTSD, violence, pollution, fracking, phone-tapping, mass incarceration, broken treaties, false flags, starvation, solution-selling, and war profiteering. It's all here and it's maddening. The desire for oil and fattening the growing oligarchy tears through me like a pipeline on sacred ground.

The most insidious of our country, the greediest and highest rung of our socioeconomic ladder, line their pockets with misappropriated funds as military personnel and hordes of civilians are maimed or killed. It's not their children out there, blinded by manufactured patriotism or lured into the service with the promise of economic stability, all with the sanctimonious blessings of misguided public consent by way of corporate, state-sponsored media. It won't be their children who are terrorized by Wahabbist insurgents tearing through city blocks and rural areas as only an ever-devouring plague could. It won't be any of their loved ones watching thousands of years of civilization unraveling like an old sweater as each thread of wool is lit on fire or stolen to sell on the black market for greedy consumers with a fetish for hijacked Mesopotamian artifacts.

The filth, the ever-lasting destruction is the furthest place we can find from the concepts of honor and integrity. There is nothing glorious or romantic about creating orphans, enabling violent religious fundamentalism, and the scent of decomposing corpses. If this what our leaders call democracy and freedom, I'm underwhelmed and unimpressed. If this is what our leaders are lending their stamp of approval, I'm enraged, and if you're breathing and have a pulse, you should be too.

Think of our beginnings: The United States was founded on violence and we have been at war much of the time we've been a country. It was drafted by white slave owners who told us that only the European male mattered and if you had a natural tan, or a vagina, you were not counted in the magical realm of equality. All men are created equal was written that way for a reason. If you were the Natives on US soil, or were of African descent trafficked in through shackles to satisfy the economic urges and consumer impulse of the new white world, or perhaps a Chinese migrant building railroads, you were not considered human enough by colonialists to be counted as a man created equal – and forget it if you're a woman of any color. Why are so few people looking back on this sociopathic narrative of history of the United States and calling bullshit, and more importantly, doing something about it?

Operation Iraqi Freedom. What difference does the word "freedom" make to someone who lost everything, from family to heirlooms to history, amid terrible violence, death, and destruction disguised as democracy? We took the word freedom, attached it to 155 rounds with the zealous blessing of extremists flooding the lands of ancient Mesopotamia like waves of body lice. We laced the term with det cord, a blasting cap, and a well-placed cell phone call. Aloha snackbar: A manufactured Jihadi dream.

Veterans being sent into unjust wars for corporate profit is a perversion of trust, at best. I found the emotional manipulation of both sides, the propaganda at play so incredibly revolting that I couldn't stand to idly wave a flag or flaunt yellow ribbons without asking serious questions regarding motive. And I knew people would hate me for it. I let go of the bars, shake my head in disgust, and turn away.

Walking away from the White House and feeling far worse, unfulfilled, and with justice seemingly out of my reach, I stumble upon the International Spy Museum, a museum dedicated to all eras of espionage and tradecraft. Something must take my mind off the validation of my amputated spirit.

While most of the Spy Museum appeared to be nostalgic over the Cold War era, or perhaps that's merely my own perception, it brings back quite a few memories of movies I've watched growing up. Between Bond movies, Pink Panther, The Inspector cartoons, and other movies glorifying espionage and danger, it's no wonder I ended up in the military after years of having danger and clandestine operations romanticized in my household.

Now, having earned a Department of Defense scholarship to study in the Czech Republic, my future seems open to the possibility of living out some of those romantic ideations. I know better, and don't hold any illusions over what government intelligence does; it's flawed. Yet, despite the current flaws, I wanted to be part of a movement to right the wrongs that haunted me.

After making it back to the hotel, I clean up, dress in business casual attire, and head toward the scholarship reception downstairs. There's a large group of students mingling and getting acquainted with others who would be in their region. On one side of the room is the Middle East group, primarily studying in Egypt, Morocco, and Syria. On another side, is South America, with some students heading for Colombia and Brazil. Another group is mostly heading to Kenya, as Swahili seemed to be of heavy interest. Other remote parts of the world surface with less commonly spoken languages to include dialects and rare languages spoken in North Africa and the Caucasus region. And then there's my group, Russia and Eastern Europe.

One of the scholarship recipients, a virginal white guy from New England who was seemingly fishing around the room for others in the region spots my nametag and quickly introduces himself. He's polite, follows his name with a warm smile, and then asks the annoyingly inevitable question for someone like me, "So, where are you from originally?"

No, this is not a question about which state I'm from in the US, this had more to do with my ethnicity. I hate having to explain to every doe-eyed individual in the US that, yes, the Mariana Islands are part of the US and no, Guam is not a country south of Mexico, Saipan is not a typo for Saigon, nor is it any part of East Asia or anywhere else one might think there be dragons. By all means, pull out any of your electronic devices with internet access and research a map mid-conversation with me about my ethnic origin. Please, do it. It'll save me the breath and trouble of explaining it and you'll have a reference point aside from my face. Then we can expeditiously move on to having a conversation where I can stop thinking about slapping you with a rolled-up parchment paper map that chronicles centuries of colonialism and exploitation that had caused these frustrating incidents to occur.

Over, and over again. Being in DC and at a conference in preparation to study abroad as a student under a Department of Defense program, I sure was not thrilled to get more questions about my ethnic origin from fellow recipients.

Ignore the idiocy and move forward, I thought. My attention quickly shifts toward another former scholarship recipient in the room, who caught wind of my interest in Russia. He tells me of his own personal nightmares in Moscow. Being of Puerto Rican descent, and dark-featured like myself, he had numerous run-ins with local law enforcement who appeared to provoke and harass him on a regular basis. Mild-mannered as he appeared, he was interrogated briefly in a Moscow subway car and was stripped naked by local police, leaving him with no choice but to make a mad, nude dash to the US Embassy after they deserted him with his clothes in their possession. Not wanting to be profiled yet again, and abroad, the Russian/Czech program in Prague was sounding even better as my final choice.

Soon after the racial interrogation and recount of Moscow police nightmares, I meet Alice, a fellow student who would be studying in Prague with me. She appeared to be Southern California chickie incarnate. The optimistic tall blonde gushes about her excitement for Foreign Service. The virginal New Englander is infatuated, as her looks fulfill his Aryan dream of kids who look like they pose for Kinder chocolate wrappers.

However, Alice was sweet, unlike what I tend to think of a privileged Los Angeleno. As a San Francisco Bay Arean myself, I'm acutely aware of my bias. We sit next to each other and start talking for the rest of the evening.

"I don't know if this is too weird to ask, but…can we be roommates in Prague?" Alice asks. Considering our conversation was enjoyable – albeit we had nothing apparently in common – I agreed.

We behave in accordance with our perception, not reality as it exists. Our beliefs can hold us back physically, psychologically, or emotionally. If you know how to reach beyond, alter your space out of your comfort zone, you can then tap into your potential. For years you could think that you're strong, then life, trauma, and chaos slam you to the ground. Iraq was all that for me, and everything I did felt like it required so much effort. This DC trip is an accomplishment I should be proud of, but nothing really gets my senses going. Before launching into this new chapter, I felt nothing. It was an act of going through the motions and acknowledging what was happening, but feeling an unavoidable emptiness.

Recalling how those senses got lost in the first place, a loss that occurred in heat, tension, and an unforgettable despair, transports me to this time last year.

Last summer, 2005 in Ramadi, Iraq was hell. However, the blistering heat paled in comparison to the hellfire my fellow troops and I endured with constant rocket and mortar attacks accompanied with daily firefights between us and insurgents on the streets.

At this point in time, I had just returned from my R&R leave which was a relief to me as the whole time I was away from Iraq, I somehow, missed it. It was a noisy, gunfire-filled afternoon, but it was a particular incident that quickly brought me back from my recently-returned-from-R&R mindset: five Marines were hit with multiple IEDs under their vehicle in front of the Government Center in downtown Ramadi. Those Marines were just a few of the infantry grunts that I had worked with at checkpoints with my buddy Jones on Team Lioness.

Sergeant X, one of the sergeants we knew from working mainly at Ramadi's Government Center came to the clinic in tears and made a beeline straight to me in front of Arnold and Jack. She was still in Baghdad en route to Ramadi from R&R – she didn't know yet. These two males – both who've given me hell the past year for being everything they hate: a minority, a different belief system, and a woman – looked at each other.

Jack rolled his eyes and gave a look to Arnold that said, "He wants to talk to the woman, of course."

Little did they know, I had worked with Sergeant X before and he wasn't merely trying to pick me up as they always insinuated. Of course, in their eyes my clinical skills had nothing to do with the rapport we had with these Soldiers and Marines.

Sergeant X sat down with me in our makeshift clinic cell and began telling me, "They're gone, they're gone, they're all dead!" while crying profusely into his hands.

His eyes were blaring red and I began to ask which ones were dead. "I'm glad you're here, at least you know…" he kept saying as he continued to identify the five Marines who were killed after rolling right over a spot in the road that turned out to be five 155 rounds waiting to detonate.

He then tried to change the subject, asking me how I was doing. I couldn't believe it, but I kept encouraging him to tell me more. He did, and the pain in his eyes spoke more than his tear-soaked words as though he lost family members. A lump grew in my throat as I too wanted to cry.

The urge to scream until my lungs fell out, to put my fist through a wall, the death of part of myself was overpowering. The devastation, crushing. I held my breath as my eyes burned, trying to console him, asking him to recall what he saw.

"He was still smiling," referring to one of the Marines whose face was still partly recognizable after detonation.

The turret gunner was blasted out of the vehicle immediately upon explosion and thrown meters away into a wall and the others in the vehicle were literally in pieces. I offered my advice, and since I knew him to be a very spiritual and religious guy, I consoled him along those lines; something I'm extremely reluctant to do in any case.

"They're feeling no pain now. They passed instantly and you did your very best to protect them. Pray for them, they're in God's hands now."

I wasn't even sure of anything anymore, not even God at this point.

"I know, I just have to trust God, you know," he said still crying so painfully and passionately.

These men are his brothers. Brothers from another mother as some of the Marines used to joke. Or sisters from another mister in reference to Jones and I. These guys were hilarious, brave, humble, feeling, thinking people. And now they're dead.

A slow montage of their smiles and jokes paraded through the back of my mind as I held back my own tears while helping SGT X catch his. I held my breath intermittently throughout conversation, a trick I've become accustomed to in order to halt any crying of my own. I had to put it away and deal with it later, I had to be strong for them now.

After all those months on Team Lioness, Jones and I made a vow to look at this war with open eyes. Seeing what was really going on, beyond what the Banana Republic vest-wearing war correspondents or newspapers said. We didn't want to hide from the good or evil our eyes and souls would encounter, so we stared deeply and attentively into the abyss.

Unfortunately, that abyss can certainly stare back, and for us it surely did. Were we unwise to stare into oblivion for so long? We stared so long into this living nightmare that it never left us, leaving us longing to be woken up. Running through the streets of this post-apocalyptic nightmare throughout this deployment had scarred us, changed us. I didn't realize the impact until we got back to the US, but it was there all along, waiting.

My eyes can no longer savor striking colors nor can any of my other senses indulge in anything I once enjoyed thoroughly – nothing, even the simple, makes sense anymore. This was our price to pay for leaving our eyes wide open in the darkness. We sacrificed our inner peace to help pull others out of hell, only to witness the horror ourselves, forever burning its image into our souls.

The next day? Another suicide bomber drove a car into a group of Humvees out in Ramadi. Two Humvees were destroyed and eight of our Marines were killed as a result. Just one of many Ramadi days I was constantly questioning if all of what we endured had any real purpose, and who was really profiting from all this pain. In Iraq, I built myself up to be a fortress, unable to cry or mourn openly. SGT X would become a metaphor for my homecoming; Americans comfort the male warrior, even when he cries. They shake his hand and pat his back. The female warrior is allowed no space to grieve, she is expected to hold it all in that psychological ruck sack or risk being shamed as not only weak, but someone who doesn't deserve any honor at all.

Every war is about money and resources, often with religious and political ideologies blinding and guiding the general public and disenfranchised. While resources can be finite and ultimately disappear, money doesn't; it just changes hands. In the meantime, innocent people die, you lose hope, and you're left among ruins to rebuild a life in the aftermath of trauma. Trauma from which you will never fully recover.

Once you've been in the thick of combat, the war never ends and is playing out non-stop in every chamber of the mind. When you're eating, you think of what you ate in war. When you're driving home, you think about driving in your HUMVEE across desert highways and dirt roads evading explosives or small arms fire. When you're performing the most mundane tasks, you think about how it should have been you in that ambushed vehicle that day and someone could have been spared, not you.

The anguish, the guilt of being alive, the regret of not being able to do more might as well be a bullet in one hand and being home always feels like you're holding a gun aimed at your own head in the other. The combat odyssey never ends; it's merely assuaged and managed through whichever coping mechanisms work effectively for you – if any. There is no magical fix, no single one-size-fits-all cure for PTSD. It is a process of discovery, and the challenge is to break the mind away from the seemingly endless war within the soul.

7 LONDON & MUNICH

Not too long before I left, my dad and I got into a heated argument. Being the staunch conservative that ironically received multiple checks from both his military pension and the VA – not for combat, but hurting his back during a leisure hike in Micronesia – he began going on and on about his support for George W. Bush et al. I, on the other hand, didn't agree and viewed his support for the illiterate gravy train-riding imbecile as a form of betrayal.

Infotainment-oriented corporate media was feeding his delusional visions of America; practically telling him what to think and giving him talking points to spew at perceived enemies, to include his own daughter. It disgusted me. War was not the glorious parade of valor he saw in movies.

He had never seen a war in his life, and actually joined the Coast Guard at the age of twenty-one to avoid the draft for Vietnam. He claimed that he wanted to serve his country, but didn't want to come back from Vietnam "maimed" or "crazy" like his now former friends as he put it. He was a self-proclaimed patriot who ran from the abyss of jungle warfare, much like the chicken hawks he idolized.

Then he unknowingly made a dangerous mistake when I mentioned Fox News was peddling disinformation about the ongoing war. He wouldn't listen to my input, but gladly nodded along with the Brown Shirts of mainstream media.

My father wagged his head at me, proudly, and said, "What do you know about war, you goddamned liberal communist?"

Something happened – I snapped. A black curtain dropped over my consciousness and I saw nothing but a target. In an instant, I picked up a barstool on my left and in the middle of my parents' home, I hurled it at my father and told him to go fuck

himself and shamed him as a misguided coward.
"At least I went to war, motherfucker! Where were you when they were calling your number for Vietnam? Hiding behind the Coast Guard recruiter, you tuna boat-chasing dipshit! You didn't have the stones to go to war, and now you want to project your regrets and fears onto your own daughter? I just get home from this clusterfuck of a war and neither of you have the fucking decency to listen to me? Fuck. You. Both."

My parents, both stood still and looked at me in shock, and without a word, I unclenched my fists and walked away. I had never, ever lifted a hand to anyone in my family and part of me was embarrassed for acting as I did, and another part of me was angry that people who were supposed to be there for me just didn't know how or, perhaps, really didn't even want to see what was causing me so much pain.

Dad's glorified Hollywood image of war was superficial flag waving, phallic stroking of a military-issued rifle, and writing your best gal until your homecoming hero welcome. That wasn't my image of war; it was completely non-cinematic. War, the taking of lives, never looks glamorous in real life. And people who do it rarely feel marvelous afterward either. It's as though the universe captures and records your inhumanity in those moments and it lives with you through eternity, reminding you of your baser animalistic ways even in the quietest moments.

Aside from clinically-diagnosed psychopaths, I have not met one person in war who thoroughly enjoyed killing. If someone ended up bragging over a kill, it was safe to assume that their story was mere fabrication or that they were one bad day away from an inpatient psychiatric ward. No matter how much someone may appear to deserve to be killed, something dies within us when we kill. It's contradictory, the antithesis of our species survival instinct.

Dad, programmed by Hollywood war films and right-wing pundit programs, sought to reduce a painful, soul-shredding experience in war to what he thought was a mere slap in the face to win a petty argument: a denial of my personal experience and branding me a Communist.

Such a word may as well be a sentence to exile in the United States, a McCarthyist-era attempt at social, political, and psychic murder. I lost respect for him that day, and I remain unmoved. A beast. I'm positive after our encounter he'll not soon forget the absence of human emotion and remorse in my eyes, the new daughter he had yet to meet until that moment. My mother apologized for him afterward. He later apologized in a note attached to a new shirt. I left it behind in a closet at their house.

Aside from family misunderstandings grating my nerves, there was a negative habit creeping in since my return. After the incident in philosophy class with the mouthy 19-year-old, I felt like drinking a lot more than I should. After coming home from class, I found myself developing a fondness for anything that mixed well with vodka. This wasn't a positive step in the reintegration process, and my mom, God love her with the Catholic guilt, pointed out to me that alcoholism runs in the family, motioning quite obviously at my father.

"He's Chief brave-in-the-house only, and still he needs liquid courage to stand up to his own daughter. You've seen a lot of bad stuff, so it's even more dangerous for you to be drinking. Tata drank after the war too. It made him unpredictable, not himself. Don't learn the hard way," my mom said, referring to her father for a vicarious lesson.

I listened, and stopped the post-class cocktail. In the few months before this flight to Europe in the summer of 2006, I wanted to drink more to ease the pain of guilt I felt through the emotional shock of being in the US. The world is broken, and I was quickly running out of reasons why I wanted to live in it.

After months of preparation, I packed my belongings into a carry-on sized suitcase and backpack and checked into my flight to London from Orlando International Airport. I traveled this way not because I want to impress anyone with my Army-inspired light packing, but because I don't trust checking my bags. Ever. Call it paranoia, call it what you will, but the one thing you won't call it is lost luggage or items lifted by TSA agents or other international handlers. Even on an airplane, I need a sense of control, and having everything I'm traveling with at the ready, and not under the plane or out of sight, is a must.

As I moved through the airport, I thought of how alien everything felt since my return and how desperate I was to be distracted. My plans for moving to Prague for a year were set and I mapped out the terrain as best as I could from the United States via videos, books, and any other sourced of information I could get my hands on and devour. Books covering the Czech language were scarce, and I had acquired one that had an audio companion complete with phrases I would need in everyday scenarios: basic phrases and greetings, asking how to repeat or explain words, buying food and the essentials, transportation, medical emergencies, etc.

Settling into my seat for my London-bound flight, I took a deep breath, put in my ear buds, turned up my music, and focused on how the past few months have not gone according to plan. Sure, I was dating someone and I won a scholarship to study a foreign language in Europe, but there was also a lot going on in my mind that wasn't quite right.

Departing the US for the Czech Republic was a needed hiatus, and during the flight to London, I did my best to focus on the positives of this journey. I loved traveling, or at least, I used to really enjoy it. Since I was a kid, I loved the smell of airports: cold metal, jet fuel, and coffee. There was always a sense of joy in the air, a frenetic energy that was contagious even if you didn't have a ticket in hand. Picking up relatives from the terminal or taking a flight myself used to be such a delight, but now everything in my life as of late inspired no real sense of happiness and felt hopelessly dull.

Looking around and appreciating the fact I'm alive almost felt like a lie I was desperately attempting to convince my consciousness to absorb. You're happy, you're on an airplane headed for London, then onto Munich and Prague. You're lucky to be alive, Michelle.

Nothing. As we touched ground in London, I still felt like a ghost, a sad phantom pretending to be a living, breathing person. Would it have been better if I never came back? Was it worth it to be misunderstood by those you love and severely judged by strangers?

While making my way through London's Heathrow Airport, I was keeping a mental to-do list over the next few days: meet with key staff members of the study abroad program; make sure important travel documents are always in the same, secure place;

take plenty of pictures; call home; and email Tony to let him know where I was as he was getting ready to return to Iraq for six months again.

After meeting the study abroad staff, along with a few students in the same program at the airport, we went to our hotel located in the Kensington neighborhood in downtown London. Before checking in, the study abroad staff member pretty much told us to go walk around and explore after handing us an itinerary for the following days. A few other students and I decided to ground our bags first then head out for lunch. I had to conserve money for this semester, so eating out was not something I wanted to do. However, I needed to try to be social.

Funny enough, the other American students predictably did not want to try anything seemingly exotic or too foreign to them, which included British cuisine. We ended up finding a Canadian pub and had lunch there.

Of all places we could've gone, the Americans end up at a vanilla Canadian restaurant. Pass the poutine.

Everyone seemed to be ready for a nap after the greasy food we had, so half of us decided to return to the hotel as others went on to explore London. I had visited London before in 2002, but now I was a bit older and over the hype of getting aggressively wasted and ridiculous. After I had a nap, I went downstairs in search of munchies, and ended up eating an appetizer alone in the hotel's restaurant and bar. Sitting alone in dim mood lights and trendy furniture, I pulled out my travel journal and started making note of what I was feeling, thinking, and doing throughout my journey as though I needed validation that, indeed, I was alive.

The following morning after a continental breakfast and a brief welcome orientation, we all got on our bus for a tour of London. Our tour guide was enthusiastic, and full of interesting trivia about various London landmarks and events as one would anticipate. I sat in the back of the bus, observed other students, and overheard inane conversations about everything looking "so European" and drinking "high tea" somewhere. I felt like vomiting all over the Trustafarian Children of the Corn, but instead I sought sublimation. Taking photos mindlessly, I drowned out the rest of the lobotomized conversations with earbuds blaring music deep into my cranium. I beseeched, implored the universe, "Let

Prague be filled with interesting people. For the love of life and all that is good, please let this trip be at least somewhat uplifting."

The bus tour was a nifty ride in spite of the company, and was an efficient way to see much of London in a condensed time slot. We passed by major landmarks, and occasionally got off at a few sites like Buckingham Palace, Westminster Abbey, Kensington Gardens, London Bridge, Big Ben, Saint Paul's Cathedral and more.

The weather was surprisingly beautiful and clear, unlike my first trip in 2002 which was rainy and miserable – but also done quite hung-over and with good friends. We arrived at Buckingham Palace in time for the changing of the guard in which the American students squealed with glee as I recorded the event and observed my surroundings. There were a few other female students talking about heading over to Ice Bar and a few other trendy London spots to see and be seen. I was so intensely repulsed by the monotony of the ongoing chats about me. The more I heard them talk, the more my skin crawled. I stared into my digital camera screen facing the guards, wanting desperately to climb inside the apparatus and disappear.

That night, I slept early and we boarded a flight the following morning for Munich, Germany. These few days were tight. The Prague study abroad official, Vera, came to greet us and escort us through Munich which was going quite smoothly until we arrived in Germany.

Yet there was one tiny hiccup. Apparently, one of the male students – a college student, mind you – was in a frenzied panic and demanded to fly back to London. He forgot his blankie, which was a raggedy blanket he's had since he was an infant. Fantastic. I'll be studying in Prague with adults who still use security blankets and binkies. Oh yes, America. These are the people we're sending abroad to represent us. Chew on that for a moment.

Luckily, Vera found a way to assuage the situation, retrieved the blanket successfully from the hotel, and later asked me about the American inclination to resort to childhood items for comfort. I told her that I could neither relate to the blankie bit nor the stunning affluence, but I sensed a lot of childhood regression in the group.

We made our way from the airport in Munich to the hostel in

the city. Munich, from what I saw, had clean streets and beautiful, ornate architecture. I had no expectations, really, but was simply present to soak it in. One of the study abroad staff members we met upon arrival in Munich guided us to the Hofbräuhaus am Platzl, a beer hall that was built around 1589.

The small group of us, a handful of students not interested in getting plastered the night prior to a seven-hour bus ride to Prague, decided to simply have dinner and a drink, then head back to the hostel for a good night's sleep. Once inside of the beer hall, laden with long wooden tables and beer steins, we decided to have our dinner in the crisp summer air of the beer garden. While the place was a bit touristy, it was pleasant enough not to come across as appearing like a soulless backpacker's hovel. We all made it back in one piece after dinner, engaging in small talk about jet lag, regional history, and places we wanted to see in Prague.

In the morning, we all reconvened; other students not so well. Most students here were far more interested in confining themselves to a bubble of some of the most boring circles of people I've ever met. You could tell, aside from vomit-inducing conversations about one's "net worth," that these students arrived from the womb of America's privileged, were predominantly and overwhelmingly white, and while they varied in their politics, they were all patriotically equal in their ability to aggravate and offend.

I planned on sleeping for the duration of the bus ride. The last thing I wanted to hear on a seven-hour trip through Bavaria were the trains of spoken thought by some of these people that would inspire me to leap off of the bus and run screaming into a field of hops.

On the other hand, the Czech staff members we met were amazing and helpful. The moment the American students found out I was an Iraq war veteran, they immediately kept an obviously uncomfortable distance that appeared to be a mixture of polite dismissal and contempt, with the exception of perhaps two to three people who were only superficially curious about my military past.

It felt like the responses I got were best summarized as "Boo! You've killed people in Iraq!" and "Yay! You've killed people in Iraq!"

Funny, no American student bothered asking me what I did, but immediately assumed and judged me in accordance with their projected fears, desires, and prejudices. As a minority female and now a veteran, one never gets used to this random, lazy judgment. Ever.

The feeling I was getting about Prague was not a good one. However, the atmosphere changed once an older gentleman with wire-rimmed glasses and a white beard from the Czech staff named Zdeněk approached me as we boarded the bus for Prague and asked me with widened eyes, “Were you the one in the war?”

8 PRAGUE, CZECH REPUBLIC

There's nothing quite so beautiful in the process of embracing wanderlust as the feeling of returning to a childlike state of awe and wonder. Being a foreigner in someone else's country where your grasp at conversation is limited, forces you to adjust fire, correct your senses, and alter your vision accordingly.

When you're not busy listening to other people's conversations, reading advertisements, or attempting to grasp nuances of that particular culture, all you're left with are the basics you had as a toddler.

I didn't want to look back on my pre-war life with a sense of nostalgia, nor did I want to look back on Iraq in a similar light, longing for chaos as a distraction from home front realities. All I desired was to spin the hands of the clock in the opposite direction away from my past, flinging time far ahead into the future, into strange places; places where I could possibly feel alive again. If anything, I wanted to end the pain, the loneliness, and my inability to feel joy. I walked forward, for better or worse, looking for clues of home and a way out of the emptiness.

To walk through unknown streets in cities where you are merely learning the language is to force yourself into a new state of hypervigilance. You are a traveler, and hopefully not just a tourist, and must appear calm, but maintain your bearings. Not to get too lost, too off course and without alternatives, without an escape plan in the event of a dangerous situation.

From the time we met on the bus in Munich and all the way to Prague, Zdeněk and I didn't stop talking. He became my gatekeeper to reality. He volunteered to help tutor me to get me out of my toddler-level Czech and into functional conversation at least once a week because all of the Czech classes at Charles

University were, as I was about to discover, merely sufficient enough to teach Americans how to order beer.

Zdeněk and the staff members all were intrigued about the details of my deployment to Iraq and what really goes on, but the American students all acted as though I were the stereotypical baby-killing soldier who's making everyone hate the US – or the stereotypical baby-killing soldier who makes eagles fly and Uncle Sam piss excellence. It was somewhat refreshing that the Czech staff members actually asked open-ended questions about my experience instead of leaping straight into judgment. While practically all of them were not fans of the invasion of Iraq, they wanted to know the objective truths of what was really happening on the ground whereas the American students in this group were simply content with their limited knowledge on US foreign policy.

Wanting to keep making a good impression as well as earn my DOD-funded year, I focused on learning Czech as well as I could. It wasn't easy. Since you should start learning what you want to know how to say in a new language first, I started off with profanity and military terminology. Zdeněk would sometimes blush or laugh at my translation requests, but he was thrilled to help me sharpen my Czech as others in the program didn't appear interested.

Before learning how to talk about the EU's economy or of President Havel, I was learning how to say, "What are you staring at, bitch?" and terms like rocket-propelled grenade, insurgency, chemical warfare, and securing the perimeter. It made conversations with DOD's linguistic oral examiner that much more interesting a year later.

Eventually I did learn how to communicate proficiently in other subjects, but you have to find your motivation somehow and from there you can take off. Profanity as an important first step in language learning, because if someone is pissed off at you and you're not sure what's going on, knowing a few choice words can give you a warning that something not-so-nice is about to happen if the situation escalates.

Upon arrival to the dormitory in Prague, Kolej Komenského, a former political prison converted into student housing outside of Prague Castle in the Hradčany neighborhood, I met up with Alice. The Kolej, considering the incoming group, seemed to be a perfect place for Americans wanting to stay captivated in their bubble. In a foreign country while staying blissfully ignorant of their own impact, they could pace back and forth in their own secure group, never having to travel too far outside of their institutionalized comfort zone. It was a psychological prison, a place with no bars but plenty of blind spots complemented by propaganda. It was perfect for this coddled bunch.

Alice had managed to secure the other bed in her room and reserve it just for me. Since growing increasingly repulsed by my fellow compatriots from London onward, I was glad to at least have someone I had a few things in common with – even if it was just the scholarship and a fondness of watching stand-up comedy.

Later in the evening, we made plans to walk across Charles Bridge, or Karlův most, and go to an Italian restaurant she was eager to try. Alice was excited to be in medieval-romantic Prague and had arrived to attend class for the summer and fall semesters. I planned on staying throughout the academic year.

So far, Alice disclosed that Czech classes at Charles University were not helping her meet the standards and she felt hopelessly behind. She, too, had to test through DOD and in accordance with the scholarship agreement. She ended up accompanying me a few times during the tutoring sessions with Zdeněk, but was hoping to maximize more of her time in another Czech class. After the first week of formal classes, I sensed that I needed to meet with Zdeněk as much as he could allow for it.

As Alice and I made our way through the first part of the Charles Bridge, I was stopped by a dark-featured man who was asking me directions in French. Being proficient, I responded. He then kept on in French, asking me how to get to other sites, and then he swapped over into Spanish, asking me how I knew French and where I was from. I was now not only curious, but suspicious of this exchange. I told him I was visiting from Florida, and then he started to ask me about Iraq in Arabic. Now completely on alert, I grabbed Alice's arm and began walking quickly away from the stranger. He reverted to French and said he wanted to arrange a meeting, and asked if I worked for a US government agency. As we were shoving past a crowd, he asked me aloud where I was going in Arabic, and I responded, "Malesh! (Never mind)," and kept on walking.

"What were you saying to that Gypsy dude?" Alice asked.

"Just keep walking. That guy was a spook," I replied.

"You mean like a ghost?" Alice looked around like the bridge was haunted.

"Shit, no. I mean like someone operating, well, clandestinely. Get it?" I said.

"Oh. Oh! Fuck! Really?! Are you sure?" Alice asked, slightly intrigued.

"How the hell would someone know by just looking at me that I have any sort of knowledge in French, Spanish, or Arabic, and know I'm familiar in any way with Iraq? Either he's a spook or an exceptionally gifted carnival psychic," I added.

"Do you think some people here know we're DOD students? Should we go to the Embassy and tell someone? That sure as hell never happened before," Alice said.

"We still have to go to the Embassy to check-in like the NSEP staff members mentioned, but let's see if this happens again or if we notice anything else weird in the meantime," I replied.

"Okay. Wow, that was freaking weird though. I feel like we're spies now!" Alice said beaming with pride with a giddy smile.

"Don't say shit like that out loud. I don't want to get detained or interrogated. I just want snacks and a good night's sleep!" I laughed.

Many of these bizarre moments between shady figures and loud American students were alleviated by intimate moments walking alone through Prague. Early in the morning as a light fog lifts from the city, I could be alone with my thoughts. Some cities seduce and charm their way into our hearts with their beauty, elegance, quiet calm amid the storms in life. Others may repulse us with vulgarity or anemia, a lifeless, plastic façade covering up lesions of inadequacy, which may send us reeling or running for cover. Prague was a beautiful woman dressed in cumbersome Medieval armor. She was a fallen Šarka, a woman warrior, filled with doubts over her own power, but filled with judgment and contempt - a natural, yet immature defense mechanism. Prague was exceptional, but she never felt that way about herself.

You could tell Prague, "You are perfect as you are," and she will tell you, "No, I am still not enough. Sure, I have so much within my reach, but I'm still so, so sad."

Prague nursed your melancholy, linked arms with you as you walked alone, and opened up a bottle of tears that you drank together as the sun set over the dark, glimmering Vltava.

"Life is hard. Life is unbearable. What's the point of being?" she would bellow through her rugged cobblestone streets like the lonesome golem she was at the core of her city soul.

While I often felt misunderstood by Prague's inhabitants, I felt that through my quiet strolls through the city, that Prague somehow understood me. While I took solace in the quiet morning hours, I felt there was nowhere to turn where I could relax the rest of the day.

Running, running, running through a maze of a city in a rat race for my own sanity. Home wasn't here, but it wasn't back anywhere I've traveled from Florida to Massachusetts. My last real concept of a home existed in the desert sands of Iraq, in my mind's eye. A wave of saudade swept over me as I realized home never existed at all. The concept of home felt far from my reach, and I felt sick with longing.

While I ran through renaissance, baroque, and gothic architecture in this jewel box of a metropolis, my mind built columns and walls of what a foundation for a new home could be. No one was going to tell me where home is; I knew I had to build it, I had to redefine it.

As I stopped to catch my breath on a bridge heading back to the Kolej, I looked out over the river and toward the city and sighed. Closing my eyes, I imagined my freezing wind-chapped skin was warmly kissed by the sun and that the sky was clear turquoise instead of the lonesome gray clouds above. I imagined that I was happy as I longed for the desert.

During bus rides through Moravia and other parts of Bohemia, Zdeněk and the Czech staff would ask to see my photos and share more about my experience in Iraq. They were saying how terrible it must be to have seen and experienced war, and were full of questions on what Iraqis were like, what the food tasted like, what was my daily life like getting shot at, doing convoys, and so on. It was therapeutic in such an unexpected way to be able to talk about Iraq without judgment through an intelligent, adult conversation. The Americans behind us droned on about shopping, beer, and everything else that resembled high school banter. The irony here was incredible.

Between an early afternoon and an evening class, ruminating over a class about Roma rights and Moravian sights in my head, a Czech student asked me to come along to lunch with a group of other American and Czech students at U Medvídků, a Czech pub. For a brief moment, I felt visible among my fellow Americans.

Blankie, the American student who left his security blanket in London, was going on and on about the wars in Iraq and Afghanistan at a restaurant with other students and began a long-winded rant that began to cross a boundary for me. He was bragging about the US kicking ass and laughing at the fact that he didn't have to go war as he was too valuable to have his life put at risk.

He was boastful remaining true to the obnoxious and loud American stereotype to the point that other Prague locals were visibly irritated in this noisy beer hall. I interjected, and explained that I had returned from Iraq the year before and that the mainstream media in the US is simply not enough to make an educated decision on foreign policy considering who owns Fox, MSNBC, and CNN, to name a few, let alone scream such ideas aloud in public in a foreign country. He was embarrassing not only himself, but everyone else present. I told him, and all of the other American students present, that while they're lucky they come from privileged backgrounds, they had far less of an idea about how damaging these wars have been and people's lives, military or civilian, are no joking matter.

He kept talking out of his rear and I knew it was due to immaturity and naïveté. But I had to stop this pending train wreck as I simply couldn't stand to hear him continue this soapbox diatribe. I know it shouldn't have bothered me, and sure, he was just some wet-behind-the-ears spoiled kid from Iowa with rich parents funding his inebriated adventure in Prague.

"Nobody asked you!" he said practically screaming at me from across the table, huffing and puffing in an exaggerated rage.

"I don't fucking care, and you've been blabbing for long enough and I can't stand to hear any more of your bullshit!" I was losing my patience and was even more appalled that he decided to get aggressive with me.

"Fuck off, bitch!" he blasted back, sitting proudly next to a female student from the University of Texas, who sat by his side saying nothing about his outlandish behavior. I laughed at him, told him he was pathetic, then decided to pack up, pay for my soda, and walked off. I wasn't having any more of this confrontation and I didn't want to engage further as I felt that familiar temptation kick in. I actually wanted him to try and make contact so I'd have an excuse to hurt him physically. No, no, Michelle. No Czech prison for you.

As I left, he followed, acting extra insulted alongside his female friend. I felt bad for her in being practically a shadow to this rambunctious loudmouth. He then ran ahead of me, stopped me, and put his finger in my face. Bad move. Time to calm down and breathe.

"Who the fuck do you think you are? You're not special? You just want everyone to shake your hand for Iraq and nobody cares about you! You're a killer! Hahahaha! A KILLER!" he screamed into the air and laughed maniacally. If I was this horrible killer, why the hell was he so eager to get in my face? And if no one cared about me, why did he bother to follow me to scream at me some more? Seems like he cared a lot about luring a purported killer into a fight. Was he suicidal?

"You have about five fucking seconds," I stepped closer to him putting one hand in his face and one hand in my pocket, reaching for my knife, "to get the fuck out of my face before I cut you open," I said, calmly and almost enthusiastically, perhaps wishing deep down that he would make the stupid move and put his hands on me.

"I don't have to talk to you! You're no one! You're nothing but the empire, a toy soldier, a pawn, an imperialist! This is why they shouldn't allow dumb bitches from the ghetto to study abroad!" he blasted as he walked away quickly with the female student.

"Why don't you go back to Iowa and suck on your blankie, you cowardly corn-fed Nazi!" I said aloud as they walked back to the Kolej and I back to class. That was the last time I would go to lunch with this group of American classmates.

Dealing with Blankie's outburst at me for being a veteran and blasting back on privilege was surreal. It took me a few minutes to wrap my head around what just happened. This went from microaggression to full-scale aggression in a matter of seconds. I later asked his friend if she was okay after Blankie blew up outside of the restaurant. She rolled her eyes at me and walked away. It feels as though once you've met an obedient female legionnaire of the patriarchy, you've met them all.

He called me an imperialist. Hilarious! He had money, privilege, and mobility; I didn't. If you could afford college in the US and get drunk in Europe, you are the fucking empire. I'm militarily expendable, indigenous, and poor. Not socioeconomically disadvantaged from a troubled, underrepresented group – just broke. We couldn't afford, nor did we have time to entertain, euphemisms in our lives. The only reason I could travel here was because of a DOD scholarship that was aided by the fact that I was a combat veteran. I originated from the side of the colonized, and Blankie was born of the blue-blooded privileged oppressor.

That's what separated people like Blankie and I. He could live high and comfortable on his invented bullshit, and poor naïve soldiers like me keep it going. The end of my enlistment marked the end of my tolerance to supporting people like him. Someone who expands, consumes, and destroys like cancer.

A privileged white male "mansplaining" and "whitesplaining" simultaneously to a brown woman to stay in her lane and to not make the other affluent white college kids uncomfortable with my viewpoints on class warfare and inane pop culture left me with a solid side-eye at this group. He reveled in his privilege and hubris. His idiocy was unchecked, and served as a painful reminder of how I got into Iraq in the first place, under false premises made by men just like Blankie.

It was a frightening metaphor for what the United States was becoming – a Titanic of rich, proud dimwits heading for the iceberg of anti-colonialist backlash. To think, thousands of miles away in a foreign country, I came so close to using my new switchblade. Not against a pick-pocket or in any confrontation with a local, but against an overly zealous and aggressive American who sought to cram his ridiculous beliefs down my throat.

9 KRAKOW, POLAND & VIENNA, AUSTRIA

On a bus heading for Krakow, Alice began asking about Iraq as I was just starting to write about my experience. I was writing an essay for a scholarship contest since I wouldn't have the old GI Bill anymore by the end of fall semester. I was thinking of different names to call my story, something that was so intimate to me but was such an idealist disaster. Much of my pursuits in Iraq to help others and the torment I endured made me feel like I was a younger, female Don Quixote. Except I was in Ramadi, Iraq instead of a fairytale town in Spain, and a product of Spanish colonialism, then German, then Japanese, and now American occupation. I was too much of an idealist before my deployment to Iraq and such hope for making positive change died hard with my spirit upon returning home. I was *Quixote in Ramadi.*

Alice asked, "Did living in Ramadi change how you see the world?"

"Yeah, your perspective changes a bit after having to urinate into a plastic bag inside of a bombed-out torture chamber inside Uday Hussein's old love shack on the Euphrates. You realize that everyone, and their well-intended advice on life, was dead wrong."

"Seems a bit cynical to look at the world that way, don't you think?" Alice responded.

"Sometimes I don't know if the world is being run by a clever group of people who are merely fucking with us or by a group of idiots on a mission. Either way, so many aspects of our lives are out of our control and perpetuated right under our noses. I don't know if that's just cynical, but I think it's quite realistic," I added.

Alice shook her head and laughed. "I hope not," she said.

As the long bus ride from Prague to Krakow would bring us to our hotel close to 11pm. We slept while we could.

A few hours into the darkness through Poland, the unexpected happened. While drifting off into sleep, I had a dream I was driving on a nighttime convoy in Iraq again with Jones. We conducted these night drives with various units, and I was always the driver. As her supervisor, I felt compelled to protect her the best that I could, and driving was my means of control. I fooled myself into believing amid all the horrible events happening around us, that I could keep us alive so long as I was behind the wheel and in constant motion. It was a false sense of security, but that wheel was the only thing separating me from reality. Taking the wheel meant control amid chaos, no matter how delusional.

As I drove, we were safe – or at least I kept telling myself that. After all, a moving target is harder to kill. No one could hurt us so long as my boot laid into the gas pedal, and I assured the young specialist every drive that we would be okay. The Marines we worked with called us "lucky charms" as our vehicle was never struck by an IED. In a place like Ramadi in 2005, this was an oddity. We were undoubtedly fortunate.

Suddenly, in the middle of this return to Iraq in dreamland, a cloud of dust kicked up in the dark and blocked my vision of the road. Jones warned that we were close to the edge of a drop and I swerved right to keep from rolling over into a ditch.

"HOLD ON!" I screamed at Jones as I could see other vehicles swerving in the darkness ahead of me as we took unpredictable off-road paths leading back to our base to avoid being noticed by insurgents on the main highways throughout the desert.

The blindness of the night was sometimes overwhelming and while such chaotic drives may rattle anyone's nerves, I did my best never to show Jones I was worried. As I looked to Jones on the passenger side, I saw the look of dread in her eyes as though she completely woke up to the horrors we pretended we didn't live through.

I saw her fully awake and I thought, "No, it's just a dream. Tell yourself this isn't real until we make it home." That look was a familiar one throughout the Iraq war. That moment when someone experienced a permanent change, a look that indicated all prior youthful hopefulness was a lie, and that the world is a terrible place filled with horrible people with odious intent. It was the moment of spiritual death, a psychic break where one can no longer reconcile the atrocious reality with any logical conclusion. We were all doing our best to avoid being crushed by war's blind boot stomp, and we were all lying to ourselves that it would never be us, that we were invincible.

"Jones," I reached out across to her in the HUMVEE as I drove, grabbing her arm as though to shake her back into the denial, the lie that everything was going to be okay once we got home, and that we would make it back to our mundane stateside realities and live life like nothing happened. I could feel myself, my hope and spirit, dying too.

"Michelle?" Alice said to me in the pitch darkness as we approached Krakow.

Fully awake, I still felt that the rumbling of the bus was my HUMVEE in Iraq. I was confused and took a moment to get my bearings, to get back to reality. My eyes were wide open and I was reaching out to Alice like I was to Jones in the dream.

"Are you okay? You look like you just saw a ghost?" Alice said.

"I thought I…," I paused and shook my head, "never mind. It was just a dream," I said. "How far are we from Krakow now?" I asked as Alice continued to look at me with genuine concern.

"We're supposedly real close," she said.

Neither of us knew what to expect in Krakow and quite a few Prague locals mostly had negative comments about Poland in general, and nothing great to say about Krakow. After we arrived and checked into our hotel, we decided to go out and hunt for food. It was late in the storybook city, but there were a few places still open and serving food.

We wandered toward the main square of Krakow, the largest medieval town square in Europe. Instead of the dirty or perverted looks I got in Prague, I got smiles and hellos. Alice, who got accustomed to far better treatment for being tall, blonde, and a racially-acceptable white female in Prague, was a bit perplexed at the attention I was getting in Krakow.

I brushed off all advances – whether with a smile in Krakow or a perverted grimace in Prague – but she kept bringing it up. It was apparently bothering her that someone dark-featured was desirable in a country where she thought she'd be getting the attention. Local men made no bones about telling me I was beautiful and to have a good evening, as opposed to something derogatory or receiving a sexual proposition in Prague.

We finally stumbled upon a Georgian restaurant in the main square that was still hopping late this night and we were quickly seated by – gasp! – friendly wait staff? This was new. People in Prague were lying through their teeth about Krakow. There were quite a few other Russian and Georgian restaurants in the area as well as a few jazz clubs going into the wee hours, but Alice and I headed back to the hotel; which was reminiscent of the interior in The Shining. Red rum, anyone?

The following day, Zdeněk took us on a guided tour, some of which bowed out to go shopping and exploring on their own, through various parts of the city. We began our walking in a group of maybe ten through the main city gate and visited a variety of churches, Wawel Castel, Jagiellonian University, and made it to the Jewish quarter as the sun set. Before we made it back to the hotel, we stopped at a nearby park to visit a statue that was seemingly important for Zdeněk to share with us.

The Dzok Monument is located near the Dragon's Den between the Wawel Hill and the Vistula River. Reportedly, the dog depicted in the sculpture comes from a story of a dog owner failing to retrieve his dog due to a heart attack. Being loyal to his owner, the dog waited and waited in the same spot and eventually died. People in the area decided upon having this statue constructed in the dog's memory to memorialize enduring love and loyalty. Thanks, Zdeněk.

The following morning took us through one of the first moments in which I experienced a familiar smell, and quite possibly an olfactory hallucination. We walked through the gates with the "Arbeit Macht Frei" writing above at Auschwitz II and all those films on the Holocaust I saw started to come back to me. We wandered through areas on our own through barracks that housed rooms filled with luggage, human skin rolled into a fabric pile to make lamps and other common household pieces, shoes, human hair, and by far the most devastating, baby's clothes. It was terrible, depressing, and a reminder of evil in the world that I knew quite well.

How easy it was to single out populations and utilize propaganda, military might, and segregation to wipe out families, communities, and races. How easy it is to justify it through fear, slander, and profit. But as we walked along the railroad tracks in Birkenau, that's when I smelled it: the scent of burnt flesh.

Not since Ramadi did I experience such an overwhelming odor, one that almost smelled like the burnt flesh of an animal, but even before you can look to confirm it, your mind, body, your entire being knows it's human. We walked through the barracks with nail marks on the wall and chilling conditions that stood in the shadows of the former crematoria. I asked Alice if she smelled anything. She said no. It didn't seem like anyone was catching any peculiar scent, or the eerie feeling of death lingering in the walls.

After Iraq, I accepted death, and was no longer afraid. As a result, I cared less and less of what people thought of me and spoke my mind with minimal filtration. There are people in this world who might appreciate honesty devoid of sugar-coating or lifeless euphemistic language, but there are some who can't handle it. Life is far too precious and short for euphemisms, filters, or not standing up for what matters.

Unfortunately for all of us, some of the people who don't like hearing horrible truths hold important political offices or leadership positions where objective facts would most likely hurt their position. Setting them free to an unemployment line would be nice, but propagandists, sociopaths, and the like will never leave quietly. They will bribe, scam, and kiss enough ass to cover their own. When you come to terms with your own limited existence on this planet, you start to see your enemies in a clearer light, and said foes will do anything to continue prolonging pain and suffering for their personal gain.

The visit to Auschwitz and Birkenau made me think about Iraq for the entire duration of the bus ride back across the border from Poland, and on through Ostrava, Olomouc, and finally back to Prague. It made me think of how easy it was to perpetuate such violence, damage, and propaganda on a massive scale. As Chamorros faced genocide imposed by Nazi allies, Imperial Japan, this visit amplified my sense of distrust for any government-imposed movement.

Closer to the end of the semester was the final group trip to Vienna, Austria. This by far demonstrated how much I had to budget, which was based on the few hundred dollars I had to spend per month. Not per day, per week, but per month. The GI Bill I had left in 2006 was not the GI Bill that came along years later that provided thousands per month for veterans, and I had to make due with plenty of ramen and actually spent my time in Vienna eating…

Vienna Sausage.

The city was so expensive that buying a soda and a pack of AA batteries for my camera almost cost me what I spent on food in Prague in a week. Lucky for me, I had canned mystery meat. Instead of going out on a shopping spree like the other students, I walked around and took pictures, then returned to my room at Hotel Alpha to eat Vienna Sausage from a can then go to bed. I was looking forward to waking early in the morning to beat everyone to breakfast. After a little research, I found that the breakfast at the hotel we were staying at had meats, eggs, breads, and pastries galore. So, before 6am, I quietly walked down to the breakfast area, which was completely empty and ate as much as I could.

While collecting and rationing food was quite normal for me as a former military brat and soldier, doing it now as a broke student abroad wouldn't appear so odd if others were needing to do it too. Everyone else around me had the ability to eat out several times a day and have money left for leisurely shopping. I thought it was so bizarre not to be in survival-mode like me, but it's a way of living I've always known.

In order to be able to eat later in the day, I packed bread and other pastries wrapped in napkins and stuffed them in my bag like military rations. Before anyone could come down and seeing me pack pastries away like a squirrel hiding away nuts for winter, I zipped back up to the room to put some of my collection of food aside for dinner, and some to take with me on the walking tour through the city.

The following morning, I attacked breakfast again with the same modus operandi of acquiring extra food clandestinely and in hopes of not getting too hungry before we reached Prague again. My mind was elsewhere – on food, mostly – as we wandered through the artists' dream, the Hundertwasse Haus, and then concluded the Vienna tour with Schonbrunn Palace. Being in

Prague was already a reminder of who were the haves and the have nots, and that I belonged in the latter. Vienna amplified that truth, and despite the beautiful surroundings, one cannot avoid such an ugly reality.

After I returned from Vienna, a trip Alice skipped in order to savor a bit more of Prague before her time in the program was done, we planned a dinner outing to catch up on our time apart. We were craving Indian food and Ivana, one of the Czech study abroad advisors, was telling us about a Himalayan restaurant near her house that she really liked and suggested that we give that a shot. When we arrived at Shalamar, there was only one other table taken upstairs, and downstairs, in a dimly lit wine cellar-like setting, we had the space all to ourselves.

Alice and I were comfortable and began sharing stories about bizarre run-ins with transportation ticket enforcement, interesting stories from locals or new friends, and everything and anything else. As soon as we ordered, an older man arrived and sat at the table next to us. He was alone, and began taking an interest in us, much to our chagrin.

As the food began to roll out, he ordered and began asking us how we liked Prague and what we like to do for fun. We kept our answers short, and perhaps it was my Iraq-inspired paranoia or Prague's general distrust for anyone rubbing off on me, but I wasn't getting a great feeling from being near this odd gentleman.

He was an Anglo-American male, dressed a bit eccentric like he fell off the set of Miami Vice back in the 1980s. He topped off the pretension when he asked if I cared to join him in an aperitif. Just a tip: if you're an American abroad offering anyone an aperitif, you sound like a boring, one-dimensional asshole who's desperately trying to come off as worldly. I declined. Alice was looking at me nervously as we began to eat. I motioned with my left hand, out of his line of sight, when I could to pick up the speed of our consumption. I hated eating fast but I didn't want to desert my dinner either. We were making great time chowing down on our meals, which were excellent but now forced.

Then he asked the question that tipped me off that it was time to leave, and luckily a server was there to issue the check at once. My hopes for a normal night were dashed.

"So, what exactly did you do during your service in Iraq? Did you enjoy your line of work?" he asked, looking at me while he delicately sipped his aperitif.

Not only was his presence making us uncomfortable enough to scarf our food, something I absolutely loathed and always have since Army Basic Training in having forty-five seconds to eat, but he was now traipsing on my sacred ground. Who the hell was he to ask about Iraq? I had no Iraq or military-related insignia on me at the time, and we weren't even discussing the topic in the restaurant or on the way to Shalamar for that matter.

"Okay, you now have my attention. What do you want?" I said putting my utensils down and looking him in the eyes, waiting impatiently for a response.

"I'm just curious if you might want to discuss a career opportunity," he said, and as Alice finished up her plate he mouthed the three letters of a US-based intelligence agency.

"Ha! You've gotta be fucking kidding me," I laughed, irate with a turning stomach.

Alice looked up and motioned with her eyes to him, then me, mouthing the words inaudibly, "What's going on?"

"We're going to go," I said while we got our cards back from the server.

He went on about contacting each other and gave me his number. I declined, then left with Alice expeditiously and caught transportation back to the Kolej instead of walking.

"This is just getting too weird. We need to go to the Embassy," Alice added. I declined, thinking it wouldn't make much of a difference. If this guy was who he said he was, that's probably where he worked.

Prague had me feeling like James Bond, but not in the cool, sexy way one might think. It was more of a solitary survival, think-on-your-feet deal.

In the military and at home, there's typically a base to go to, a unit or home in which one could return. In Prague, I was on my own, and Alice was a bit too green to be of any help. Intel agencies attempting to recruit, unknown dangers lurking around the corner and the absence of weapons forced me to create escape routes, resources, and contacts. Out of necessity, I created my own network, safe houses, and designated people, often unbeknownst to them, as my insiders to places I typically wouldn't have access.

This was like Iraq+, where I was relying less on firepower and armor and more so on wile and adaptability. Prague became, unexpectedly, the unspoken next level of survival.

The need for adrenaline, camaraderie, and purpose were the three main points I had come to identify as motivational necessities. If I didn't see all three in my midst, I knew it was time to move on. But if I couldn't leave, I found ways to make situations work until I could successfully depart. From the time I came home from Iraq, and felt abandoned by those I hoped who would help me, I knew I had to start defining my personal boundaries for my own safety as well as others. There were noticeable lines I didn't want others to cross with me, and I had to figure out every other boundary that may potentially lead me into danger, or to become dangerous to someone else.

Boundaries exist to maintain self-respect and self-care. Without boundaries, we potentially allow people to cross lines of respect, safety, and sanity. With boundaries, I can free myself from the confines of external judgment. I'm liberated to be who I want. Boundaries are guidelines in how you want to be treated, and I encourage you to have your boundaries, to build your safe zone, your sacred space within. Altar your space by declaring what you want and need, and you will find your home, a sacred area to feel safe no matter where you are. Eventually. In the meantime, and until then, I kept running through this strange city in search of the ever-elusive safe home.

On the last week of our stay before winter break, Alice and I had stayed up late one night watching stand-up comedy on my laptop, then trailed off into other circular banter. It got quiet as both of us were drifting off into sleep as snow flurried into the city.

"Michelle?" Alice asked.

"What's up?" I yawned.

"What did it feel like to come back?"

We didn't talk about Iraq much aside from our chats with the Czech staff, but I knew she was curious. I paused and looked up at the ceiling and took a deep breath.

"Initially," I said, "I was angry that I didn't return home in a coffin. I was jealous of those who died because being alive feels a lot like purgatory, sometimes hell. Often, it feels as though I'm locked in an asylum and completely cognizant, almost too conscious, of my situation, while I watch everyone else lick the windows and twirl in delirium. It's hard to justify one's own existence in that state, and dying doesn't sound so bad most of the time."

She was quiet for a moment. I could feel her eyes peering at me through the darkness as I continued to stare upwards, not wanting to engage in what could turn into a longer, emotional conversation. Then she said, "I hope you don't feel that way anymore, Michelle."

I closed my eyes. I couldn't say no, that I didn't feel that way without lying to her.

"Good night, Alice."

10 PRAGUE 8

Travel can sometimes push us to lose ourselves and find ourselves at once. The shedding of old prejudices, dead skin, and the opening of one's eyes is far better than what any mainstream news outlet could ever tell you. After Iraq, I felt compelled to remain in motion, mobile, on the go in perpetual voyager status. Coming back as a war veteran left me feeling like a nomad, a refugee, one without a country who was a constant moving target escaping death.

After making it to Prague, I caught a cab as the sun was setting to head to my new apartment in Prague 8, a residential area in the north. This semester, I switched to a different school, the Anglo-American College in Mala Strana. From what I could tell, the student body was quite diverse, and classes were certainly not going to be dominated by American students.

It took about forty-five minutes to make it to my new place and like the last time, I packed light: one roller carry-on suitcase and a black backpack. Upon my arrival, I met my three new flatmates in the two-bedroom set-up, named Betsy, Sara, and someone we came to call Hurricane Hattie.

Hurricane Hattie, with whom I of course was sharing a room, was, well, a fucking disaster. When I walked in, there were piles of stuff everywhere, to include my side of the room.

"Oh, so sorry about that, let me take my clothes out of your storage area!" she chirped, as she began shoveling her belongings onto an already large pile on the floor.

She had completely made herself at home, no doubt. I quickly unpacked everything into the shelves of the rolling garment rack, clothes already neatly folded and still done in accordance with Army regulations of rolling and storage. After putting up some pictures next to my bed of Tony and I, unloading a few toiletry items onto the skinny white shelf above my IKEA single bed, I was done. Hurricane Hattie looked perplexed at my side of the room.

"You're one of those military neat-freaks, aren't you?" she asked, appearing a bit self-conscious and twiddling nervously, while going on about her habits and peccadillos.

"Kind of. You can arrange your stuff how you want on your side of the room so long as I have my own space. That's all I ask," I said smiling, hoping to assuage the palpable anxiety.

"Sure! Great!" she squealed, "So, can I show you something, now that we're going to be roomies?!" she asked brimming with excitement.

Please let it not be a stuffed dead pet. I was getting that unstable vibe, but kindly agreed. She then pulled out what appeared to be a self-made passport booklet, but instead of the word 'passport', it said 'sexport'. Oh. No.

She handed it to me and I opened it before her, hoping beyond all hopes that a used condom wasn't going to fall out. Luckily, no prophylactics. However, there were hand-drawn flags of countries all over Europe. Oh. Hell. No.

"So, every time I visit a new country or meet a cute foreign guy, when we hook up, I put a stamp of their flag in my sexport!" she said laughing hysterically.

Her best friend, who was studying in London at the time, was doing the same sexport deal and they were competing who could leave Europe with the most flags; or with more STDs.

I was now a bit apprehensive of getting to know Sara and Betsy who shared the other bedroom near the entrance. But, I walked out anyway and started talking with both of them in the living room. To my luck, they were friendly. Betsy, a peace-loving environmentalist from Wisconsin. Sara, a creative artisan and anthropology major from Michigan. We immediately discovered a shared love for international cuisine – no matter how intimidating – and a variety of other interests in books, music, art, etc. Since Alice was already gone and I wasn't at the noisy, brat-filled Kolej anymore, I was relieved to have a place to stay in a quiet neighborhood on Nad Hercovkou in Prague 8 with people I already liked.

To conserve money, since I had no more GI Bill funds and was relying on savings, I mostly ate at home and went out after class only when I knew I had enough to spend. Often, I continued my cost-free solo walks through Prague. Later, Sara and Betsy started to go out exploring with me, going out to Bohemian tea houses and bizarre art shows.

This time around in Prague, despite Hurricane Hattie, was a bit easier. I continued studying Czech with Zdeněk, and on occasion, Betsy would join us in the lessons. The racial tension was still there in the city, of course, but I was happier to be making friends with a more international crowd at the new college and being able to return to a place that was comfortable and filled with people who didn't treat me with contempt.

Tony was supposedly returning to the US shortly since his time in Iraq was ending. However, I had noticed a few odd things online in his interactions with other women, one in which posted love letters supposedly from Tony. I took screenshots of the proclamations of love, promises to see one another, and it made me feel that this person who I thought was tender, real, a friend in such a lonely time in my life was a fraud.

We were arguing for days and he denied any flirtations were serious. He claimed that he didn't mean to lead other women on, but I wasn't convinced. He seemed to be in a bit of a rush to get married, and I was getting increasingly nervous. His fellow Marines buddies in Iraq called me, wrote me, reassuring me that these love letters were a farce and nothing to fret about.

If anything was causing stress during this semester, it was him, but I did my best to focus on learning Czech, going to class, and enjoying Prague as much as I could and with what little money I had.

Most nights I couldn't sleep. Insomnia was returning in addition to stomach problems as I tried to figure out ways to calm my mind and the nausea. At around 2am, I heard strange noises coming from near the front door and then in the kitchen. While Prague was relatively safe, I was suspicious of any unfamiliar noises and grabbed a knife I kept near me at all times. More noises were coming from the kitchen so I quickly shot up out of bed. I flung the door open with a knife in my hand and switched on the lights, illuminating the small living room and kitchenette space.

Blood rushed to my face as I muttered the words, "You dirty fucker."

Across the room from me in our kitchenette stood Sara with a spoonful of chocolate just millimeters away from her mouth in one hand, and a jar of half-eaten Nutella in the other. For the first month in Prague 8, there was a disappearing Nutella conspiracy. An unsolved mystery. No one owned up to it. I had come home from nights of being harassed and treated like garbage by Czechs in the city and would often look for comfort in a piece of dry toast and Nutella and I had typically found emptied jars that were obviously scraped clean and put back in the cabinet. I just needed chocolate on the bad days, but it was often MIA. Blasphemy. Just fucking blasphemy, Sara.

"Busted," Sara said with a sheepish smile.

I rubbed my eyes as it adjusted to both light and disappointment. "Just buy two more jars, dude," I mumbled as I walked back to bed. "And stop Bogarting all the damn chocolate!"

I really liked Sara and Betsy, but we all loved bad-day chocolate too.

Throughout the semester, everyone would travel to another country or head to a small town in the Czech Republic to go exploring. On occasion, we would go together to places like Čáslav, Karlovy Vary, Plzeň, to name a few. We'd take pictures, share food, and generally just enjoy the travel. I didn't feel compelled to explain myself, and felt happy not being interrogated or judged by them. We were considerate of each other, except for an ongoing Nutella war, and were simply enjoying the present.

Hurricane Hattie was gone almost every weekend, and mostly I think she was yearning to find herself. A week went by near mid-semester since Hurricane Hattie returned from her trip through Italy. She took the train down and followed a Rick Steves-narrated travel guidebook that took her through the Italian countryside and small towns that ultimately led her to Rome. She was beaming when she returned, showing us all the treats and souvenirs she had acquired in Italy, to include an Italian stamp in her sexport.

Fantastic, another graphic story is on the way. She was bursting at the seams to tell us about her Italian adventure that involved finding one of the bartenders that Rick Steves gushed about somewhere in Emilia Romagna or Tuscany en route to see the film setting of "Under the Tuscan Sun." Hurricane Hattie went out of her way to chat up this bartender and then slept with him that same night. Apparently, things went south after quite a bit of aggressive anal sex and while she was glowing in her supposed bragging rights, you could tell by her expression of smiling teeth but confused eyes that her night did not sound as sexy as she had imagined.

"Wow," said Sara, apparently appalled and not wanting to encourage Hurricane Hattie's behavior. But like everyone else who saw her, she was a train wreck that you couldn't stop gawking at in horror. Just when you thought she had maxed out her ability to rape your psyche with her outlandish stories, she pulled out the excavation crew via vulgar spoken word and took you that much deeper into her depraved, attention-starved rabbit hole. Needless to say, my hope for her to find herself, at least a bit, in her travels was dismal at best now.

Hours later after her fireside chat about getting reamed by an Italian bartender, I wandered over to our restroom where I spotted the largest bowel movement I have ever seen in my entire life. It was already a long week, and part of me really wanted to weep in sheer frustration, but then I started to laugh. Mind you, Czech toilets have somewhat of a shelf where your "business" can sit on top and not get fully flushed. Sometimes, you must cover it up with toilet paper and push it along with a plunger or toilet brush.

That was awful enough, but witnessing the elephant-grade turd in the toilet, sitting quite high enough that it practically peeked out of the toilet like an over-baked loaf of bread that was ready to be cooled is what really set it off. It was a Pringles can-sized excrement and it was the most disgusting display of a rough sexport weekend Hurricane Hattie had ever shared other than occasionally foul vaginal odor.

There was no keeping it together after that point. We have gone way too far down this portal and I couldn't simply keep quiet anymore. I then called Sara and Betsy to take a look. They appeared concerned that I was calling them to the bathroom, thinking something was wrong with the toilet or piping, until they laid eyes on the big brown Kraken.

"The bartender!" Betsy gasped, and all three of us burst out laughing. We laughed loud enough that Hurricane Hattie overheard and asked what we were talking about.

"Uh, Hattie, you've left us a souvenir from Italia!" Sara said, struggling to keep the laughter under control.

"OH MY GOD!" Hurricane Hattie exclaimed as she bolted down the hall toward the bathroom as we stood outside the door doubled over with laughter.

"I'm so sorry you guys! I'm so, so sorry!" Hurricane Hattie said, obviously mortified, but aware of her carelessness on a whole new level.

"I was having such a shitty week and I'm sorry you're embarrassed, but I think we all needed a good laugh!" I added.

"Does it hurt?" Betsy asked, sounding genuinely concerned for Hurricane Hattie's colon.

"Seriously, that shit didn't even seem human," Sara said.

In a matter of seconds, Hurricane Hattie was over her embarrassing episode and continued on with the other sexcapades she had encountered while in Italy, Germany, and most of Western Europe. Hurricane Hattie spoke miles a minute, gushing about her interactions with random dudes, beaming with pride.

I know I may sound like a judgmental asshole – which I won't deny in most cases – but I was concerned about Hurricane Hattie's low self-esteem. Albeit her stories were horrifying at times, but it made me wonder what it took for her to care so little about herself to use sex as a form of currency to buy counterfeit love. This wasn't about mere sexual adventurism; this was about approval. What determines your outcome is heavily influenced and dominated by your most powerful belief about yourself. We behave and act in accordance not with our real potential, but with our perceived self-worth. The lesson here, I suppose, is to really evaluate your self-worth and learn to like who you see in the mirror – or else you might find yourself getting boned by a guidebook bartender.

Spring Break:

Airline tickets, passport, packed bags. I took pause at an airport café inside Prague-Ruzyně International Airport before my flight to Brussels, then onto JFK in New York, then finally, Boston Logan. Hovering over my travel journal, I doodled mindlessly while chewing on a day-old sandwich in the early morning hours of my spring break from classes at Anglo-americká vysoká škola, attempting to avoid storm cloud feelings of doubt.

The wheels in my head turned as I tried to ignore the obvious. Tony had purchased an engagement ring not long before I discovered a trail of romantic pursuits he sought out online. My insides twisted, and it wasn't just about love letters to other women. There was something else about him aside from my fear of his philandering, and in spite of it all, he proclaimed his love to me with tears in his eyes. When we arrived to a snowy, frozen pond outside of his parent's home near Worcester, Massachusetts, he pulled out a ring, officially asking me to marry him – and I said yes. As snow swirled around us, I railed against my intuition by giving him a second chance.

His mother seemed to be a bit uneasy about the ring, and made an odd comment that my ring was bigger than hers. How that was Tony's problem, I had no idea. But the initial interaction from the smiles I got his parents changed to what looked like anxiety. The week flew by in a blur with Tony heading back to Camp Lejeune and I back to the Czech Republic.

During a weekend where the approaching summer weather brightened the skies and caused us to shed the layers of clothing we wore in winter and spring, we boarded a van with Sara and few Czech staff members and headed for Čáslav, Zdeněk's hometown. Listening to the calm narration of Zdeněk in Plzeň, Krakow, Vienna, and Moravia often felt like guided meditation. I got lost in his passion for history, language, food, and his eagerness to learn about everything and everyone around him. At a picturesque picnic in the forest, I finally had a chance to relax before we were scheduled to leave the Czech Republic.

Upon arrival to this sleepy area, the trees embraced us and welcomed us to a river where we barbecued sausages and drank wine and beer until the evening.

"Do you like my hometown, Michelle?" Zdeněk asked.

"It's gorgeous, and to have grown up around all this natural beauty must make you homesick while you're in Prague," I said.

"Yes, sometimes one must leave and go into the nature," Zdeněk replied.

Czechs simply don't say they're going camping or spending time outdoors. They say, in Czech, that they are going "into the nature" as though nature, příroda, is beyond a place in the woods or other forms of terrain, that nature was a state of mind and had the ability to reverse the crippling, chaotic aspects of life.

In Zdeněk's mind, příroda was this beautiful forest with clean, cool water cutting through, as the sun shone down through fresh leaves on this quiet, idyllic paradise. However, my sense of příroda was drawing me back to an unusual place: the desert.

When I dreamed of the desert, it wasn't just Iraq. I was in a place that was dry and rocky, with clean air and high altitude. In my mind's eye, I saw sand, cacti, visions of surreal beauty that transported me to unusual places in my mind that were pushing me toward creativity. When I woke, and my příroda was gone, I carried a sense of sadness within that I couldn't quite explain.

In the midst of my saudade, my wanderlust and irreverence remained symbiotic. I've naturally been curious about the world around me, and even with my post-war cynicism, there is still a sense of childlike wonder that is always looking around me as if it were the first time. Perhaps there was a sense of duty within me to do so as others who didn't make it back from Iraq will never have such a luxury again. I knew I needed to force myself to continue moving, closely examining the world while praising innovation and mocking anyone or anything via art that would cause us to backpedal. As I've observed some of the most bizarre and sidesplitting works in Prague, I've accepted that nothing is sacred – from checked baggage to shit stacks. If my work ever appears to insult, know that it is not because I threw the first punch, but my creative endeavors will serve as a gadfly to provoke change where it is needed. As much as it pained me to get back into creating art on a regular basis, since Iraq sapped my creative mojo, I knew I had to eventually take the leap and get back to work.

As the semester came to a close, I had new friendships with people from all over the world and other areas of the US, more photos, and better experiences that really opened another door in my consciousness. Repacking my belongings with no regrets, I knew I made the right choice in leaving my comfort zone in the US. Now, I was far more prepared to keep writing my experiences from Iraq down and letting some of those traumatic events out of my system. I wasn't sure where to start aside from writing things down as it was the only thing outside of travel that was helping, but at least I knew something was working.

Before my departure back to the US, Zdeněk invited me out for coffee at the 1920s built Café Imperial on Na Poříčí in Prague 1. Saying goodbye to Zdeněk was a must above all else. Some of the stories I shared about Iraq and him of WWII and Soviet occupation proved to be mutually therapeutic. He told me that he loved me like his own daughter and hoped I write wonderful things one day about my travels in a place I could truly call my home. He knew why I was traveling and that it wasn't mere wanderlust or youthful curiosity. He grasped my hand and told me to be easy with my heart and one day it would be whole again.

"Even with all your military toughness, you are sugar on the inside," he said laughing. I could see him start to tear up through his silvery hair-lined glasses, as his muscles twitched around his white beard.

"Don't let the world make you close yourself off and be cold. You're a good girl who really cares about others. When you find your příroda, go to it quickly, and be happy again."

As numb as I thought I was, my eyes welled up. All that we had shared over the past year was some of the most healing aspects of my time abroad. There wasn't anything beautiful enough, no words sufficient to express my gratitude. In this blink of an eye in time, Zdeněk pulled me back into the world by sharing his world with me. No judgment, no malice. Just kindness and compassion. I hugged ol' Papa Smurf Zdeněk after our coffee and as I boarded the tram, I waved good-bye to him, holding myself together as I saw him waving and wiping away his tears.

11 SAIPAN, NORTHERN MARIANA ISLANDS

The last time I was in Saipan was in 1998 to see my dying grandfather Enrique, "Tata" as we called him. I didn't pay any heed to another uncle's words as my mind was made up and I would enlist in the US Army a few days after my 17th birthday. I just focused on getting to Saipan. Being a large family, we all either slept in the available beds or woven mats laid out on the floors of other rooms. My mother and I slept in my grandparent's room.

My grandfather, still a tall man at eighty-six years had withered away from leukemia to barely ninety pounds. A survivor of the Japanese occupation and brutality on the Chamorro people in WWII, he was in line to be beheaded after he had been accused by the Japanese for concealing the whereabouts of American troops. The Japanese had so mercilessly slaughtered the Chamorros and put them into internment camps, but no one is more stubborn than we! As Shinto shrines were erected, indigenous Chamorro Animist and Catholic sites burned and a list of dead Chamorros rose like chimney smoke as Imperial Japan was succeeding in modeling their occupation and ethnic cleansing methods after Nazi Germany.

Tata had witnessed heads rolling on the ground in the execution line in front of him in Marpi, Saipan, being ordered to dig their own graves, all the way until Japanese troops were scrambling as American troops landed to capture and liberate the island. As I sat up writing and keeping an eye on Tata throughout the day, I remembered him looking right at me, and perhaps right through me, for hours. Occasionally I'd look up, smile and nod, ask if he was okay, and other times I'd just quickly return to my writing. My mother, curious as to what he was thinking about, asked why he stared at me as he did and he replied in a labored breath, "Suette." Lucky.

In Chamorro culture, there is a belief that before we die, we can see the fate of our loved ones, who they really are and what they'll become and what lies before them. When Tata called me lucky, I had no idea what he meant. Lucky to be alive after spending a year in Ramadi, Iraq? Lucky that I didn't get court martialed for mutiny because I had a penchant for keeping a travel journal in my cargo pocket that documented my unit's corruption? I walked around with a rucksack of guilt for being alive and while I knew that I should be grateful, I wouldn't exactly call what I was feeling lucky.

In the US, schools barely touch upon WWII in the Pacific, and in the end, we feel sorry for the Japanese. But no one in American schools talks about what the Japanese did, and how they were wiping out indigenous people of Oceania and torturing the rest of East Asia. Imperial Japan was brutal, inhumane, and their alliance with Nazi Germany was evident in everything they did and everywhere they went. They were serious soldiers who were excellent at genocide.

Before Tata passed away from Leukemia, my uncle Danny, a typically stoic and silent Army Ranger who had deployed around the world like many of us in the family, asked if Tata could ever forgive the Japanese for what they did. It was an important question, one in which involves the deepest hurts and trauma. It was the first time I had heard anyone ask how he felt outside of vaguely disinterested requests for recounting old stories for my cousins' school projects.

Mind you, there are no Chamorro holocaust museums or lobbyist groups to counter Japan's narrative, or lack thereof, when it comes to war crimes; we are in a very similar boat with Native Americans, preferably silenced. Tata said he had forgiven the Japanese. He was at peace before passing, even though there was no apology for anything the Japanese did, no reparations, not a thing. He forgave them. It wasn't worth his time to hold onto the anger.

Yet in that valiant forgiveness comes a vacuum of accountability on the part of imperial invaders like Japan and Spain. Like rapists, they forced themselves onto the indigenous, fucked them violently and mercilessly, and then denied any accountability. It must be nice to do as you please with minimal to no consequence – free of remorse. Tata still forgave them.

If you attended high school in the U.S., Manzanar, the California-based internment camp for Japanese-Americans, was usually discussed from a position of compassion, along with Hiroshima and Nagasaki survivor stories. On the other hand, you would be hard-pressed to find anyone in the world - let alone the U.S. - who's heard of Matansa. In fact, you would be lucky to find anyone who believes there is any Pacific Island not located in the South Pacific instead of the North Pacific, which is anything north of the Equator. South Pacific. You know, that musical that apparently ruined Oceania's geography for millions of Americans. Essentially, whether you're familiar with Julie Andrews fuckery or not, we've had little control about how our history, culture, identity is handled and communicated throughout the world. Hell, few people know we exist.

Matansa. It means massacre in the Chamorro language, and is a nickname for the village of San Roque in the northern part of the island of Saipan that endured the most brutal slaughtering as a punishment for Chamorro resistance by Imperial Japan in WWII, which was part of an ongoing ethnic cleansing campaign that almost completely wiped out the Chamorro population from the face of the earth. San Roque is my family's village.

They hacked relatives and non-relatives with machetes and threw people into pits, doused them in kerosene and lit them on fire. My grandfather, who was previously working as a machinist and farmer when the Japanese arrived, was taken prisoner by the Japanese, and was a typical unarmed Native. Like many other Chamorros who were put into concentration camps, they were tortured and interrogated over the whereabouts of American troops who were hiding during reconnaissance of the island. Marine Navajo Code Talkers along with their fellow troops with 2nd Marine Division invaded on the day that my grandfather was scheduled to be executed, June 15, 1944. If it weren't for the Navajo language (Diné), Chamorro people would have been wiped out by the Japanese through their use of torture and concentration camps modeled after the Nazi design. And they were pretty close.

Unfortunately, the film *Windtalkers* entirely dismissed and overlooked what happened to Chamorros and deleted us out of the picture all together. *Windtalkers* was handled, quite ignorantly, by Hong Kong film director John Woo. The film did, in fact, lightly touch upon the racial persecution Native American code talkers endured during WWII and how they played a crucial role in US military victory in a hard-won Pacific campaign, which is barely discussed in the realm of US history in grade school or at the University level for that matter. Anyone who's attended public high school in the US can attest to the European theater of WWII dominating the discussion, and quite disproportionately.

The film featured fierce combat between Imperial Japan and the United States, and showed exemplary courage and humility among Native code talkers. However, Chamorros – who endured ethnic cleansing at the hands of the Japanese on the island of Saipan, where the battle took place – were completely absent from the film. It was as though the entire indigenous population of the island that almost disappeared due to Imperial Japan's Nazi-esque ethnic cleansing agenda, well, didn't even exist at all. The film practically called Saipan a "Japanese Island" which of course erases roughly seven thousand years of indigenous, Micronesian Chamorro history in the Marianas in one thoughtless, inhumane sentence for billions to see. WWII may not have rendered us exterminated as an ethnic group, but John Woo sure made Chamorros feel that way via film.

When you're persistently deleted from history, media, and any other channel to access information – or that information is distorted – it's far worse than physically killing someone. It, instead, induces a form of psychological death. How can you truly be alive, how can you genuinely breathe, when everyone around you believes that you either don't exist or are dead?

However, as a Chamorro with generational trauma from multiple attempts at ethnic cleansing by Spain from the 1500s to the late 1800s, Imperial Japan during WWII, and having faced racial persecution in Iraq, I can only hope that putting the pieces of lives shattered by trauma back together can result in a stronger American-made fabric. We are all, no matter our color, part of the same Americana quilt. I'm drifting off to sleep.

On an island, I saw myself in a white dress as a little girl. I walked with my family to the seashore where a boat was waiting for us to board. As I watched family members pack up our belongings, I knelt down in the shallow waters of the beach and cleared sand off of a beautiful shell. It looked like the inside of an oyster. Sea foam, pearl, and flashes of turquoise danced in my eyes. Splashing in the water and singing with my beautiful find, a woman who appeared to be my mother called after me to hurry up. She looked distressed. Before getting into the boat, I turned and saw white plumes of smoke rising from the island's volcano. This was an evacuation.

"We have to go!" the gentle maternal voice insisted as she held my hand.

As the boat took off from the island, I waved goodbye as the volcano reacted.

"Pagan," my mother said, when I woke from the dream. Chamorros are serious about their dreams, and often insist messages from the spirit world await us in the fog of sleep.

I told my mother about the strange dream, and she told me it sounded like an actual time when her mother, Ignacia, and her family left the island of Pagan in the Northern Marianas for Saipan. Nana, as us grandchildren called her, was a woman of few words. The dream puzzled me, but in Chamorro dream interpretation, this is meant to be a forecast, a premonition.

"Maybe Nana's showing you something, a sign. Pay attention to what you saw. Those are your clues," my mother said during the long journey from Florida to Saipan.

Shortly after my return from Prague, we found out Nana was dying of a variety of medical conditions. My maternal grandmother had been hospitalized and her condition was considered terminal as her heart disease and diabetes was now affecting her ability to walk and her circulation became so poor, amputation of limbs would have been the next step if it weren't for her frail cardiac condition.

My mother and I took flight from Jacksonville to Newark, then a 16-hour flight over the North Pole and Russia to Hong Kong, stopping briefly in Guam. My dreams of Nana continued on this flight and my mind wrestled with the symbols. The flight from danger, happiness found in unexpected moments, the discovery of beloved people or places when we aren't trying so hard. I dreamt of the seashell, symbols, archetypes, the colors, the subtle appearances of iridescent pearl and sea foam.

As we boarded a rickety propeller plane bound for Saipan, I looked out past the cliffs of Guam toward the sea and thought of all the beauty and pain of the Marianas. In places like Oceania, conquerors, whether from Europe or East Asia, seem to lose their polite disposition upon reaching our island shores. When Spain colonized the Mariana Islands in 1521, they easily swung into full-oppression mode when met with people who actually embodied the community and social generosity of Christianity's supposed core that they were so desperate to shove the cross in the faces of the indigenous populace. It was a distraction great enough to keep one's eyes off property, resources, and land.

That seductive aroma of unchecked power was more than enough to commit genocide and mass sexual assault while unashamedly carrying their nation's flag draped around a crucifix. People completely devoid of introspection, flaunting their entitlement and a self-importance that masked an endless pit of dejection that demanded more gold, land, and power. The Spanish crown was a plague of miserable dimensions for Chamorros.

Colonizers used up resources, exploited people, raped the land, and when they were done, it was onto the next one. I thought about the upcoming wedding the whole way, and why I had a sinking feeling that I couldn't shake off. Perhaps, deep down, I was afraid of someone trying to "conquer" me, to lay claim to me as an object, and not a person. To be used, and not loved, or to be exploited, not fulfilled. Metal parts clanged around us as doubt consumed me.

"OH, GOD! Is this how you felt in Iraq?" she asked as she clenched my hands as we waited for take-off.

"No, this is scarier," I laughed and continued to hold her hand as she buried her face into my shoulder praying the rosary.

The flight, operated by Cape Air – also known as "Cape Scare" among fliers who have no other choice than to risk their lives with what feels like a coffin with wings – which has a monopoly on flights going in and out of Saipan, was rough to put it gently. It was a turbulent ride that made you question your life choices from birth to present. I tried not to show the slightest bit of anxiety in front of my mother who appeared to be on the verge of a nervous breakdown. As we approached the coast of Tinian, I took my camera out to snap pictures of the north side of the island and the ocean between the island and Saipan.

Craggy coastline embraced by deep sapphire waters appeared along with what I liked to call “the old Pizza Huts,” Saipan International Airport, with its reddish, hut-like rooftops covering the white sand terminal.

Upon landing, my brother Rodney was waiting along with his three younger kids to greet us. We went to his house to shower and have lunch before heading over to the hospital. He had caught a few parrot fish that morning and waited for us so he could cut it open, put some sea salt and lemon, and then grill it. We had that with steamed rice and finadene, a spicy Chamorro dipping sauce made with tiny fiery peppers, lemon, and soy sauce. That buttery taste of parrot fish, the spices, the ocean breeze flowing through the open doors and windows of the house carried a faint scent of flowers and mangoes. It was good to be back.

When we reached the hospital, my mother used humor to shield her fear, which was surprising to me as she had spent the past thirty-six hours on the edge of a meltdown next to me.

She greeted Nana, who barely recognized her. I was unsure of how this was affecting her as she continued to joke and laugh with Nana, acting as though she weren’t terrified of what may happen next. My mother then helped Nana to scoot over, and then climbed onto the hospital bed with her. I paused and took in the sight of my mother and grandmother.

My mother, as ill-tempered and anxious as she may be, was like a little girl clinging to mommy’s dress right before my eyes. She was holding Nana’s hand and put her head on her shoulders, telling her jokes as Nana smiled and chuckled through apparent physical pain. I was used to seeing her vulnerable in a PTSD sort of way, but this is the first I’ve seen of what appeared to be the most obvious sign. Perhaps much of her anxious and fearful behavior was partially childhood regression, unresolved wounds from decades before as in her first marriage that involved intense physical and emotional abuse. Dealing with both Nana and Tata in their post-war processing must’ve been hell too. Despite her smiles and laughter, my mother looked helpless and alone. We’re all children in the presence of our parents, no matter our age.

As my mother set up camp with Nana, my brother and his

family filed in and greeted a few relatives already in the room. We overcrowded the room and began telling stories to each other as though we were a traveling troupe to entertain our dying matriarch, to keep her smiling and engaged. Not too long after, everyone prepared to leave and my mom left briefly with my aunt to go talk somewhere else in the hospital. I stayed in the room alone with Nana.

Nana began squeezing my hand, motioning me to massage her hands and arms. For Chamorros, massage is not exactly meant to be erotic; it's meant to heal. When I stopped massaging her hands, she'd twitch as though to tell me to continue. My mom used to do the same thing as her non-verbal cue to tell me the massage wasn't over. By the age of ten, every Chamorro kid is a freelance massage therapist.

In the US, being an herbal healer or anyone who believes in spiritual healing can be labeled quickly as a shaman, witch doctor, or something tacky that actually condescends to or cheapens the practice. Being a suruhana (female healer) or suruhanu (male healer) was not anything you could learn in a book, online, or anywhere else without becoming an apprentice. Nana's mother taught her, her grandmother taught her mother, and so on.

"We're proud to have women warriors coming back now. This war was not right, but you had no choice and were brave. You now know things no one else does and you see life differently. That's a gift and a curse, just know how to use it wisely," a distant uncle said.

It was funny how I had to make it all this way from across the globe to hear that women warriors are deserving of respect. I didn't feel that way back in the continental U.S. Pacific Islander culture is used to the idea of fierce women, and the transition into being a combat veteran was not farfetched in the minds of Chamorros.

As an Iraq war veteran, I've developed a much stronger awareness to others who often go unheard, ignored. Hell, I'm a bisexual Chamorro female combat veteran. If the VA decides to wake up and process a claim, add disabled to that list. If that doesn't scare your closest human resources department, I don't know what will.

With my family coming from what seems like the opposite end

of the Manzanar experience, I can see that through the telling of our stories, that no matter where we are in the traumatic pain spectrum, we all have permission to share - and to the betterment of our society. War shatters lives in more ways than the bloodied battlefields tell. Yet through effectively verbalizing and expressing our pain, no matter the source, we can give ourselves and others the room to grieve, process, and eventually heal. Nana and Tata, like many other Chamorros, dealt with the aftermath of war with little to no assistance in recovering their broken lives.

One thing I recalled about Nana was that she never smiled. Or at least I knew of no one who had witnessed her smiling. Ever. She laughed. I recall her tremor-like laughter that would shake the table and such laughter was usually directed at other people. Her laughter came with minimal commentary or a judgmental huff. She didn't need to say anything. If she was laughing at you, it was for a reason. Like a weathered infantryman, she had endured war and was ever-aware of her surroundings as well as the idiosyncrasies and behavior of others. Before having to depart for the mainland, we stopped by to see Nana at home to say good-bye.

As we walked out the door we both stopped after putting our shoes on and turned around to look at Nana one more time. She slowly raised her right hand and bent her fingers down and up, down and up. As she was waving good-bye, she was smiling. It was the purest, most innocent smile from someone whose life was so incredibly difficult, filled with pain, and spent in service to others in the village using local medicine. We saw peace in her eyes and in that instant, our hearts sank together to the bottom of the Marianas Trench. We returned her wave as it hit us like a tsunami. We stood there drenched in the last adios.

As we marched through the dark and back to the car, we were silent. Rodney's wife waited for us in the driver's seat and asked if we were okay. That's when my mother broke down sobbing like a toddler who couldn't find her parents, "Let's go. Please, just drive."

12 FROM BAGHDAD TO BEIRUT

"There are storm clouds up ahead," I told my mother as we started prepping everything in the house for the rehearsal dinner and the arrival of friends and relatives for the wedding.

My mom looked at me, looked down, and asked if I really loved Tony. I said that I did, but I didn't tell her of the arguments we were having while I was away. Pictures of him and other women that I found, and how he cried and begged for me not to leave him, and that he said he would do anything to make me stay. I forgave him, and asked him, above all else to just be honest with me. He agreed and promised that I would have his full attention, for the rest of our lives, if I'd still marry him. Colonel Platoni, who worked with me in Ramadi was on her way, as was my other battle buddy from Iraq, Jones, and Sara from Prague.

After everyone arrived, I relaxed and lost myself in the process of cooking Chamorro dishes. I overheard talking to some of his friends who arrived for the dinner party.

"There are only perhaps 250,000 Chamorros in the entire world – and I got one." Tony laughed.

"I got one?" I asked myself.

What was I? A children's fast food surprise toy, a collector's item? An indigenous collect-the-whole-set edition of Micronesian womankind? I felt wildly uneasy. At the time, so much was going on that I didn't even fully process how Tony was objectifying me, quite proudly, in front of friends and family as though he had just dragged Pocahontas to England to meet the "civilized" world. Not a partner, a spouse, or even a friend, but a conquest.

Then the real fun started. Tony's parents came to the house and started to make rude comments to my family when I wasn't present. His father made comments to my Godfather, who is of

Irish descent and married to my Chamorro aunt and Godmother, about my dark-skinned nieces and nephews looking like monkeys and that unless a child was white, blond-haired and blue-eyed, that they'd never be beautiful and certainly not a true American. Other relatives overheard this, as did one of my brothers who then told my mother. No one wanted to make a scene the day before the wedding. Although I wished that they had told me. Tony's mother and brother went on to make comments about Chamorros and asked if we were civilized people and poked fun at stereotypes about Islanders living in huts and acting like savages. Tony's family was acting very proud of themselves, and I had no idea – until a few days after the wedding.

That night, Platoni, Jones, Sara and I went out to a hookah place and had dinner and smoked like we did in Iraq and how Sara and I did in Prague. We all had a nice evening out, and preferably not a loud bachelorette party.

Before the end of the night when everyone but Jones and I turned in, she turned to me as we were laying on wicker furniture in the patio watching a lightning storm.

She asked, "Do you really want to do this, Brookfield?"

I smiled, and looked onward at the lightning spreading out over the sky with flashes of purple and white.

"I do, but I have to admit that I'm worried," I said.

"Well, no matter what happens, B, we'll be here," she said.

The next morning came and as I got suited in a beaded $1000 last minute dress, my mother began to cry before we made it out the door.

"Are you sure you want to do this?" she asked.

"No turning back now, I guess," I said, smiling.

"You can. You can cancel everything right now if you want to," my mom said with tears in her eyes.

"I'll be okay, don't worry," I said, kissing her cheek.

The wedding went smoothly. Jones and Tony's sisters were beside me with bridesmaids as Tony was in his USMC dress blues with his friends and younger brother on his side. As we entered the reception hall a few blocks from the church, my mother pulled me aside. Apparently, my brother's wife brought a box of wedding favors with a bunch of human hair attached to the table centerpiece.

To explain this in a bit more in detail, in Chamorro culture, one would get human hair from a corpse and attach it to someone or a personal item belonging to the individual to put a curse on them, to dissolve happiness and good luck. I didn't make a big deal of it, and just shrugged it off. Everything was going well so far, or so it seemed at the time. Even my father's side of the family who showed up were acting somewhat personable, which the exception of a few aunts leering at me from across the room and whispering to each other.

Then something strange happened. After the father-daughter dance where I ended up playfully leading my father through the song My Girl, Tony and his mother stepped onto the dance floor. Immediately, as Celine Dion crooned, Tony's mother pulled in Tony tight and they began slow dancing like two teenagers at a middle school dance. I'm surprised that the priest didn't step in and say, "Leave some room for Jesus!"

It was terribly uncomfortable and I was wondering if everyone else was seeing what I was seeing. Tony's mother was caressing his neck, whispering in his ear, stroking his back and had her arms wrapped around his neck. It was creepy and incestuous-looking. I thought to myself, "Did I just make one big effing mistake?"

During the dance, Jones and another friend came to sit by me and asked what I thought of the dance.

"Holy shit, am I the only one seeing this," I asked them.

"Um, no," they both said simultaneously. They were equally freaked out and feeling a bit sorry for me. This wasn't good. This wasn't a subtle sign that something was wrong, but a blaring warning siren. I looked down at my wedding ring, and then up at my new family.

After the wedding, I went with Tony to North Carolina where we spent a few days relaxing and hanging out in Wilmington.
Tony paid for his family's airfare and hotel by selling his motorcycle, and they contributed nothing to the wedding claiming they didn't have any money, but were heading to Disney World in Orlando after the ceremony.

I couldn't relax and asked Tony about the strange dance. He denied anything was out of the ordinary and dismissed my concern as mere overreaction. As Tony had to head back to work, I drove back down to Jacksonville alone and ended up having a conversation with my family.

Apparently quite a few more bizarre incidents happened with Tony's family and I was getting to hear an earful from multiple witnesses.

"You couldn't tell me all of this before the wedding?" I said.

Most of the incidents were racist comments, sexually suggestive behavior by Tony's dad, and general racist animosity. I called Tony later in the evening when I had calmed down and when people went home. He denied any wrongdoing by his family, even though he wasn't present for at least some of the behavior. He denied everything and didn't question his parents or the possibility that something was wrong. It wasn't mere defensiveness, but a robotic series of no's. What was happening here?

"You tricked me. I didn't sign up for this," I told him, feeling regret for marrying into exactly what I wanted to avoid, a family of bigots. Talk about a military flashback.

Tony eventually apologized and took me up to Massachusetts to see his family before his next and final 6-month deployment to Iraq. His family never apologized, but his mother went on babbling about Catholicism and his father handed me a dated, and quite racist book on Pacific Islanders written in the 1950s as though he was the aficionado on Oceania now.

What does this even mean? I'm kinda sorry? Ha-ha, fuck you some more?

His father's next spiel on minorities at the dinner table seemed like something out of some racist novel of the old South. He spoke with such assured ignorance, and even seemed quite oblivious to the discomfort he was causing. He really believed, that in spite of his own faults that by ethnicity he was better than anyone in my family, and certainly above me in every way. It was not what I had bargained for in a father-in-law, and I could feel that the bond of marriage, this tying of the knot into this family has turned into what I now felt was a noose.

Never force someone to make a space in their life for you, because if they know your worth, they will surely create one for you. It felt that in Tony's family, there would never be space for me, and I ruminated over the recent debacle wondering how this was going to work.

After all the bizarre moments from the wedding and the recent uncomfortable trip to Massachusetts before Tony left, I received a message from an old friend, Eugenio. He's the soldier I met who fawned over me while I was facing trial at Ibn Sina in Baghdad. For some odd reason, even when I was in exile in a tent on the other side of the city, we kept on running into each other. Romance, obviously, was far from my mind while battling mutiny charges. How strange that in the middle of wedding drama that he finds me again…

Before Veterans Day, I met a young aspiring journalist from Beirut named Maya who was writing for the University of North Florida newspaper. We agreed to meet at a café in the town center where she would ask me questions about my military service in order to write her article about Veterans Day, which was still over a month away.

Years have passed, death anniversaries, suicides, and being back in the United States felt like purgatory with chain restaurants. I couldn't imagine what I would be able to say to Maya that would make any difference in how I felt, and I couldn't imagine talking about the stereotypical aspects of being a veteran or invent fairy tales about how I felt honored to be back.

With numerous cups of coffee, cigarillos for me and cigarettes for her, I told her everything. Not just snippets here and there of life and death in Anbar Province. I told her every last detail from the time I met the racist chain of command, the severity of corruption in leadership in Baghdad's Green Zone, how Army mental health was failing, and how I was moments away from committing homicide several times while in theater. I told her of the gradual breakdown of my psyche, that being surrounded by senseless, and even justified, deaths had taken every bit of quixotic idealism I had and buried it deep in the desert sands of Iraq.

Maya listened, took notes, almost dutifully, even though we both knew there was no way in hell UNF's newspaper would publish any real veteran account of life in Iraq, especially not that of a woman who performed successfully in combat operations. No. UNF, as most mainstream media outlets, wanted the Johnny-comes-home-from-war-craving-mom's-apple-pie rubbish. Not the real shit that makes your toes curl and your skin crawl. The types of true life stories that tell you that often there is no happy ending, innocent people suffer and die, justice remains missing in action, and how many a conscience has gone AWOL.

In one night, which was supposed to be a trite Veterans Day tribute, we ended up going in depth about what really twisted my soul. While the paper rejected my story and kept the piece palsied and predictable, Maya ended up taking in the whole Quixote in Ramadi story herself. It was the first time I had told the story from start to finish, every gory detail of deaths, suicidal and homicidal ideations, cover-ups, muzzled whistleblowers, false flag operations, media distortion, and other surreal conspiracies that were actually proven to be true. So much had happened in Iraq right before my eyes and I came home to people who had never been there tell me the war was all about freedom and democracy. Maya listened not because she had to, but because she felt no one else was telling this story, not from a soldier's perspective at least.

With Maya, I divulged the background of my angst and how I exploded in theater. From dealing with memories of childhood, imperial conquest, and ethnic persecution, I told her the story of an indigenous female soldier under severe pressure while facing unexpected catastrophes and military corruption. While my command leadership laundered money, mistreated personnel, and even denied services to soldiers in Baghdad, soldiers like me were sent out to the worst outposts as the unfavorable ones, cannon fodder. In Ar Ramadi, I thrived, much to the chagrin of those who wished to see me dead. I didn't merely provide support as many would want to suggest, I performed in direct combat while working checkpoint operations, personnel searches and house raids with Marine infantry units in addition to losing friends, earning the trust of locals, and responding to military suicides and homicides in the region.

In the meantime, the narratives I read on war were mostly watered down tales, and the most whitewashed versions of the war got the most air time. I had no chance to speak up because there was already a culture of media commitment to selling one version of the story, the version that was dedicated to yoking it out for the state and not the people. And if you speak up, you have to be ready for slander, backlash, and veiled or overt threats. This wasn't new to me, but to Maya, it confirmed many of her own fears of how deep and depraved the Iraq War rabbit hole truly was.

As I told her my story, she interlaced my narrative with stories of her own in her native Lebanon. Stories of war, trauma, and dancing the night away in clubs in spite of air raids, bombing campaigns, and violence creeping in through every crevice of her beloved Beirut.

I adored the talks with Maya. As we drank espresso and smoked through the wee hours, she would tell me stories of her family, of partying hard on the rooftop bars of Beirut, paying no mind to explosions of war making its way through the city.

War. Nightclub music therapy to soothe the war-damaged nerves of local souls, dancing on the edge under the moon to forget the world plunging into eternal night. Trendy shops, whispers in Arabic, English, and French intermingling in international crowds amid cigarette smoke and top-shelf alcohol. She described a gilded, hedonistic, and cosmopolitan life alongside religious, conservative neighborhoods. With bomb shelters used for all-night ragers, war couldn't cramp Beirut's style – but seemed to strengthen it. She believed in living life like there's no tomorrow, something which I could understand after Iraq.

"Some of the best partying you could do in your life is in Beirut. One day, I'll show you," Maya said, beaming with pride over her beloved city.

I'd love to go.

Before taking off to Beirut, Maya insisted that I push the story into publishing. Maya and I had spent months before her departure talking about politics, love, war, and everything in between. She was one of two people I completely divulged everything that plagued me, and it reminded me of the only other person I had shared this much with: Zdeněk. One Lebanese and one Czech confidant. Getting an American to give this much of a shit seemed like a stretch by now, and it seemed apparent that in order for anyone to believe what happened in Iraq, they were probably not going to be American – at first.

It's sad to see people fall for predictable warmongering time and again. With Maya, my message was understood, but I saw so many other people around me eat up everything the media served with a smile. When jingoes beat the war drums, it's not them or their children that will be sent into war. No, no. Chicken hawks don't fight. So, fellow veterans, there is no need to bark when these fraudulent cowards push us into another war, a war that we witnessed tear lives apart on all sides, wars we still live with long after we come home.

Follow the money, not the emotional, pathos-packed pandering you see everywhere, but to do your homework. Dick Cheney, one of the architects for the Iraq War as well as the 7-country/5-year plan, is also suing veterans that sued his company for poisoning military personnel overseas.

Recalling that bright orange water from Ramadi, I thank Cheney/KBR. Our so-called water was dirtier than the Euphrates. Wonder why so many vets now have renal and pancreatic issues? Don't let some power-hungry chicken hawk blind you with meaningless flag-waving, push them out of the way and read the fine print of their bank statement.

My writing was not romantic, a glorified testimony to the endless lust of combat. It wasn’t too long after that I started sending out queries to literary agents and publishers, but the general consensus came to be that my story of mutiny and colonialism was not exactly acceptable in the US military genre. A ‘thanks, but no thanks’ that persisted for years while books about Iraq and Afghanistan were peddled from white perspectives or were written by white women and men covering perspectives of color, but rarely any stand-alone minority voice – let alone one that had anything critical to say about the war. It reminded me of the soapbox the US Ambassador to Yemen stood on at Harvard.

People like her owned the microphone. Not me.

13 NORTH CAROLINA

After Tony returned from his final six-month deployment, we moved in together to a small, old brick apartment complex outside of Camp Lejeune, North Carolina.

Camp Lejeune's surrounding area left much to be desired. Directly outside of the Marine Corps base were the typical makings of military installation periphery: strip clubs, pawn shops, and auto dealerships. The enlisted Holy Trinity. Our place was a few miles away down Wilmington Highway and everything in between consisted of a Wal-Mart, a small shopping mall, and a few chain restaurants. Other than that, it was a country-fried wasteland of uneducated, bizarre, prejudiced people mixed in with military personnel and retirees who found great deals on housing prices.

At first, things were great. We were finally alone together and in our new home. There was nothing materially impressive about our apartment, but it was ours. We didn't have much, but we had each other after two and a half years combined time in Iraq; it was like prison time. We soon bought a futon sofa, a TV, and a workstation for the computer. I brought in a dining set, kitchen items, and bedroom furniture. In a matter of months, I finished some remaining courses to finish my bachelor of science degree and set out on looking for work and trying to live a normal life.

As we were leaving the apartment one day, Tony asked me if I gained some weight since Prague. Perhaps about 5-10lbs from eating bread and cheese on a tight budget, but not that I've noticed.

"Just for the record, I don't want a fat wife," Tony said one afternoon.

After he said that, I felt another wave of doubt. Did I make a huge mistake in marrying him? Or should I give him a chance, and that comments like this were a fluke? After a month, the newlywed luster wore off, and a new tone set in. Tony came home with stories about his coworkers, one in which was a frequent mention, a Marine they called Dee-Bo, who had a wife who was half-Mexican, half-Caucasian.

"She's only half white, so her pussy is only half as good," Dee-Bo reportedly joked. As Tony relayed the story to me, he was laughing, seemingly in agreement with Dee-Bo.

"So is that how you feel about me? Only half valuable because of the white side?" I said.

Tony accused me of being too sensitive, I told him he was acting like the inbred yokel Dee-Bo was. He knew how I felt about racism and that it was my trigger in particular, but he seemed unfettered by my reaction. It seemed as though his coworkers enjoyed mocking their spouses, berating them, and these women seemingly put up with it. I, on the other hand, wasn't so enthusiastic about the apparent spousal PSYOPS campaign.

Resentment surmounted, and I felt distant with Tony. He didn't respect me, and seemed more interested in pleasing his peers than relating to his own wife. His detachment from me and lack of attentiveness was not simply a sign of omitting any internal struggle, but a monolithic sign of preoccupation.

Weeks went by and I wasn't able to find work. I applied everywhere, and got nothing until a bookstore called me back. I was asked by the manager at the bookstore during my interview, holding my resume in her hands, if I was able to handle pressure. The pressure she was speaking of was the pressure in dealing with irate customers and a busy, fast-paced environment. Looking around the store, it appeared quite relaxed in the middle of the day and barely had an audible hum to it. I respectfully held in my laughter. Was she joking? I dealt with people who wanted to kill me on a daily basis, from Saudi insurgents to the racist WASP officers in my own unit. Iraq was a fast-paced post-apocalyptic nightmare. Could I handle pressure? Was she being condescending or did she not read my résumé?

Instead of relaying my inner monologue like a radio transcript, I smiled kindly, and said, "Absolutely, I have confidence that I can be of great assistance here. It would be a great opportunity to be part of your team."

She sent an email about a week later saying that they chose another candidate, but after revisiting the online listing and calling the store, I confirmed that the position was still open.

During this lonely period, I began talking to my Army buddy, Genevieve, again.

She was the only one I could confide in on a regular basis while here in North Carolina. I felt stuck and while I had thought that Tony would be there for me, he was absent from conversations we should have been having.

Tony was also giving me mixed signals and evidence that something wasn't right. I asked him if there was anything we needed to talk about, if he was seeing anyone, or if he was just unhappy, but he was at ease in his denial. He had seemingly changed from a warm, loving person to this one-dimensional droid, devoid of any thought, feeling, or remorse. It was almost reptilian in nature. For a moment, I wondered where my loving partner and friend went. But it occurred to me that perhaps this was the case all along, and just maybe I only saw what I wanted to see in him.

While this didn't absolve him of his shortcomings, it did leave me holding a share in the accountability in the way things transpired in our marriage. I didn't take action on those initial red flags and our marriage turned out looking like a false flag leading into a war.

While suspecting infidelity and revisiting life decisions, I heard from Eugenio again. Before a full year passed in his marriage, Eugenio was having difficulties with his wife ranging from mistrust to full-blown infidelity and physical confrontation. Eugenio kept me apprised of the situation and I did what I could to be a good friend, listening to him from afar. I was already getting a shaky feeling about my own marriage as Tony was beginning to do what Eugenio's wife was doing when he first saw the signs: the avoidant behavior, carelessness in one's spouse's feelings, little red flags popping up progressively faster than one can think.

It wasn't that I didn't want to make any friends in North Carolina, it was that no one talked to me, and when I tried reaching out, it was clear that my presence was unwanted. Most of the Marines Tony worked with were friendly, but their wives were a whole other story. Most of the female Marines in Tony's unit would just glare at me when I said hello. I didn't know what else to do, and when I'd ask Tony why everyone was in such a bad mood, he claimed he didn't know. There was one exception, a Brazilian expat named Faustina.

During laundry day, I found another woman's underwear in the basket. Tony was stone-faced and denied everything. It was a painfully evasive display, as though he wasn't actually exerting himself in any strand of effort, and simply turned on autopilot. He was doing what he wanted and would admit to nothing, even if the dishonesty was killing us. This wasn't his first offense. This was just the first time I had started thinking about leaving. It was then that I finally recognized just the type of person I had married. After calling me disgusting for discussing bisexuality, I put up another wall. Feeling trapped after that first month, I had been going through the motions ever since. It had shifted from marriage purgatory into marriage hell.

Tony eventually started to drink even more after he came home from work. He went from being a social drinker to having a gin and tonic every day after work as he tuned me out to play Xbox until bed. One night, I decided to drink with him. We were watching movies and he seemed like he was actually in a good mood. He started to tickle me and then wrestled me to the ground. I told him to stop and that I was tired. He wouldn't and kept grappling with me. Something inside of me kicked on.

Training kicks in when your instincts are alerted. My mother taught us that if someone puts their hands on you, you put them on the ground, and if you lose, don't come home. Funny how those words echo years later and I found myself putting Tony on the ground like a rag doll. A Marine who prided himself as a physical fitness stud gets clobbered by a small female veteran who hadn't seen a gym in months.

I recalled the fear in his eyes and in a split second, I felt the ecstasy of power and domination, an opiate of being on top and instilling a sense of dread and fear. And as fast as the adrenaline rush of victory came, a wave of guilt followed. Sure, my countering Tony was warranted. I asked him to stop and he didn't, so now we're here. What bothered me was I had tackled my spouse to the ground like a rugby player and, in turn, petrified him. I felt ashamed. I wasn't sure what love was at this point, even after marriage, but I was positive that it wasn't this.

The next thing I knew, tears were streaming down my face, and I bolted to the bathroom and began vomiting. I started to think of Iraq again.

Anytime someone pushes my buttons and alcohol is involved, I seem to gravitate toward grieving; grieving for the dead, feeling guilty for being alive. It was disappointment in myself and what life had become.

I remember seeing his face before blacking out, and it was a look of a stranger. He had slowly been making himself a stranger to me, but now the metamorphosis was official. I matched the level of his carelessness and lack of consideration with an unabashed aggression. He never forgave me for it, and I lost respect for him. Never again did we speak of that night.

Tony continued to drink alone and I would go to bed after staying up late writing. Writing about what I felt, writing about Iraq, writing about how depressed I was and gaining weight no matter how much he pressured me to be some stick-figure ideal he had of female anatomy. I hated myself for being here, and the first thoughts of suicide were a lot closer as we slept with a Glock under our pillows – sometimes under his, sometimes mine.

One afternoon I received a call from a woman who watched the documentary Lioness that I briefly appeared in and wanted to reach out. Her name was Eleanor and she ran a veterans nonprofit in Massachusetts.

We talked on the phone for hours, and in the end, she asked if I'd consider working for her up in Massachusetts. I spoke to Tony about it. He wanted to move back up to Massachusetts after he got out of the Marine Corps, which would be in six months. So I took the job, packed up my clothes and books, and kissed Tony good-bye.

We hadn't been intimate in months and even in spite of him body-shaming me, I had stacked on quite a bit of weight which I'm sure was a bonus from the severe depression I felt in North Carolina. He wasn't apprehensive, and appeared to have no reservations about me leaving – and neither did I. There was no last-minute clinging, no teary-eyed request to stay in spite of hard times, nor was there any apology for how I had been treated since moving with him to North Carolina. It was just me, my GPS, and the open road ahead. As I drove away on that grey, overcast morning, I didn't look back. I felt free.

14 MASSACHUSETTS

Driving to Massachusetts in tail end of winter was gloomy, cold, and somewhat depressing – exactly what I felt of my marriage to Tony this far. Eleanor had offered me a salaried position as well as a room in her lakeside house near Winchendon, Massachusetts. I accepted, and was grateful for her hospitality and openness with me knowing my background. She was looking for someone to run an Iraq and Afghanistan program in her nonprofit, and seeing Lioness convinced her of my adaptability. One of the people in charge of the construction site of the proposed facility actually watched the film first and shared it with her as a recommendation to hire me.

Eleanor appeared to be a kind woman who had went through her share of hell, and seemed to be a free spirit. Her husband, Fred, was the nonprofit's grant writer and while he remained quiet for the most part, his right-wing perspectives would surface every so often. On occasion I would share in cooking, and of course, anything Eleanor needed, I had no qualms in helping. After all, she had opened her home to me. I thought she was a saint!

During this transition, I would visit Tony's family, mostly as a courtesy. I'd cook for them at times since they seemed to like Chamorro food or any other dish I made, and it didn't appear that anyone else in the house was cooking very often either. In addition to Fred's occasional rant that he regurgitated from right wing radio shows out of Central Massachusetts, I got to hear Tony's dad foam at the mouth over his love of Ann Coulter, Bill O'Reilly, and other right-wing pundits. It became apparent that he also wasn't a fan of my combat service that his son lacked, and started to make snide comments that I never really belonged on the "front lines" anyway.

Not too long after moving into Eleanor's house in the upstairs portion while she slept downstairs, I had to start making solid decisions with Tony on where we were going to live. He suggested that I should stay with Eleanor until he moved there so we could at least save money. However, I noticed that the money in our joint checking account was beginning to disappear into an outside account, in which I began to question him. He was also a bit MIA in social media, and strange pictures began to surface of him dressed up and having a great time with whoever was holding the camera. I asked him who he was with, and he would just say with the other Marines. Funny, it didn't seem like he'd be giving the bedroom gaze to one of the guys, but I could've been wrong.

Eleanor and I would talk about this and she wasn't very optimistic over my situation, but she also encouraged me to do what I felt was right with my life no matter which path I took. She seemed a bit lonely on the inside, as on the outside she looked like she had quite the full life: a beautiful home, a supportive spouse, successful children, her own business, and an active life in the veteran community. I really looked up to her and it was easy to do so, as much as it was to talk with her like a close friend. She invited me to stay as long as I wanted, and to figure things out, and living with her actually made it easy to say yes.

After about a month in Massachusetts Tony was calling less. A sneaking feeling of impending doom manifested. Something wasn't right outside the apparent lapse in communication. Thankfully, I had Eleanor cheering me on. I didn't know anyone in this state, in spite of my father's side being originally from Boston. However, he warned me not to contact any relatives there, saying that unless I wanted to meet real life characters from the film, "The Departed," it would be wise for me to stay away.

My situation with Tony was on shaky ground, and I did my best to keep busy. Eleanor and I had a scheduled trip to Washington DC to attend a veterans coalition summit. During a panel on veteran mental health, I spoke up when a national spokesman for Iraq and Afghanistan veterans, whom I'll call Saul Jerkoff, began spouting what sounded like Army mental health palaver that must've been spoon-fed or scripted. It was the same motionless rhetoric I heard while in uniform that covered the ills of military mental health and it alarmed me that similar principles were being proposed to VA and veterans nonprofits.

Speaking up even though it wasn't exactly en vogue to question a billionaire's protégé, an Aryan good ol' boy who was packaged to be acceptable to the general American public, to say everything MSNBC wanted to hear and to act non-partisan even though the primary modus operandi was to lobby.

I asked Saul, and the rest of the panel in the mental health discussion, what were the proposed strategies on aiding veterans of underrepresented minority groups, and particularly women – like me – who were not being adequately addressed or helped as their Anglo-Saxon counterparts.

Saul stared blankly with an eager smile, then said, "We're going to support the troops, storm the hill, and take no prisoners until we change Washington DC. Mental illness is a normal response to an abnormal situation, and we're going to fight for our brothers and sisters for a successful reintegration."

The audience erupted in applause. I, on the other hand, was not impressed.

"Saul, you still didn't answer my question," I countered, "What are you planning on doing to aid underrepresented veterans who are facing homelessness, institutional violence, or suicide? I haven't heard one clear objective on how that's going to be addressed other than a vague, blanket statement that sounds like a campaign platform."

Then, a pixie-like US Army officer skipped into the room. It's been a while since I had seen full lack of military bearing in full view, but this time it was some chipper General, the head of Army Behavioral Health. This General did what looked like a cheerleading routine to cover the inefficacy of Army Mental Health processes with catch-phrases and euphemisms that only added to the repulsive lip-service from Jerkoff. Seeing her prance around like Gidget was the manifestation of why veterans kill themselves: community and leadership denial, faux support, minimizing trauma, overmedication, and sociopathic staff. Looking at the zombified Stepford Wife of a General affect made me want to rip my veins open and drown her with my own blood. People like her, women like her, made rank simply because she wasn't a threat to the most insidious leaders of the establishment. Her routine was a mockery on any and all women's progress in or out of the military.

No one else bothered to comment, save one female veteran who said she "didn't know how to approach the minority issue." Every person on that panel was white, all women with the exception of Saul. This was the developing expectation I had of other veterans: nothing.

One of my least favorite memories since returning is that particular trigger of mine. While at a conference in Washington DC, a group of women and I were discussing our experiences in the military, life since being back from Iraq and/or Afghanistan, and everything under the sun from good restaurants in the area to books we've read recently.

When someone asked about my experiences with racial discrimination in the military, as well as in life in general, they followed after my response with, "You must get mistaken for a lot of ethnicities you're not even associated with, doesn't that get annoying?" I laughed and explained how one of my best friends and I met. In high school, Hafiza approached me, stated her name, and then asked if I was Afghan. I said no, but that was our ice breaker and we've laughed about it ever since. It was an innocent inquiry, and gender and race are the first things people see; so long as it's not vindictive, I don't care.

All of a sudden, a white female veteran immediately chimed in and exclaimed, "That's ridiculous. You obviously look Chinese, maybe even Hazara," then laughed aloud.

This was someone who actually participates in quite a few veterans discussions and she attempted to use race to undermine and belittle me. My reliable trigger. Women who use race to put minority women down, keep us ostracized and believe that making us feel that we don't belong will always be garbage to me. There is nothing more inherently dull than playing to the crowd of one political party or the other, regurgitating textbook party politics hoping someone will think of you as brilliant.

Women who engage in such microaggressions are, in my eyes, of the same stock of exploitative men in veterans nonprofits. If they can't fuck you one way, they want to fuck you in another special way. This supposed fellow woman veteran targeted my race for her personal pleasure.

If you're a woman who is a minority and a combat veteran, you really have limited avenues to turn to for help. Later, I met another woman veteran who claimed she was the reincarnation of an ancient Egyptian pharaoh and that Pocahontas was her great, great, great, great grandmother.

She didn't look Native American nor have any evident ties other than what her dad reportedly told her. I've heard the typical "Cherokee grandmother" legend that guilty Anglos like to use, but Pocahontas? Really? Wonderland. Yep, I'm still here. I excused myself from the conversation and go searching for a way to mainline Pinot Noir to forget where I was.

Women veterans meetings in my DC rounds didn't appear to be the great networking opportunities I once thought them to be before I started attending. In these meetings I found white women veterans talking in cliques and often staring down their noses at women veterans of color.

This didn't always happen, but it was a recurrent theme throughout these conferences where a white female, military veteran or not, would seek to "correct" me on something, seek to label me, seek to put me in a box, seek to shut me up.

It wasn't that they didn't see my budding empowerment, it's that they didn't want it to exist. Whatever issues they were dealing with were often projected onto me, and I kept having to remind myself in spite of seemingly personal, scathing attacks, that it wasn't about me. It was that they were unhealed, and leaking all over me.

During this conference, the fact that veterans and the like are coming out with books on Iraq seemingly sooner than their redeployment briefings left me feeling unsettled. I couldn't understand giving away such intimate accounts of horrible events so soon, if they occurred at all. Veteran organizations are also here popping up like weeds screeching, "Support the troops!" when it all really seems like an extravagant meeting at a plush, overpriced hotel where white people who've become far too savvy of the nonprofit system come to drink coffee during the day, and get shit-faced by night, then go home to do as little as possible.

All the while, things we should be fighting for, our civil liberties and rights that are slipping through our hands are on the back-burner. I felt worried about the complacency in the room, but it was easy for others who were taking advantage of grant money and generous, but ignorant, donors.

It's all too easy to wave the American flag and proclaim one's love for God and country, but it's also an effective tool of propaganda covering up issues we that should be worrying us. When fascism takes root in the United States, it will look a lot like this: A Swedish-looking Jesus draped in the American flag, carrying an AR-15. But there will be no flag pristine enough, no religious symbolism beautiful enough to cover up the permanent national scars resulting from atrocities committed by this country both foreign and domestic. We have yet to truly face our demons, let alone heal.

Before heading back home from the Washington DC trip, I stopped by Tony's family's home to say hello. It turned out that his mother and sisters were fighting right before my arrival. His mother asked me if I would mind taking Tony's younger sisters for the weekend. As I drove his younger sisters, ages thirteen and fifteen, toward Eleanor's house up north, they began to disclose the details of the fight they had with their parents before they left. Apparently this was common. I had noticed the more I came over, the more the two girls opened up and were wanting to talk and spend more time together. Being that I live almost an hour away, that usually limited my interactions strictly to the weekends.

On one hand, I appreciated the company and of course called Eleanor and asked if it was okay. She was thrilled and suggested we have burgers, watch movies, and have a girls' night. However, the two girls were different now that they weren't around their parents. Tony's parents adopted these two at the ages of two and four, I believe, and had been with Tony's family since.

They were usually pretty shy, home-schooled, didn't speak much, but were certainly the sweetest and kindest kids you've ever met. In the hour it took to get to Eleanor's, they had told me what I already knew: Tony's dad thinks I'm a communist, non-white people are monkeys, and white supremacy is the American way. I already knew these comments were said from overhearing Tony's dad shout them over the phone and Tony would simply comply, never really sticking up for me, which caused some of our arguments while we were living together in North Carolina.

While the girls told me about constant arguments which occasionally turned physical in the household, I had suspected it before. This was, however, the first time anyone had openly admitted it. Every time I was at their house, Tony's dad was seemingly biting his tongue, his mother looked afraid, his brother was usually gone, and the two girls would mind their own business and daydream. Something was wrong, but who was I to insinuate, even on a hunch?

As we made our way inside, Eleanor had already bought some goodies and we started cooking away. It was a great night back from Washington DC so far. During the movie, My Life in Ruins, the girls got a text message from Tony's father.

"You know how I was telling you daddy is a little weird sometimes?" the younger one said as she handed me the cell phone.

I looked down at the messages and couldn't believe what I was reading. Tony's dad had sent these girls sexually-charged texts about his penis or "fucking" their mother during the movie. I felt nauseous, and turned to Eleanor and gave her a look. She could tell something was amiss, so I took the girls outside to get more food on the patio as they talked more.

"How long has this been going on?" I asked.

Tony's two younger sisters told me their father had been physically and sexually abusing them for years. I, then, by both moral and legal obligation, had to report this. Eleanor, whom I worked under was liable as well, especially since she joined in the conversation. One is liable if they don't report child abuse but even if I wasn't a mandated reporter, I still would have taken them to the police station anyway. We called Tony. I assured the two girls that they would be protected, and told him what they said.

When he picked up, I then handed the phone to the oldest where she reiterated, shaking, everything she told us.

Tony snapped at her, and she handed me the phone as her eyes welled up. Oh, no. I then asked Eleanor to stay with the two girls as I walked to the next room to speak with Tony in private.

"Your sisters need you right now, what are you doing?" I asked.

"I don't believe them! My parents would never do such a thing! They're fucking liars!" Tony growled.

This was quite an odd reaction for someone who often referred to his sisters as perfect angels. Now they're liars? During his bout of cognitive dissonance, I told him he needed to take a step back and rethink his approach with his sisters. He hung up, and I was devastated for them.

Aside from the suspicion of infidelity, he was now committing another unforgivable act, but this time it was siding with a child molester.

The next morning, I took them to the police station and they filed a report on their adoptive father. Tony continued to demonstrate disbelief as his mother acted totally clueless even though she even let slip a few words about the physical confrontations a few times. Tony's mother reportedly manipulated him into thinking that I was intentionally trying to destroy the family. I shot back at Tony over the phone saying it was only doing the ethical, right thing and that if she were a good mother, she would've protected her children. So Tony started calling even less, even ignoring my calls, and I had a sneaking feeling he was making his move into another relationship as more photos of him traveling to Texas with another woman surfaced.

Prior to this event, it was already declared I was unwelcome in the family, but I don't mind being an outcast if a group of abusive pedophiles are the ones judging me. Tony was actively looking to replace me, but didn't have the balls to initiate the divorce. Clearly, he had the martyr complex like his mother, and told others around him in North Carolina that I was the villain in this story. I noticed mutual friends we had in North Carolina, mostly just acquaintances I knew from his unit, distance themselves from me.

The few times we spoke since that night he was incredibly nasty. I begged him to go through counseling with me, or counseling by himself.

This wasn't normal and our marriage was officially on the brink. He kept acting out until I told him I was tired of him taking his bullshit out on me and that he was too much of a coward to face his family troubles. He said nothing but a repeated series of "No's" like a robot. Nothing was making any sense with him. I felt like I was talking to an ATM and his refusal to work on our marriage or seek help was now being ignored by his unit. I had been branded the "crazy bitch" who was doing their Marine wrong. If only they knew – or did they?

Out of sheer frustration, not to mention the pain this was causing his sisters and reminding me of abuse I've endured, I asked him a question that would decide the fate of our marriage.

"If the Worcester DA discovers, beyond a shadow of a doubt, that your father is guilty of sexual misconduct with your sisters, would you allow your own children to be alone with your father," I asked, knowing what was coming next and preparing myself accordingly.

"Yes, yes I would! I love my father!" Tony snapped.

"You would allow your own children, your flesh and blood, to be alone in a room for any amount of time with a pedophile? Is that your answer?" I asked, now trembling with fury.

"YES I WOULD!" Tony yelled defiantly. That would be his final stand, a stand he took in defense of a pedophile.

"I WANT A DIVORCE!" I said, starting to tear up and dig my nails into my hands, tearing at my skin.

After all he had done to make me feel worthless, invisible in our marriage, he really pushed me to a hopeless point. It devastated me to get divorced after only two years of marriage. If he condoned his father molesting and beating his sisters because of his own impulse issues, then he can't be trusted if we ever had kids. I feel like I married an indifferent stranger, and even though it's heartbreaking, I feel confident that I've made the correct decision.

Indifference is the worst kind of response when love is expressed. Hate is not the antithesis of love; it's the nonexistence of feeling, a pervasive apathy. When hate is present, so is love. It's passion gone sour and fueled by pain, but, nonetheless, passion and love is apparently still alive. Yet when indifference seeps into our spirits, an emotional numbness and permitted scotoma takes the place of any passion – whether it's love or hate – and resigns in a new state of being.

After an investigation was conducted, it was determined that Tony's father was guilty, and that the girls were telling the truth. The Worcester DA was ready to roll through until the younger sister recanted. Apparently, and accordingly to the older girl, Tony's mother had been pulling them aside nightly, after the father was forced to leave the premises, and told them they were hallucinating, imagining things. She proceeded to bribe them and pressured them into recanting with promises of new clothes, a better home life, and gifts of their choosing. The older sister stuck to the story and wanted to leave, but social services kept them with

Tony's mother. What a horrible mistake. Since one of the girls recanted, the charges were dropped.

In the process of filing the divorce paperwork, I was noticing strange movement in the woods when Eleanor and I came home.

"There's something in the woods. I feel like we're being watched," I told Eleanor.

"It's probably a deer," Eleanor said, not paying it any mind. But this movement and feeling of being watched continued. It wasn't the sound of deer. Every time I looked up, I noticed the movement becoming carefully quieter or would stop all together. There was a person watching us.

One afternoon when Eleanor and Fred went out for a day trip, I was at home alone with their dog, sketching to keep my mind off of stress. All of a sudden, the dog started to go nuts. Eleanor's house has large floor to ceiling windows on three sides, and the dog was running around and barking at the woods. By the time I got up, I couldn't see anything.

It was a different bark, one of distress, that I've never heard. Something was wrong. I started to wonder if the movement in the woods was Tony's father looking for revenge. A shameless narcissist, I exposed him for who he really was and I wouldn't be surprised if he would try anything stupid to assuage his fragile, pedophile ego.

I grabbed two butcher knives and hid behind a door with my cell already to call 911. Finally, the dog calmed down but I heard the breaking of glass coming from the street. While grateful the dog alerted me, I was also concerned about it giving my position in the house away. It would bark and run across the house then circle me. The butcher knives I held onto were being gripped in a way I held my rifle in Iraq. Ready to do damage, but I was alone again. Facing some potential psychopath outside and wondering how I'm going to continue living this way.

When Eleanor returned, I told her what had happened and I wanted to check on my car which was parked in between trees. She had Fred follow me, and we discovered my car with shattered windows. This wasn't a ball coming through or any other object. Talk about a confirmed PTSD paranoia moment. I was being stalked and now my car was vandalized.

I've pretty much reached my wit's end pretty quick with my in-laws as their racist, passive aggressive antics were far too reminiscent of what I went through as a kid. Tony knew of all the things I have gone through and he still didn't get it. But that's not the catalyst for the divorce. Having his sisters confess that not only they were being molested and physically abused by the father, they've already demonstrated suicidal behavior, e.g. cutting, writing letters. Tony's mom wrote it off as being goth or emo.

His apathy toward his sisters is what did it, not how he disregarded and disrespected me. It took seeing him doing it to others to react, to respond, and I kicked myself for not opting out the first week we were married.

I've been through way too much to have to deal with this again. You think someone is potentially normal and you give them the benefit of the doubt, then one day they rain the crazy in on you while you're sans umbrella. I was drenched with Massachusetts.

While Tony cheated, he painted himself as a victim, which is what sociopaths do. They don't thrive on merely inflicting pain, they thrive on generating pity and sucking people dry accordingly. And now I can officially tell you that his real name isn't Tony. I just changed it to Tony in honor of the Tony Awards, because he deserves an award for the song-and-dance number he put on for me throughout the duration of our relationship.

Divorce. Even when it is warranted, desperately craved to cleave yourself unto a blank page and away from an emotional vampire, it's still heartbreaking. Supposedly 1 in 2 marriages end in divorce in the US, but this didn't make me feel better, as though I had transitioned into the vanguard of divorcees of America marching toward newfound freedom.

The impact of divorce, even though my conscience was clean, made me feel like I had failed. The impact was worse than I expected in terms of how it affected my health, self-esteem, happiness, financial stability, communication, and ability to feel intimacy. I already struggled with all those things before, but it felt like Tony dropped me further into a hole I wasn't sure I could get out of in time.

His mistress later became his wife when all was said and done, a hair stylist whom he spoiled accordingly, treatment I never asked for and never received when we were married. All he wanted was a woman asleep at the wheel in life, someone who would shut her eyes to all the blaring warning signs of his shortcomings and decorate the house with country kitsch and predictable Americana. When Tony realized I couldn't be conquered as he saw fit, he sailed toward new territory and planted his flag anywhere he could.

15 KAZAKHSTAN BY ME

Before I headed to North Carolina to retrieve the remaining items I left with Tony, I spoke with Faustina, who ended up telling me about Tony's club-hopping and going off with different women around Jacksonville, NC. This is why he wasn't calling. She didn't want to start any trouble, but I had wished she told me the first time. As the day came for me to fly out, Eleanor gave me a pep talk, told me that there would be a cake waiting for me to celebrate my fabulous divorce. I laughed in my familiar, numb existence.

Upon my arrival into that miserable town in North Carolina, Tony picked me up and with a feigned sad expression. I treated our interactions like it was strictly business. When we got to the apartment, there were some other woman's trinkets lying around. I shook my head and asked him about it.

"I dunno," he said. That was his answer for everything. No integrity, no accountability.

As I saw the wedding photos lying face down on the shelves something happened inside of me that erupted like a volcano, but with tears. He used me. I was just the cook, the maid, not a person. Just an exotic animal he collected and I felt my heart sink to an all-time low. He came toward me and hugged me. I allowed it for a second, then was filled with such intense disgust that I pushed him away and stormed off toward the other room. After that, he stood aside as I gathered books and extra clothes that I didn't take the first time I drove away from him. I told him he could have everything else. The dining set, our dishes, our bed in which he probably slept with many other women. I wanted nothing from him and nothing to remember him by. He had the nerve to ask me what to do about the wedding photos and gifts, and I told him to burn it. I wanted nothing. No memories, no trace of the lie I lived with him.

Before finishing boxing everything up and taking it to the post office, I called Faustina and asked if it was still okay to sleep over at her house. She told me to come on over immediately, and I waved Tony off as Faustina led me inside. I dropped my bags and she saw the look in my eyes.

"I don't know what you saw in him, but I'll tell you the truth: He never deserved you," she said as she held me tight in solidarity.

"It doesn't matter anymore, does it? I sure don't deserve any of this now, and still I have more bricks to carry. I'm getting too tired, too sick of bearing this weight on my back," I said.

Faustina held my hand through the evening, telling me that everything was going to be okay and helped keep me calm until it was time to fly back to Massachusetts. She showed me a photo of Tony's mistress, and mentioned that they knew each other supposedly since high school. I didn't care anymore, all the lying, the cheating, and now standing on the side of disgusting child predators. There was nothing that could ever make me feel for Tony. It was never a marriage; it was a mirage, a complete illusion.

While in North Carolina, I gave him the chance to be honest with me, to level with me about what our marriage might have lacked. In the end I discovered there was nothing I could do to prevent our matrimonial demise. You simply cannot have only one person in the marriage putting in effort, disclosing oneself honestly; it's just too much of a burden for one person in a couple to carry. And the user will, in turn, take more advantage of the situation and continue to lose respect for the other who is tolerating the abuse. I wouldn't have been so quick to sign the divorce papers if he had been honest with me. It wasn't the infidelity alone or him siding with his father in an odd and dangerous family feud, it was the fact that he took my ability to choose away from me. That was the greatest betrayal of trust. He did what he wanted and negated my right to select whether or not I wanted to stay or go, whether I was okay with our circumstances or not. In the end, I had to initiate divorce as he was never with me from the start. Semper Fi, fuck the other guy – or anyone other than your wife in this case.

A month later, Tony came up to Massachusetts to attend the

divorce hearing. Tony tried to tremble his lips and act like he was about to cry. Pathetic. I paid no more attention to the show and turned my eyes on the judge. The judge heard both our sides and then looked to me. He looked sad, as though there were a moment of silent understanding of what I just went through as though he had seen it a thousand times over. Perhaps he had. He then signed off on the divorce, and Tony and I went our separate ways.

Afterward, I thought of Tony's hypocrisy and sociopathic behavior, his materialistic attitude, that stupid gape mouth he made in pictures, his lust for luxury cars, his envy of wealth and dreaming about power were more than enough to encourage me to leave, but I stayed until something horrible made me drop the hammer, and shattered any and all illusions completely.

I held him as he cried, a Marine who never took part in direct combat. I was bandaging his inner wounds when mine were festering, while I was being ignored or slandered by other male-dominated and predominantly white veterans groups. I didn't fit in; not in those groups, my environment, school, or in holding my husband together. I just didn't belong, and I didn't know how to verbalize it and tell anyone. Even if I could, I feared that it wouldn't be enough to remove myself from the vast loneliness I felt while Tony cried in my arms. Everyone around me was allowed, permitted to fall apart; yet I had to think twice. I couldn't bear to take another dip into an ocean of solitude for another taste of ostracization. I felt I would die. So I kept my mouth shut in order to survive on this seemingly alien plane, constantly looking for an exit, a wormhole back into another time, where life made sense.

I thought back, often of the desert. Iraq wasn't simply carnage in my mind, it was devastatingly beautiful. Vast open space, wind caressing your skin causing the fabric of your uniform to ride slightly on a cushion of air while inhaling that scent that resembled the smell of old parchment paper and eucalyptus. It smelled like that until weapons started to fire and bodies were charred and left on the side of the road to rot in the sun. Then it smelled like hopelessness, carbon residue, and death. The apocalypse already came for Iraq, everyone else was just too stupid to notice, but now another world was ending here.

There were very few people I could relate to, and Tony stood out for being someone who appeared to understand me. I was wrong. With him, I thought that I had an ally, someone I could trust in a world of strangers. However, with him, I've never felt so isolated and alone. I wasn't living in North Carolina when we were married; I was on an island. Marriage was just another status to acquire in building his image. I needed more than a label. You can stick on and peel off labels. What I wanted was someone who didn't blow away like a leaf, but someone who would grow with me like my own roots.

Before the divorce was finalized, I had already moved into an apartment in Gardner. It was an old mill that had been converted and updated into cozy apartments with high ceilings and large windows. I wasn't expecting to live alone in such a snowy winter wonderland, but I accepted that this is where my career was taking me, and that I had no other real options.

In November, I ended up being nominated for an award by the State of Massachusetts for Outstanding Woman Veteran of the Year. It was a great ceremony, but no one from the office attended. Eleanor was out of town for some reason and no one knew about the event, except Eleanor and Fred, until after the fact. This was around the time that the temperature with both Fred and Eleanor began to change, and word of misused funds began to surface. I started asking questions about the nature of where the grant money and donations were going as plans for my designated workplace in Gardner were still unclear, and much of my inquiry was met with contempt. Much like Tony's infidelity, I had that uneasy, impending trauma feeling again.

Before Thanksgiving, I was invited by one of the people who helped build the veterans center in Gardner. Let's call him "John." He was a Vietnam veteran and a former Special Forces soldier, but he was also the person who watched Lioness and referred it to Eleanor. After Eleanor watched it, he reportedly suggested for her to hire me. As much as things fell apart here in Massachusetts, I was grateful to have a job and a place of my own as well as supportive people like John encouraging me to push past painful experiences.

John lived in some remote location in New Hampshire, remote enough that I ended up using grid coordinates to find it. When I reached his house, his wife was in the middle of cooking and other family members were making their way over. John and I ended up sitting out in the living room and started chatting about some of the collectibles he had around the house. Indigo dye, Indigofera tinctoria, in authentic oriental rugs? Hmm. I recalled that he did a stint in Saudi Arabia as a general contractor, but judging by the coloring, shapes and design of the rug, it looked like something one would see in Central Asia.

John went on about other trinkets and items around the house, telling me about his travels in Iran, Afghanistan, Turkmenistan, Azerbaijan, and every other country that ended in –stan. Much of this took place after the Vietnam War of course, but when these travels took place is what caught me off guard. He was in Iran and Afghanistan in the 1980s. He was all over Asia in this period. He knew Farsi. Okay, what's the deal?

"What do you mean?" he asked smiling slyly.

"You didn't think I'd come over here and not notice all of this, or delve into your past and not be curious?" I said.

"So, what did you think I did? I was in the business of energy!" He said.

"Like an economic hitman?" I laughed.

Not quite, but he did tell me, much like the aperitif-offering American in Prague.

"I knew it," I said now wondering why the hell he really brought me out here.

"Have you given your future any serious thought? Is this really what you want to do?" he asked earnestly.

"I enjoy helping out other veterans. Am I happy right now? No. But then again, I just went through a divorce and I don't have any friends in Massachusetts," I replied.

"That's not what I asked," he said smiling, knowing I was skirting a vital point here. He spoke for a moment about needing to get war out of one's system, and that while I was handling the veterans program, he knew I wasn't telling anyone my story. He mentioned Lioness and that if I didn't get help for what I saw like he did, it would eat me alive.

"No, I haven't given my future serious thought. I'm not sure about having much of a future. I'm not in love with my life and Iraq gave me an additional, incurable melancholy that I can't escape. So, I don't care about living and I've lost the fear of dying, really. There's little giving me the will to live and if things don't turn around by the time I'm thirty, I hope to bite the bullet and say yes to an offer and stick to that until I die, which will hopefully be soon," I said.

"I thought so," John said.

He continued to outline why he ended up doing what he did. To never accept an offer through the front door, to never be too armed but to spread weapons and hide resources, to keep behaving like I did in Prague in networking and having an exit strategy in every circumstance. That it wasn't wrong for me to think tactically, and to be flexible, to adapt – even if it meant faking it.

Before we started dinner, he offered to connect me to an old friend who was looking for "contractors" in Kazakhstan. I said I'd think about it. He said he'd give me time to think about it before I left, but I simply thanked everyone for the lovely Thanksgiving dinner and drove back to Massachusetts. I was having a hard enough time processing this transition as I had to prepare for another. While disappearing into Kazakhstan was tempting, I felt there was something bigger out there. Something bigger than taking some spook job.

There had to be something more than this.

16 WINTER IN NEW ENGLAND

Snow, piercing wind, gray skies, white out, black ice. I wondered why so many people here complained of the terrible winters but choose to stay. One should love the place they call home. Then I looked back on my divorce and asked myself what I was waiting for, and what took me so long to leave. I betrayed myself by downplaying my instincts and in the end, I found that such subconscious nudges were red flags burning right through me.

The supposed love Tony and I had didn't die naturally, but by asphyxiation. It died because no oxygen was available to breathe, to be myself, to be loved with the freedom to love back. In time, I grew weary and he had conquered me as a territory, instead of loving me as a spouse, a friend, a person. After my energy well had run dry to try to get him to see me as a human being, I was empty, and he had long since moved onto the next oil reserve to drill.

As I sipped hot cinnamon tea, I peered over the window ledge of my apartment, the 4th floor in this space filled with ghostly industrial ambience. Looking down upon the blanketed snowy ground below, I saw myself lying there. With glassy eyes and hardened blue skin, the dying self of my imagination enveloped in the winter nothingness told me to run. This was not an insecurity of life itself, but an insecurity of my icy environment. I knew who I was, and when I clearly was not doing well. All of that was apparent. It was that my concept of home was uncertain. It created a vacuum of security that left me feeling restless and constantly wanting to leave the cold. However, that road map didn't exist yet.

Before I made the move from the headquarters office of the nonprofit, inter-office politics were getting intense. After Eleanor and Fred left for the Bahamas during December and January, it marked a turn for the worse with the CFO, Laura, throwing daily tantrums and bullying a new employee.

Microaggressions are designed to cut a person down - not with a swift blow to topple them, but to engage in slow murder with thousands of tiny lacerations. It's simply too much to ask for someone to merely get over multiple, daily attacks, to simply get over a lifetime of wounds. How about we just stop hurting one another in the first place?

This was not the first time Laura has bullied someone in the office, i.e. when she made Susan cry after returning from a relative's funeral in September or Laura getting in my face while discussing a simple task in regard to Gardner. She came to my desk and ended up putting her fingers in my face, yelling, "FOCUS!" Belligerent, condescending freak-outs, getting into a shouting match with Fred before Thanksgiving – the list goes on of stupid, petty attacks.

My interactions where I've gotten angry all have to do with the same thing: when I ask someone to stop pushing me to argue. A good example of this is when Fred started an argument in early November where he brought up Iraq talking points from the news. He kept pushing me to engage even when I told him that I didn't want to discuss it because it makes me upset.

He got my attention when he said, "Well, what have YOU done for your country?" This incident took place the day after I got my award from the State of Massachusetts. It's funny how men who've never served in combat feel so comfortable questioning my service and have less trouble taking my military past and defecating all over it while waving the American flag. God bless America.

Fred went on to explain to an employee who asked why no one in the office was there at my award ceremony that my award is "no big deal" and that "Eleanor gets big awards all the time, but she just puts them in her desk and shuts up."

I wasn't making a big deal of it, the other employees and Susan were the ones apologizing for not being there to show their support since they didn't know. That's when Fred jumped in and interrupted the conversation to belittle and insult me. While I may be viewed as the combat vet with PTSD in the office as both Fred and Eleanor have joked, I don't care for someone utilizing my veteran status against me. I wanted no further harassment while I worked there.

Laura flaunted her work for this veteran organization, but continued to treat me, a combat veteran, with plenty of malice, insults to my intelligence and emotional stability as a combat veteran despite the numerous tasks I've been able to tackle. I was coping just fine on my own, even with horrific memories. She even commented not too long after Eleanor left that she shouldn't have hired me and I was a mistake. I didn't want any interventions or anything else that would cause Laura to touch my paycheck – something she's threatened to me personally that she's capable of – or do anything to jeopardize my position in this hostile hole. No one in this office deserved the harassment that she doled out. For someone who constantly threatened, even flippantly, that she'd sue, she had a lot of cause to be sued herself for several EEO violations.

I just wanted to be able to do my job without someone harassing me or pushing me into an altercation where I am needing to defend myself against aggressive attacks and/or outlandish statements that are not only offensive, but cruel. I'm just fed up with having to put up with a bully in the workplace. I feel sorry for others who are going to have to continue to walk on eggshells while working with this nonprofit. While I've verbalized the interactions during trips with Eleanor before, she told me that I was being sensitive or to get over it.

So, I got over it and filed a written complaint. After I relocated to my new office to Gardner, the lines went silent with Laura.

Not too long after opening the Gardner facility to four veterans living in the detached houses outside of the main center, I was approached at the front door of the facility. Two men from a local veteran service organization inquired about recruiting veterans at the facility in which I was in charge, handing me brochures and sign-up forms to pass onto the group of male veterans living on-site. They kept mentioning how proud they were of the "men" who served our great nation and how it is everyone's mission to support our brave "men" fighting in Iraq and Afghanistan.

"It's great that you're doing so much for these men, but what about women?" I asked, completely not expecting the immediate, thoughtless responses.

"We have a women's auxiliary," said one of the men.

"Well, what's the difference between being a regular member and being a member of the women's auxiliary?" I asked.

"The women's auxiliary is for the wives of veterans, they participate in bake sales and other similar events, baking cookies and such to raise money for the men," the other responded proudly.

"I'm not a wife of a veteran. I'm a veteran myself. And why would I want to bake cookies? I just want to be treated like the veteran that I am," I responded, expressionless.

Both men stood in front of me as wide-eyed as a deer facing the headlights of a semi. They looked at each other, almost appeared embarrassed, until one of them nervously stated, "Well, you could join. I guess we never thought about having women join...You were in combat? How?"

From this interaction alone, my interest in joining had gone from "mildly interested" to "I'd rather die, thanks."

My time with the nonprofit here was not improving, my support system was dismal, and as my marriage dissipated, so many other illusions were dismantled as well.

I started to receive strange phone calls from various parts of New England warning me about Eleanor. Some of this bizarre new information and other stories were confirmed by current employees via casual small talk. Figuring out where grant money actually went started to worry me, and my questions about it were perceived by Eleanor as absurd. However, it was one call in particular that got my attention.

A woman called me one night after I got home from work. She looked up my home phone number, admittedly, and felt the need to inform me that I was in danger. From money laundering to insurance fraud, she mapped out a series of events for me that indicated the company I was working for was rife with corruption. The caller told me to keep her name anonymous, but for me to make plans to leave. But where? I had no one, no home I knew of where I could go to feel safe. I was in winter wonderland with a bunch of crazed elves.

Leaving the main office where Fred and Laura leaked mental hell, I felt that in coming to Gardner, I'd be happy to get away from the drama to my own office. Essentially, I would be doing some good? With every story the caller provided, which went on for two hours, I listened in horror and asked questions that were often left unanswered by the company. It was making me fear I was in yet another untenable situation.

Initially Eleanor seemed like a youthful free spirit, but she was clever when it came to shuffling money and hiding pertinent information. I soon saw that in the process of running veterans' programs, they were intent on keeping veterans as long as possible. Sick veterans, not rehabilitated ones, generated the money, so there was no apparent profit in seeing anyone recover. I felt sick.

I wondered who this caller was in all this chaos and how she knew so much, but she claimed to be too afraid to share details regarding her identity. I told her I understood her concern, but what was I going to do with all this information?

"It is despicable to think that someone who is supposedly all about the troops and collecting donations and grant money for such a cause should live such a lavish lifestyle and attempt to charge veterans to stay in programs that were previously advertised as free of charge," the mysterious caller said.

To add a nice touch to my holiday story, Eleanor called me a day before Christmas. She had a different tone to her voice, and jokingly ask if I had killed myself yet in reference to undergoing divorce this past summer. Knowing I was in Massachusetts without any close friends or family, I failed to see the humor in that statement. Nothing was funny about my life. Just plain pitiful. Empty.

Sensing my wallowing in a puddle of misery, Susan asked me over for Christmas to participate in a White Elephant party, which is a gift-swapping game where you bring a gift and then pull a number at random to receive an equally random gift. Susan had a large family, and welcomed me into the mad get together where good food, alcohol, and bizarre gifts mixed. As I looked around the room and observed the happiness of family and friends who knew each other well, loved each other, and were involved each other's lives, I made a mental note of this scene before me. One day, I thought, I'd like to have this in my own house, to feel love around me and feel welcomed to be myself. Susan then nudged me to stop looking so sad and to smile.

After the party ended, Susan invited me back for New Year's Eve, "You're not going to be alone for New Year's. I don't care how tough you are, you are coming over and that's the end of the discussion."

I tried to get out of it saying I didn't want to drink and drive.

"The more the merrier in my house! You're staying in a room upstairs. It's settled. You're sleeping over!" she commanded.

Susan, a seasoned federal penitentiary nurse who had moved to the veteran hospice side of the house, was making a concerted effort to keep me in her line of sight. Her brother, whom she was extremely close with, was a Vietnam veteran who passed away years ago. She remained by his side through the aftermath of war, and others in her immediate circle knew of veterans who suffered similar physiological and psychological ailments. I knew what she was doing, but it's difficult to acknowledge or accept help when so much of what's been in your environment were problems, catastrophes, or threats. She knew this, and kept drawing me in no matter how I tried to break away.

Before the clock struck midnight on New Year's Eve, Susan, her family and dozens of friends, and I were happily smashed. I had unfortunately engaged in somewhat of a drinking contest before the countdown and what was a steady buzz turned into blackout mode after downing a bottle of champagne – or two? All I could recall at the time was that when everyone around me in Susan's house cheered, something inside me turned off. I wasn't happy to see another year, and in many ways I was angry about it.

Looking down at one of my empty glasses, Susan's husband began asking why I looked so sad. All I could remember saying was, "I don't deserve to be here. I didn't want to come home."

After uttering those words, I blacked out. Supposedly, and according to Susan's account, I was crying after I said that I didn't want to be alive. Susan's husband and a few others started to cry as well. They all knew someone like me, and being there perhaps reminded them too of people who died young, or took their own lives to achieve what appeared to be a more desirable outcome after a failed homecoming. After bawling my eyes out with people I barely knew, I made my way upstairs and passed out in the guest bedroom. Others followed suit to their respective rooms and homes.

When I woke up, I found myself drenched in a puddle of vomit that fortunately mostly landed on my winter jacket. I was covered from my hair and face to down my chest and back. Some of it made it onto the guest room blanket. Hung-over, hurt, and pitiful, I spent early morning hours in Susan's house washing all of her sheets in sheer embarrassment. Aching all over my body, I quickly showered after completion, then made my way downstairs to thank Susan for allowing me to stay.

Wondering what the hell had become of my life after nearly pulling a Jimi Hendrix on myself, I walked up to Susan at the dining room table. Before leaving, I got a stern talk from Susan who made me promise to never kill myself. She cried and talked about her brother who passed, someone who suffered the ills of war and combat trauma, someone she loved dearly and held his hand through his own personal hell until the day he died. She told me she loved me and that she knew I was alone in a way that no one understood.

Happy New Year.

PART II

17 A VISION IN THE SONORAN DESERT

In January 2010, I had grown tired of the snowy, wintery abyss of the Northeast, a condition with which I could commiserate with Eugenio in Germany. Rufus, one of the Iraq war veterans that I met in DC had apparently kept my contact info and called me one afternoon. He offered an all-expenses paid trip to attend a workshop for veterans in Tucson, Arizona.

"What's the catch?" I asked, secretly hoping for once that there wasn't one as I stared out into the bleak, snow-filled forest outside the clinic window.

"There's no catch. You don't owe anyone anything. You're an amazing advocate for women veterans and we would be honored to have you part of our workshop. Maybe teach us a thing or two about what Lionesses go through?" Rufus said endearingly.

Pausing for a moment, I rolled my eyes in tedium. Then I looked back out of the window into the winter Hades of my present circumstances, and replied, "When do I leave?"

After driving carefully on icy roads and heading toward Boston Logan International Airport at 2am, I arrived a few hours later on what should have been a forty-five-minute drive. The roads were so slippery and heavy snow was coming down for over half of the commute. I was early for my flight by a few hours and the ticket counter wasn't even open yet, so I bundled myself in my car and just let my mind rest. It felt like I was about to get out of prison.

The time came to get my tickets and I gleefully hopped onto a flight headed for Arizona and kissed the winter void bye-bye for the weekend.

When I arrived in Phoenix, I stopped for a moment en route to my next gate and just stared out at the sandy mountains resting in the afternoon sun. Aside from Iraq, I had never lived in a desert, but something about being in this part of the country felt invigorating. All around me there was a sense of strength and a comforting solitude that relaxed my jingling nerves and thawed my blood. I've only been here for a few minutes and I could already feel the innocuous desert warmth seeping into my soul.

Upon arriving in Tucson, I met up with a group of other veterans from other states who were on their way to the same event, which was located in the Painted Rocks area of Northwest Tucson. It was a forty-minute drive or so from the airport to this place called Redemptorist Renewal Center, a retreat site that caters to spiritual groups and corporate functions. I had no idea what to expect, but so far I was soaking in the surrounding mountains that seemed to embrace the city like a womb. It felt as though I had been dropped onto another planet.

We arrived at the site as the sun began to set when another veteran exclaimed, "Turn around and look at the mountain, quick!"

As a few of us turned, our eyes were met with beautiful, brilliant colors. The Santa Catalina Mountains were bright pink and accented with shades of purple.

"I'm going to move here," I said to myself.

As romantic of a notion it may seem, something about being in the desert again – sans IED's, small arms fire, and the like – brought me a sense of peace that I hadn't felt in quite a long time. I wanted more of it.

Watching the mountains change colors flipped a light switch in my brain. I wasn't happy living in Massachusetts, working for a questionable organization, dealing with the aftermath of my divorce, and generally rebuilding my life in an environment where I perpetually felt like an outsider. Massachusetts didn't offer what this place seemingly could.

One afternoon during the workshop, a group of us war-weary veterans climbed up the side of the mountain next to the retreat center. We made it to the top of this peak that provided us an illuminated vista of Tucson. I breathed deeply, taking in every bit of cold arid desert air into my lungs like the first gulp of clean water after years of contamination. Then, looking around me, at the affects of my fellow wanderers, I saw a moment of hope and peace in their eyes. Crazy beautiful desert landscapes swallowed our heartache, even if it was just for a moment, and gave us a glimpse of what life could be like if we could just loosen the death-grip of our violent pasts.

I fell in love with the place, which was ironically Eugenio's hometown. Before leaving that weekend, I went up to the central Virgin Mary statue, surrounded by Saguaro cacti. In complete darkness, I looked at it with my own emptiness. I didn't exactly look at her in the traditional Christian, Catholic sense; I looked at her as an embodiment of what I projected all of my hopes. I wanted to be whole again and being here, something inside me was piecing itself together. There was something surreal and peaceful about sitting alone at the foot of sandy mountains of the desert in this seemingly secluded retreat center that meshed Zen Buddhism with Roman Catholicism – roll that around in your mind a bit – with a vast blanket of stars strewn across a sapphire banner sky. A dreamland of sand, wind, and solace. I needed to be here. In this desert I felt more alive than I ever felt since being back. This treasure I've been searching for, home, is here somewhere.

When I returned to New England, I had one of the most lucid, surreal dreams I've ever experienced. I dreamt that I returned to the retreat center where a mysterious woman told me that I needed to leave Massachusetts for Arizona.

Above me, a cool, cloudless cobalt blue gradient sky flowed into turquoise and warmed up to a pinkish orange hue hugging the purple mountains, providing a tranquil backdrop for the neon green saguaro cacti living on the earthy, golden sand. It was difficult to distinguish the earth from heaven. I am present here; the most present, the most human, here in this magnificent desert. Before my arrival I was just a ghost. The will to live again began coursing through my veins, as my heart beat faster, a steady drum in the desert.

Then I saw her. A woman warrior standing in the same spot as the statue from the clandestine Buddhist-Catholic center. I didn't know what she was exactly. I moved closer to her, examining as I did the statue in Tucson. Then she spoke. I panicked; the statue was alive.

As I ran as fast as I could toward the apparent safety of the neon cacti-filled mountains, she scolded me, "Stop! Turn around, and come back here."

Like a remorseful child to its mother, I returned to her upon her request with eyes cast down out of both fear and respect. She resembled an indigenous Virgin Mary. Tonantzin manifested. However, she lacked that silent, solemn nature one expects in a traditional deity. She spoke with me and was blunt, but caring; stern yet emanated a sense of love that couldn't be explained but only felt. She told hard, painful truths to me without an ounce of vulgarity; she didn't need it. She didn't mince words, and spoke a refreshing honesty. I longed for this honesty.

This Desert Warrior told me that I needed to pack my belongings and come to Arizona, and that she would bring me to Tucson where good things awaited me.

“Sometimes in life you have to leave home in order for you to find it again. Your life has been in perpetual motion and you’re becoming the person you’re supposed to be. You will continue to learn, on a deeper level, about how to live again. Truly live. You will have new life taking place inside of you, and you will learn to love again,” she said. That was music to my ears, to love again.

“You will continue to travel across the country, meet people who will guide you to your destination, and finally you will rediscover your spirit. You have this one chance to take and to make things right with your life, and it won’t be easy, but you need to begin your journey soon,” she stated in a concerned voice.

I really liked the sound of this as terrifying as it may seem. I was excited, enamored with the idea of leaving everything behind, giving up all the trivial material nonsense I’ve acquired and getting on the road to a place where I could love again. What a beautiful thing it is to travel, to move, to change scenery, to go somewhere and discover something new. It all made sense.

“Have no worries about anything. You will be alone a lot – at first. You will continue to find peace in solitude until the time is right, when you’re ready. Don’t overanalyze. Trust yourself. You will find home and you will be forever changed,” she said smiling.

A sense of warmth came over me. I was to experience solitude in a place I’ve never lived and trust my instincts and people I’ve never met. She continued to look into my eyes, and cloaked in an iridescent sea foam and pearl color that glittered in the moonlight above us, stars encircled her in constant motion. She told me that we would meet again.

“How will I know it's you when we meet? Will you still be

you?" I asked.

"I am who I will be," she said. I had no idea what that was supposed to mean.

"Is there anything else I need to know?" I asked, wishing that there was more time to talk. The conversation was coming to a close as I could feel myself waking up in my room in the seventh circle of wintery hell in New England.

She smiled, and said, "Take care that the voice of God and the Devil sound one in the same in the desert. Trust your instincts. You were not put on this earth to be naïve, blindly optimistic, or passive; you are here to be vigilant, to survive."

Before our conversation ended, I hugged her. As I held her in my arms, I felt like I was holding a little girl, and I embraced her with a love I had never experienced in my lifetime until this dream. She smelled like warm sugar cookies and love.

Then I woke. What the Desert Warrior said in that beautiful, surrealist desert resonated with me and I knew what I had to do. I wasn't sure if I had some sort of spiritual, transcendent experience or it was my unconscious mind pulling out the last few biological survival-mode stops to keep me moving in a direction where I'd be motivated to live again. What I can say is that it left a great enough impression to act on it, to take the steps necessary to find the will to survive trauma.

At times, I've wondered since returning from Iraq, where is my home? I don't mean it in the sense of an actual physical structure or even the place in which I remove my boots and take off the Army-issued socks that I still wear. As I type this, I pause to look down at my feet and see the same issued socks that have proved to be somewhat of a comfort item. Perhaps it keeps me grounded. No matter how glamorous I may feel in feminine clothes, these socks remind me that once I was dusty, dirty, and in the same uniform for days without having an opportunity to wash them in an empty oil drip pan.

Returning to my apartment in central Massachusetts, I recalled the dream. Getting back to sending out resumes with cover letters, I remained locked onto the computer screen looking for answers, looking for a sign, searching for a way out of here.

Two months later, I received a job offer in Phoenix. Apparently, while sending out an inquiry to the State of Arizona, the women veterans coordinator, Gabe Forsberg, recognized my name. She had seen the Lioness documentary and seemed tickled pink that I was considering moving to Phoenix. She promptly recommended me for a position in veteran's education. The hiring process would take a while and she encouraged me to be patient and that all would work out. I took out a postcard of a saguaro cactus I bought in Tucson, gripped it tightly, and wished myself into the Sonoran Desert.

While keeping my eyes fixed on images of the desert, I still had a job to do. The dream was fresh on my mind throughout the workday and I felt a sense of urgency to do something, anything to make a change in my life. The dream itself wasn't like a jarring hallucination of a fallen comrade, but it pulled me right back into the Chamorro idea of dreams as foretelling. All my life, I've been taking care of other people. From operating as a Lioness in Iraq to running this center, my work has always been about helping people find their path, their way through the worst of life. It was time I did that for myself.

Maintaining the veterans' center with no help, I ended up getting pulled aside one afternoon for a newspaper interview. Apparently, Eleanor had told a local paper that the center was staffed with therapists, doctors and wonderful medical professionals of all kinds. I merely told them that it was patently untrue.

Something really bothered me in this moment. I knew that we had the money for the veterans' center, but I also knew where it was going and it wasn't toward veterans. I thought it was ridiculous to charge homeless veterans to stay in housing after telling them it was free. I was blind-sided by what sounded like a scheduled and forced soft story about waving flags and tying yellow ribbons, and it made me absolutely livid.

Soon after, I faced backlash for speaking out as expected. Although I resigned, Eleanor and Fred made sure that the newspaper published a piece that said that they fired me and basically called me inept and lazy. Because that's what happens with inept and lazy people, you leave them in charge of a multi-million-dollar LEED-certified veterans rehabilitation center.

There were others online and via phone trying to reach me to give me a virtual high-five for standing up to a powerful business that uses veterans for profit under the nonprofit banner. Others side-stepped me and analyzed why I did what I did like a case study, attempting to speak for me. Be my ally, listen to me. But please don't be my voice.

There was a group of white women veterans who were spreading the Gardner story like wildfire on social media, and with smug intent. There's the trigger. It wasn't insisted that my standing up to the powers-that-be was any act of courage, they were calling on others to mock the fact that I was getting slammed by my former employer.

Being a gadfly in the veteran community can make you unpopular, but when you're a woman veteran of color, you are at the mercy of the pitchforks of these types of colonialist Americans. This felt as though they intended to exacerbate my suffering, and they enjoyed the attacks thoroughly. A few people sent me emails, called me, and then I felt like others were on my side. However, I felt liberation in standing up for what I believed in, albeit alone.

There was something else that occurred to me about Eleanor and other women I've come to know over the past few years: I was needed by them. Not for anything spiritual or deeply meaningful. They wanted me around for a transfusion. Their blood had thickened with an excess of superfluous, artificial fillers of their own life and was clogging their arteries. They longed to live vicariously through my life, absorbing my dreams, passions, interests, my will to survive and more until the line between their reality and mine became blurred. It was a parasitic, vampiric drain on my psyche.

That was it. They were psychological vampires. In their seemingly flawed, empty worlds, they weren't enough. While I was observed to live freely, unbothered by the opinions and judgment of others, they thrived to take from me in some of the unhealthiest ways to patch up the holes of their own sinking spiritual vessel. Although my world was just as flawed as theirs, by living through me, they could breathe – yet it was my oxygen they were stealing.

Eleanor's desire to deconstruct and squeeze everything to death was painful to watch, but I no longer had compassion for her and what she was doing. Through me, she got to vicariously live the life of a combat veteran that she never was, to be the indigenous woman at the mercy of America that she never was, to be a mental health practitioner in a war that she never experienced. It was a depressing state. She wanted to be me, and she resented me for what I did, no matter how many times she claimed to honor veterans for their sacrifice. The emptiness people like her feel will only continue to strangle her and she will, in response, grab onto others for air as she slowly drowns.

Why is there such an intense compulsion in contemporary North American culture to latch onto something good and drain the life, blood, and passion out of it? Why does everything need to be exploited to death, turning even the most sacred human virtues into buy-one-get-one-free gimmickry? Why even bother to call passion by its name when it has a bargain sticker attached to it on a clearance rack?

Susan, on the other hand, disproved that suspicion. Nothing that felt as suspicious as a friendly white woman; and it seemed almost unwise to trust one if I was going off personal life experience alone. I didn't want to treat her like I had been treated, and I'm glad I had accepted her hand in friendship. She opened her heart to me, made me feel like I was a member of her family, and kept calling me, nudging me, bugging me every chance she had until I left.

The following week, post-newspaper debacle, I had my final phone interview with the State of Arizona. The phone interviewer, after speaking with me for over an hour finally asked, "How soon can you be here?"

When we least expect, life provides a test for our willingness to change, to grow in a new direction; when that time comes, there is no point in denial or declaring that we're not yet ready. Life won't wait, and it will roll on with or without you. There was no hesitation; I decided then and there.

"Give me two days to clear out my apartment and a week to get out to Arizona," I responded.

"Great, we'll give you an extra day to recover and the following day, meet us at our office at 12pm," my potential new supervisor replied.

I leapt out of my recliner and bounced around the apartment like a kid on a sugar high. It felt like a prison term was over and I was getting my life back. Susan immediately volunteered herself and her family to help me empty the apartment.

"How much do you want for this?" Susan said referring to miscellaneous items I had aside from a TV and a queen-sized therapeutic foam mattress.

I paused. "Just take it, all of it."

Susan looked at me with a mixture of pride and sadness. I was just grateful to not have to haul furniture across the continental US. I took only what fit in my silver compact sedan, which was over-packed with all of my clothes and books. That's all I needed to leave, as was the case everywhere else I've left in a hurry. Clothes and books.

That night when we concluded emptying my place, Susan and her husband took me out for dinner at an Italian restaurant and laughed at all the fun memories we've made, as well as the road that lies ahead. Before the night was over, walking to our respective cars, Susan gave me the biggest hug and started to cry.

"We love you so much. Go, and don't look back. Follow your dreams, and find your home," she said tearing up. I smiled, and held back the tears, waving good-bye as I kept walking forward. So much of the suffering I had endured alone came to a beautiful silver lining before I left Massachusetts where I was shown so much love that it illuminated my own private dark sky that much more.

You can't become immune to life's pain and suffering. You can't simply acquire courage or the will to live, it takes constant practice and no matter where you are on the healing spectrum, like a muscle, you must work it out constantly or lose your inner strength. From our youth, we're taught to believe in the world as a meritocracy, that if you study and work hard, your dreams will come true. That if you're honest and kind, you will be rewarded. And when you're continually screwed over in life, you're told that you will be rewarded in heaven and that God loves you so much which is why he is throwing the weight of the world on your back. But this simply is not true. You get betrayed, slighted, and find yourself asking God to love you a little less and cut you a break.

While I don't believe that all misfortune is part of some divine plan or cosmic realm completely out of our control, we have to remind ourselves that there are things we can control and things we can't – but we'd better focus on the former and just prepare for the latter. How we respond to trauma and life's ills determines our survival rate and our happiness. Horrible things happen to great people and great things happen to horrible people, but there's no sense in grinding your teeth over it. We are here to be vigilant, to survive, and instead of ruminating over the motion in the tall grass, we must get the hell out of the way and run toward our haven, where we can survive instead of ignoring danger and what can kill us in the long-run.

The challenge I made to myself here was to make the trip out on the open road and into myself, challenging myself to shed the dead skin of depression and have a deeper, more intimate spiritual life. The reward of being able to live a life I've wanted is worth it, and I'm ready to face what lies ahead.

When facing destiny, words alone don't suffice. I've met quite a few intelligent speakers over the past few years who are great with advice yet simply didn't practice what they preached. People who read about life but don't experience it, or are too afraid to take any risks, lack substantial life advice – or at least the advice I'm interested in hearing.

I really can't stress this enough. If you want to make an impact, don't simply sit idly by and 'hope' for courage. Courage is not the absence of fear, but rather the decision made in determining what's more important than fear. There was a newfound wisdom to be had that just wasn't in this environment, but thousands of miles away.

In travel, I found sublimation. I'll be hitting travel hard and putting the pain into something productive, a survival mechanism to avoid a splitting of the ego. Sublimation redirects a painful experience into a positive experience. It's a defense mechanism against turning inward and losing my bearings. The desire for perpetual motion was my key to staying alive.

It's a mistake to imply wisdom through age alone and without any practical knowledge, and you sure can't read about the world without actually living in it. The dream of the woman warrior in the desert appeared to me as an inner longing, a pull to go westward. It inspired me to abandon the opinions of the fearful and meek, in search of my own happiness and sense of fulfillment in the fog of the unknown, toward that shining mountain in the desert.

18 ON THE ROAD

Road trips can teach you a lot about life. For example, what's the biggest window on a car?

The windshield.

If you spend all your time on the road examining everything in your rear-view mirror or the back of the vehicle, you're not only going to miss everything in front of you, but your likelihood of crashing increases exponentially. Keeping focused on the view through the windshield, everything in the present and down the road, is imperative to success and survival. Bottom line: It's okay to glance at your past, just don't stare.

Blind spots can get the best of you, too. If your fears, prejudices, and inhibitions cloud your vision, you will miss the bigger picture on account of these unnecessary and dangerous distractions. Road trips are a physical and mental journey, and this long trek across the continental US was some of the best therapy I could ever get. No judgment, no rejection, no implications; I was free to be me, flying down the road and keeping my heart fixed on finding "home."

The home that my soul thirsted for, ached for, was somewhere out there. My dried up spirit longed for the refreshment and rejuvenation that the desert so willingly provided. It didn't sound very conventional to others in my family, who apparently thought I was crazy to have left a desert in Iraq filled with madness to move to another unknown, unpredictable desert where I didn't know a soul. Instinctively, I felt that in order to become whole again, I would need to completely open up and expose myself to the unknown, the new, and embrace this chapter in my life with a determined, keen curiosity.

Like driving down a desert highway in Iraq, I was eagerly searching for signs. Now is the winter of my discontent. As you embrace the new, you become dissatisfied with the old. Your comfort zone, stasis, is death. It's all too easy to come back to a familiar place or some insular bubble where everyone looks, acts, and thinks like you – the you that existed before the world fell apart. That's exactly what I didn't want – but I never had such a luxury in the first place. In my case, my comfort zone was in a rut of depression. I intuitively knew that my comfort zone would kill me, so I began my drive from Massachusetts to my parents' home in Florida, then the journey would take me from Jacksonville down Interstate 10 to Phoenix, Arizona.

The night before leaving, I stretched out on my inflatable mattress and wrapped myself in a blanket I bought in Iraq. It was indigo and so incredibly warm that I felt like I was back in the womb. Ridiculously happy and at peace, I was finally leaving a place that had given me so much heartache and disappointment, a place that felt so cold in the soul. While I was thankful for people like Susan and others I've met here, I was also very weary of the dense population of flag-waving sociopaths and bigots in my vicinity. It was scary, and I was grateful for the opportunity to leave it all behind.

Before sunrise on April 15, 2010, I woke up to place a few items on the street corner to be collected, extra decoration and foodstuffs. When I came back for another drop-off, the first pile was already gone. I placed what little remaining items I had left in my apartment – clothes, books, and my laptop bag – into my little silver 2002 Kia Spectra, which filled up the space so much that I couldn't see out of the back and barely through the passenger window. The plan was to place everything I would take into the hotels with me at night on the front passenger seat for easy access, which was a large black Army backpack and my laptop bag, while the rest of my belongings were hidden under my Iraqi indigo blanket or in the trunk. I was ecstatic.

With an open mind and an open heart, I set out on the open road toward the unknown in Arizona. As soon as I started my poor little car, heavy with everything I owned and had left to my name, I felt the butterflies kick in. There were still little patches of snow on the ground as I drove away from Gardner and down past

Worcester. As I crossed the Connecticut border on highway 84, I let out a war cry of heartbreak. It was a ceasefire of spiritual warfare after a season of soul-crushing, post-divorce madness. In this thunderous scream, I felt the exhalation of torment, and inhaled the promise of a new life.

From New England, through anger-inducing traffic in New York City and the enormous slog of driving through Washington DC, I found myself drifting through the Carolinas. Here lies a wounded, unhealed soul with a nasty colonial past much like other Southern, Bible-belt states. I wanted nothing to do with their past. I didn't want to have anything to do with anyone's past so long as they were in deep denial.

You can't help people or places that don't want to be helped. You just have to keep driving forward, taking care of yourself and being the best you can be if you want to help others. I knew deep down that I was no help to anyone so long as I wasn't looking out for my own health, safety, and sanity. So I kept to the one direction I knew had always helped: forward.

With chips, fries, or nuggets in hand, I had turned eating and driving into a delicate art form that could be choreographed with music – and it was. I had my music connected and blaring as a soundtrack for my adventure.

South Carolina soon gave way into Georgia, and seeing nothing but green foliage and highway, speckled with little towns here and there, left me feeling a bit hypnotized, so I was eager to make it to Florida to keep from falling asleep. As soon as I crossed the border from Georgia into Florida, a new level of excitement hit me. I was now facing the next longer and more rigorous part of my journey: Interstate-10.

My stay in Jacksonville, was extended by only an extra day. I knew my parents wanted to spend some extra time together, and they were waiting in the opened garage of their house as I pulled into the driveway. We went out and had dinner that night, and talked about the rest of the journey awaiting me that week. Later that evening, my mom and I stayed up late talking about the move. She was asking how I felt about everything, and if what I was doing felt right. I was positive, and I could feel the difference in going this distance after my dream. There was a desert filled with mystery at the other end of the highway and I was determined to see it through. She didn't say much else about my move after that, and began talking about her favorite TV shows, gossipy relatives, and how her arthritis was acting up with the rain.

On April 18th, I started my drive from Jacksonville, Florida to Baton Rouge, Louisiana. I had planned my stops according to the hours spent on the road. I had a few thousand dollars saved up, paid my rent for the new apartment in downtown Phoenix, and I was ready to roll. My parents walked me out to my overstuffed compact car and hugged me, telling me to stay safe and call them when I make pit-stops. I assured them that everything was going to be okay. Waving good-bye to them standing in the garage as I made my way toward the panhandle. My drive across the Mathews Bridge into downtown Jacksonville toward I-10 was shrouded with an overcast sky as I felt the weight slowly being lifted from my spirit. I was leaving my past behind and making my way into the unknown, mile by mile, with unbridled excitement.

Between Jacksonville and Tallahassee, as in much of the US Southeast, there's an unforgettable humidity, the smell of trees, freshly mowed grass, the sounds of crickets, and the constant sense that an alligator might be hanging out nearby. Humidity really wasn't my friend, and I recalled how well I was able to breathe in that arid Arizona air. I fantasized about Tucson as one would over a long-lost love or as a secret admirer.

The sense that I got in passing Pensacola and into Alabama was somewhat eerie. I recalled moments where I lived in Daphne, Alabama en route to Mobile, and what it was like to grow up in an environment that was rampant with abuse and bigotry. My paternal grandparents, estranged to me, still lived in Daphne, Alabama. My father had asked, with full knowledge of how I felt about our family's past, if I was going to stop by and visit them. The thought of their entitlement sickened me, and my parents were still aching for their approval. It disgusted me that numerous times I was made to be cordial with them in spite of years of torment, secrets desperately buried to save face but slap mine. It made me feel pain for a broken world I wasn't inclined to root for. As an adult, I was choosing to draw a boundary line. I knew that I wanted to live, so I declined, and kept driving intently out of Alabama.

It began to rain as I crossed over the Mississippi state line. The tree-lined 1-10 stretch running through the southern part of the state was hardly visible as buckets of rain poured onto the car mercilessly. So many tears have been shed here throughout colonial American history as well as my own.

This was a place of sadness, injustice, and the breaking of spirits. Having my spirit broken here in this part of the country and at such an early age left me cold on through adulthood, but Iraq and the transition home left me spiritually amputated. I had little fight left in me, but there was still an urgency to keep swinging. Moving past these southern states was a victory, a physical movement through a violent and merciless past in which I never received an apology, or witnessed any apparent remorse. I was moving on in life, and passing through these parts in apathy with an eager spirit to leave it all behind at long last.

After caving into my craving for spicy chicken, dirty rice, and biscuits outside of Baton Rouge, I found my hotel and repeated the cycle of carrying everything in my front seat into my room, and happily ate alone as I messaged family and friends that I had arrived in overcast, humid Louisiana.

The next morning, April 19th, I woke up early to pack everything in my car after my night of fried chicken comatosis. It was worth it. The next leg of my journey was to drive from Baton Rouge, Louisiana to San Antonio, Texas.

Leaving Baton Rouge began with weather as experienced the day before: muggy, gray, and miserable. But it was happy time for me on the road; I was excited. This wasn't the prettiest part of the journey, but knowing I was closer to the finish line had ignited exuberance and joy within. It was reminiscent of a time I actually remember being genuinely happy. I can't recall when's the last time I felt this type of emotion, but it was sometime well before Iraq.

While making my way across the border into Texas, I laughed at the numerous, egregious displays of Texas flags everywhere and recalled my time in San Antonio. Texas is much like a foreign country located within the boundaries of the United States. You see more Texas flags than American ones and every Texas "expat" I've ever met outside of Texas has a flag, an armadillo, or a Longhorns sticker just lurking somewhere – and quite possibly a collection of all three. The love for their state is a form of mania in which they are all proud.

Houston's traffic: a state of purgatory for all living creatures on Earth to witness. The intertwining interstates, drivers who seem to lose all sense of direction when it begins to drizzle, and an overwhelming sense of ennui and hatred for life sets in when attempting to reach the other side of I-10, getting one the hell out of the city.

Overall, it took me nine hours, due to Houston's traffic, to make it to San Antonio. The trip really should have been under seven hours, but that added congestion on the highway left me exhausted; even more so if I had spent a few more hours driving. Stagnation drained me, movement kept me feeling alive.

San Antonio finally appeared and I grimaced at the signs pointing to the old Army base I was stationed at in my first years in the military. It was still sunny outside and after securing my belongings in the hotel room in downtown San Antonio. I meandered over to the River Center near the San Antonio Riverwalk. There were so many memories here.

While I was attending medic and mental health school in my younger days in the Army, we used to come here quite a bit. I was eighteen, still impressionable, yet still headstrong and determined. During my stay in San Antonio, I recalled going to bed late, getting up in the morning and being ready for a company run at 0420hrs. Eating at 0800hrs, getting out of training at 1600hrs, and often getting to bed at midnight – and repeat daily. I had spent nearly a year in San Antonio due to the former pre-requisite medic certification before mental health school, which had an additional clinical component.

While I could wax poetic about sightseeing, food, and the great shape I was in at that age and how my knees didn't crack then like they do now, I was reminded more so of things that disturbed me while I was here. It was in San Antonio that I got to see corruption among various US Army leaders in full bloom, ranging from sexual assault to racial discrimination. It was merely a taste of things to come for me in Iraq, and I felt naïve for thinking those incidents were isolated. You see, it's not that the Army, or any other US military branch, lacks regulations; it's that there's little enforcement and few people with integrity to act upon doing the right thing.

After grabbing a coffee inside the San Antonio River Center, I walked through the streets outside near the Alamo.

That's when I heard someone scream, "There's no basement in the Alamo?!"

It came from a tour group standing outside of the Alamo, and I nearly pissed myself. Growing up watching Pee-Wee's Big Adventure, hearing that line near the Alamo never got old. A woman standing close by heard it as well, and started laughing with me. Out of these hundreds of people swarming the Alamo, we were the only two that laughed. It's funny how we can sometimes feel so invisible, but a laugh, a smile, a friendly nod can reconnect us, even briefly, to the world of the living. I floated away.

One could walk through so many cities across the world where no one knows your name and for a second, you can be reminded quite easily through a familiar phrase, sight, sound, smell, taste, sensation – in spite of feeling alone and alienated – that you're part of the world too, and it's not so lonely after all.

During sunrise on April 20th, I left the La Quinta on Blum Street in downtown San Antonio to make my way toward Las Cruces, New Mexico. The Tower of the Americas appeared lonely, yet stunning as the sun was starting to light up the sky. There were quite a few memories made here in San Antonio, some good and some bad, but it was a lovely return to a place where I could compare the changes in the eighteen-year-old version of myself versus the one ten years older. Although I had been through my fair share of hellish moments, rollercoaster events, and those bastardly learning experiences, I was pleased to see how far I had made it and that, in spite of all obstacles, I was here and I had survived. Time to keep moving forward.

As I drove past the limits of the city of San Antonio at sunrise and the Bexar County line toward Segovia, the landscape changed to a cool, foggy, almost mountainous ground with a mist gently kissing the hills as I drove past. One of my pit stops was near this area of Segovia which had a gas station, a country store, and diner attached. I acquired my munchies and bought a few absurd black and white redneck humor postcards and a colorful greeting card that had Guadalupe on the front. I loved the warm tones and vivid imagery; it reminded me of my dream and why I was here. Still here.

Miles before reaching El Paso, the sky and landscape really open up through the wild and restless Chihuahuan Desert. There are hundreds of miles of road, and this is where I truly began to feel that I was light years away from pain and bittersweet memories. While still in the United States, I felt like I was on foreign soil and my homeland simultaneously. Although I had never lived in the Southwestern US, I felt like I belonged. An unspoken embrace came over me as the warmth of the desert sun. The heavens opened before me here in the West, welcoming me back, and told me to follow the signs to paradise.

Traveling westward, seeing both the US city of El Paso on your right and Ciudad Juarez, Chihuahua, Mexico on your left gave a sharp contrast of the two border cities and the lives lived on both sides. On the right with El Paso, it was far more developed, modern, and was home to a large US Army base, Fort Bliss, home to 1st Cavalry Division.

On the left was heartbroken Juarez. The poverty visible even from I-10 was overwhelming. I had friends stationed in El Paso at various parts of their career to include more recently relocated contacts, and they all had something to say about the increasing crime and violence that had besieged Juarez over the past decade. Crossing the border for any reason was considerably safer years ago. Now, drug cartel violence and corruption was so rampant that it was considered an "enter at your own risk" zone by locals on both sides. Beheadings, kidnappings, and other horror stories reminded me that places like Iraq were not too far away, and we had our own troubles of similar nature on this side of the world in which many also turn a blind eye.

El Paso and Juarez look like a divorced couple forced to live as neighbors. The two cities are separated by a barely motivated Rio Grande and they are so close to one another you could watch someone talking on the phone on their balcony in Juarez from El Paso. Juarez is one of the most dangerous cities in the world and much of its middle class and above have fled with everything to El Paso, with few ever wanting to venture back across the border.

After a twelve-hour stint on the road, part of me wanted to stop in El Paso, but another part of me simply didn't want to spend any more time in Texas. I've seen quite a bit of Texas for the past few days and I was more than ready to greet New Mexico, the Land of Enchantment.

After finding another reasonably priced hotel to spend the night, I made my rounds to another fast food drive-thru and gathered my meal for the night. I wasn't interested in spending any time in public, having to possibly deal with anyone looking to bother a woman sitting by herself in a restaurant. I preferred to eat alone in my room, updating friends and family on my whereabouts, having a good shower, and a much-needed full-night of sleep. As I threw off the comforter and dove into the white blanket, I stared up at the ceiling and smiled. Tomorrow was the day I would enter Arizona and begin my new life; in a place I've never lived and growing with people I've never met.

April 21st arrived and I was up before my alarm sounded. With much anticipation, I packed my bags, grabbed a large cup of soda from a gas station convenience store accompanied with junk food for the drive, and got back on the road to the rest of my life. Adios, Las Cruces, New Mexico. Here I come, Phoenix, Arizona!

As I drove away from Las Cruces, the sun was just starting to rise. I snapped a photo out of the window behind me. The sunrise over the desert was gorgeous and traveling through it felt like I was wandering through heaven. The dry air in this part of the country felt different on my skin; I felt lighter, nimble, welcomed, happy.

Before leaving the state to enter Arizona, there was a Border Patrol checkpoint line backed up on I-10. As I approached the checkpoint, I was asked, with quite the heavy car, by two agents if I was a US citizen. They looked at my car front to back, another agent had a German Shepherd nearby. They looked at me, and said, "Have a nice day."

The dream of the Desert Warrior became more vivid in my mind's eye as I passed Deming, New Mexico and onto the border of Arizona. My heart started beating faster, butterflies in my stomach went crazy, and a smile overcame me as I passed the line and sign that said "Welcome to Arizona."

That's when I let out the loudest, happiest scream. I yelled until my lungs hurt, my heart pounding joyously. It felt like I was crying with happiness for the first time in my life.

The desert may not be everyone's cup of tea, but from West Texas and on through New Mexico and Arizona, it's a desert wonderland. To me, this landscape is breathtaking, inspires me to paint, write, do more. Why I didn't feel this on the East Coast or elsewhere in the world is a mystery to me, but I just know that the desert and I, somehow, speak the same language. We understand the same music of the wind caressing the sand and mountains like blood traveling through one's veins. It was paradise. My paradise.

That dream of the woman in the desert, the inspiration months ago in snowy Massachusetts woke me up and brought me here. I was so grateful, for whatever it was – and I won't pretend to know or understand it – was enough to pull me here. It's amazing how clear my vision had become for who I was and what I wanted simply by listening to my own needs and wants. I had been looking everywhere outside of myself for an answer, for resolution, for justice and wasn't close to recognizing it until I looked within.

Paying attention to my instincts nudging me, and someone finally telling me in my dreams to move forward was a gift. For so long, I looked outside of myself for those temporary illusions of fleeting love, moments, and people. It wasn't until I listened to my heart that I felt alive again. The pains and horrors of yesterday neither encompassed me nor owned me. Today, I don't wait any longer for destiny, I create my own path and I decide who I shall become.

As I zipped through Willcox, Vail, and then Tucson, I snapped a few photos and looked out toward the Santa Catalina Mountains sitting warm in the late morning light. All I could feel was gratitude, and I promised myself if there were any openings in Tucson, I would move here immediately.

The drive up the last part of I-10 took me through Marana, Eloy, Casa Grande, and on into Maricopa County at last. My GPS took me through a fairly smooth route that led me to my new apartment on East Van Buren Street in Downtown Phoenix. I walked, nearly skipped, into the leasing office to pick up my keys. Thankfully, I didn't have to sit through a mountain of paperwork since I had prepaid and took care of everything online prior to my arrival. The leasing agent showed me to my new home and shook my hand, welcoming me to the complex. As I walked through my new, empty, one-bedroom apartment, even on that scorching Phoenix afternoon, I was on cloud nine. Finally.

Later on in the evening after carrying everything from my car to my new apartment, I drove to a nearby Safeway to buy groceries for the week. As I loaded my items onto the checkout lane, the cashier started chatting with me about her day and how she was looking forward to getting home to her kids. She was kind, and seemed to be that type of person who would talk to anyone without a care where they were from or what they did. Unlike the suspicious glares I got in the Northeast, I was treated like, well, a person. I told her I just drove across the country from New England to make Phoenix my new home.

"Wow! You've come a long way, lady! Welcome home," she said smiling.

"Thank you," I said, as I secured my bags then headed home.

That night I had another vivid dream. I envisioned the woman warrior in the desert. She wasn't too far off in the distance, standing among radiant cacti and cloaked with stars. I could see her smiling, as though to validate the worth and necessity of my journey. I stood there, as though I needed to observe the distance and that the journey, even though I had arrived in Arizona, was not over. I waved to her, feeling both gratitude and love, then I woke.

After getting myself together, I went out on the balcony of my downtown Phoenix apartment, and looked out toward the swimming pool a few floors below. The sky was cloudless, clear and turquoise. The air was warm, dry, and quiet. The sun lit up the pool and sparkled. A hummingbird then flew toward me on the balcony. As it flew all around me, I observed it. I felt calm, present. Its wings vibrated in infinite circles and got closer to my face, seeming as curious about me as I was about it. My new little visitor hung around for only a few seconds more, then flew into the desert sky.

19 PHOENIX, ARIZONA

Traveling throughout Europe after returning from Iraq was about running away from reality, hiding in the midst of the unknown, the risks, and in a place where anonymity was a cover for the monster I felt I became. Taking hold of my journey behind the wheel of my old silver bullet of a car, traveling was now about finding home and redefining it on my terms, where my soul could finally open up and rest.

Travel was never about accommodating old habits as I knew the old ways of living could not mend my new problems of dealing with post-war trauma. Finding a new treatment, a potential cure for my malaise was a journey of trial and error, and one where I had to put my faith entirely into the process and hope for the best.

Looking at a world map tucked inside my travel journal, I realized something ironic about my gravitation toward Phoenix. Baghdad, Ramadi, and Phoenix exist on 33 degrees North Latitude. I knew there was something oddly familiar about Phoenix, but I didn't realize that this dusty desert city was that much like a few other dusty desert cities I've worked in thousands of miles away. It's funny how we're drawn to bizarre places on the map for seemingly no reason, only to find that strange, unexplainable comfort. In dreams and reality, the desert was calling.

Upon arrival to Phoenix, my world certainly seemed far brighter and blurred the lens into my past in Massachusetts. My world in the Northeast was indeed bleak, but with the appearance of Gabe, things changed. Gabe had been communicating with me from the start of this selection process and was an ardent advocate of my hiring. Now, I had to prepare for the final interview. It wasn't a guarantee that I had this job. I came out here knowing I had taken a huge risk, but I had to do everything I could to stay.

Arizona. The gold sand, the wide open space, rugged mountains that turned violet at sunset while the sky lights up in the colors of orange juice, turquoise and indigo. There wasn't any other place in the world I wanted to be, so I prepared myself as best as possible to study everything I could about my potential new position and bring my best to this interview. After reading the instructional email, I made my way to the office and had my final interview with two higher managers. Both of them appeared to be pleased with my experience. One of the other men took one look at my resume, then looked at me again, and laughed. He asked how someone who looks like me could be in the Army, and called me a 'beauty queen." I laughed it off, and waited until I was far, far away to let a good rolling of the eyes and gagging to occur.

Finally, keeping my composure after that creepy interview ending, the hiring managers then introduced me to the State Director.

"Are you Native?" the State Director asked.

"Native to the Mariana Islands, sir," I responded.

"Hmm. What would you call your tribe?" he asked, slightly squinting at me as though he were trying to make sense of my face.

"Chamorro, sir. We're Micronesian," I replied.

He stared blankly for a moment, then asked, "What's that? Is that like Polynesian?"

"Close. Polynesians, Melanesians, and Micronesians are all indigenous Pacific Islanders. We're often erroneously lumped together with Asians," I said, noticing some of his Choctaw emblems and Native art around the room, "but we left the continent of Asia thousands of years ago like you. We just took canoes."

The State Director, who was flanked by two nervous-looking white men in trying-too-hard turquoise bolo ties, paused then laughed aloud.

"You're okay, soldier," he smiled. "So, you were in the Army, is that correct? Served in Iraq?" the State Director asked. He was a 2-tour Vietnam veteran, Army as well.

"Yes, sir. Served in Ar Ramadi, 2004-2005, in the Army, but served mostly with Marines in theater," I replied.

We spoke for a while about our respective deployments, PTSD, and how important it is for indigenous peoples to help one another on the path of healing and success. The two white men in the room appeared increasingly anxious and slightly irritated, but being subordinate to this State Director, they had to conceal their contempt.

"We have to stick together, my Islander sister. You were raised to be a warrior, like me. And that war ain't over when we get home," he said, smiling with his teeth, but his affect was somber. The men around him appeared to be those he could trust, but only out of necessity. In a way, I began to feel an uneasiness creep through. I agreed.

After that meeting with the State Director, I was hired and told to come in the very next day to begin training. Amid a few kind faces, there were plenty of shadowy characters. One of the men I interviewed with was particularly suspicious of me. The name on my resume, apparently didn't match my face. He looked up and down between the document and my face several times as though he had been duped – he was expecting pure Anglo-Saxon female and got me. One of the men I worked with on a small team was not exactly fond of my presence either and constantly condescended to me. I wasn't going to let these people kill my buzz.

While I was happy as a clam during the day, my sleep was still quite disturbed as it was in Massachusetts. I was happy to be in Arizona at last, and felt ready to take on work challenges, but the nightmares kept getting worse. One night I decided to revert to an old Chamorro method for alleviating nightmares where Western religious methods proved to be insufficient.

The first few nights of the nine-day ritual were hellish. Apocalyptic scenes where I was one out of very few survivors in a global holocaust, and scenes where the worst parts of my deployment to Iraq surfaced. I would wake up drenched in sweat, panting as though I had been running and evading capture for miles. On the fifth night, I had a dream where this creature was watching me. I had my mother with me who was frightened, and I was protecting her from this creature. It looked as though it were a hybrid of some dog-like being and a human, with eyes darker than anything I had ever seen, beyond pitch black and abysmal. Its face was long and resembled a coyote or a similar animal, but had the body of a tall human. It was a quiet presence, but one of misery, despair, and helplessness.

The creature pursued me relentlessly in the dream. As I ducked and dodged its grasp, I was shielding my mother and myself from capture. Once again, I woke up drenched in sweat, and it wasn't the Phoenix heat. The AC was on and I had thrown everything off of me, and was exhausted once again, but this time I was furious. I was tired of nightmares revisiting me anytime they could and was determined to return to sleep at once and face the negative presence that lurked in my subconscious, whether it was this creature, Iraq flashbacks, or anything else that plagued me. I wanted to destroy it.

As I closed my eyes, determined to face the pain, it was waiting for me. Instead of lurking high in the trees and staring down at me, it was standing right in front of me, apparently seven feet tall, and a grisly sight to bear. It breathed, said nothing, but smiled as it opened its arms, cloaked in shredded animal skin, and lunged toward me as I braced myself for what was next. I prepared for things to get far worse.

Before the creature could reach me, a Taotaomo'na, a pre-Spanish colonization Chamorro spirit, appeared. The Taotaomo'na, a traditionally feared but respected entity, walked out from behind me. One doesn't speak directly to Taotaomo'na unless you are asking permission to enter sacred land or take from nature – or to apologize for any disrespect. It appeared larger than the abysmal creature. In an instant, the Taotaomo'na grabbed the creature's skull and crushed it as it shrieked in pain and horror. It was a terrible sound of bone-crushing and screaming. It stopped me in my tracks as I watched the creature fall to the ground, dissipating into a dreadful pile of skin and bones.

"Saina ma'ase," I said, thanking him in Chamorro for coming to my aid.

He nodded, and embraced me in what felt like sympathy, as though a relative were finally reaching out to say they were aware of what I had endured. Out of all the scary ghost stories I've heard about our ancestral spirits, what the Taotaomo'na did in my dream was unexpected, but I was indeed grateful. After this dream with the intervention of the Taotaomo'na, I never had an Iraq-related nightmare or creature visit again.

A renewed sense of joy infused my daily routine, and I decided to tell my mother that I had a dream that the Taotaomo'na helped me through a nightmare. She was frightened. As a child, she had an encounter with Taotaomo'na that required an intervention from a suruhanu that lived in the mountains of northern Saipan. She never forgot the encounter, and was scared of the thought of anyone having any sort of connection to a Taotaomo'na. I told her it was okay, but she urged me to stay away. I wasn't scared. I felt understood. Perhaps the closest someone could come to understanding the anguish and wrath I felt is someone who experienced genocide and never saw justice. Taotaomo'na's knew this firsthand from Spain wiping out indigenous peoples. You don't hear much about that in history books outside of the Marianas – not at all.

This newfound freedom from nightmares instilled a sense of happiness only I knew about, and kept this new gift close to my heart. However, workplace assholery took the place of the shadowy creatures at night. It seems to happen anywhere I go. It's not just me, but other females who aren't shrinking violets. But I refuse to change. I refuse to dumb myself down or act far more meek and mild than I really am around insecure people. Staying true to myself is important. Being empowered, motivated, and good at what you do is just what insecure people hate.

In effort to at least get to know people outside of the office, I joined meetup groups and went to a few veteran functions. It wasn't easy making friends here at first, veterans or not. I just wasn't feeling any real interpersonal connection. However, there was no shortage of flirty or even sexually aggressive advances in Metro Phoenix. Some would approach me with cheesy pick-up lines or tell me that they weren't accustomed to being attracted women who wore size three jeans – too fat apparently. Somehow, that was meant to be a compliment. While out with a small group of friends, a guy twisted my arm after telling him I deployed to Iraq in effort to show me he was stronger. I was more so creeped out and told him if he didn't stop, he was going to get stabbed. He let go. I was one dick pic away from sticking with women exclusively.

When I felt ready for an actual date, I said yes to a Navy veteran who asked me to dinner. He took me out on a lavish date, but wouldn't stop talking about his ex. Needless to say, we didn't go out again. Another time at a bar in Chandler, a guy started chatting with me and was actually keen on the idea that I was a combat veteran. However, his supposed best friend wasn't too enthusiastic about my ethnicity. He was mixed like me, and his friend began to pry a bit too much about Iraq, asking about killing innocent civilians as though it were for sport. Of course, it ended up really pissing me off, and I got to witness this guy allow his white friends shit all over him. I stood up to his friend, who was making racist comments toward his best friend. He went on insulting my service, and nearly punched me before the guy I was chatting with held him back. While there were plenty of opportunities, once again, none were fruitful.

Luckily, in between bizarre moments of my astronomically comical love life, I kept busy. I was asked by a Native American women veterans group to speak with them on my experiences as a member of Team Lioness in Ramadi, Iraq. The woman asking me was enthusiastic that I accepted the invite and was willing to travel to speak with them. Even though a few of the WASP, wannabe Natives from my office protested, I accepted and got back on the road.

20 FARMINGTON, NEW MEXICO

A few weeks later, I drove about seven hours to Farmington, New Mexico and while I was taking in the scenery and historic Route 66, there was a lot of time for me to think. These desert drives were celestial gifts that gave me chills and left me wanting more. Perhaps it's a form of safe exposure therapy for me as I drove on convoys in Iraq and here in the Southwest, I'm surrounded by desert and luckily not being shot at, ambushed, or attacked in any other way - unless I'm meandering about certain parts of Phoenix. I had a lot on my mind outside of my busy work schedule, mostly having to do with processing this adventurous year so far.

After hours seven of driving, I arrived at the hotel and find a beautiful Anasazi-print blanket, a wool-covered planner, and a card thanking me for my service. Shortly after my arrival, I contacted Charlotte, the event coordinator, who then invited me out for dinner. We met up with a few of her coworkers, and we relaxed for a bit before heading out to pick up a few other guest speakers, Dr. Moseley-Brown and Major Breslow from Lioness. While waiting, we chatted about life, the military, comparing Dine' and Chamorro words, and so on. I noticed around the outside of Farmington's little airport that it looks like a very familiar place that I immediately recognized: Al Asad, an airbase in western Iraq.

The conference the next day went well, the screening of course always inspires quite a few memories, and the panel discussion was great. There were quite a few amazing people there and I'm grateful for such an experience. Most of the audient consisted of Native American women, many of whom were veterans. Everyone at the screening was welcoming, understanding, and asked insightful questions in addition to expressing their solidarity with us.

No matter what their experiences were, civilian or military, you felt connected to others in the room through the expressed compassion and without judgment. I felt, well, like I existed again.

In downtown Farmington, there's a cool little brewery that Charlotte, Major Breslow, and I went out to with excellent grub called Three Rivers. We talked for hours and toward the end of the meal, a new friend of mine I met in Phoenix, Joe, called from Albuquerque saying he was en route to Farmington and should be there soon. We were going to meet up and hang out for a while after I dropped off Charlotte and Major B, but as soon as we got back to my car to start the engine, I heard that awful noise that no one wants to hear, tick tick tick - then nothing. This had never happened before and of all places it happens in Farmington where a tow truck needs to take at least an hour to get here. While waiting for the tow truck company to call back, Joe calls.

As I'm telling him what's going on over the phone, I hear a loud, hyena-like shriek coming from the street. Joe offered to come and help me out after going back and forth over the phone as to what may be wrong - the starter, the alternator, the battery? As soon as I hang up, the shrieking continues and Charlotte and Major Breslow are laughing. It turns out that a group of local guys in an SUV were trying to holler and get our attention.

I quickly turn to Charlotte, who lives in Farmington and ask, "What the hell was that?"

"Oh, that's the Indian Love Call," she said.

We all burst out laughing and start mimicking just the same long after the SUV of over-eager males drives around the block.

"I'll have to try this on Joe to see if he recognizes this call," I said to Charlotte.

"You better watch out, he might like it!" Charlotte said as Major Breslow stood there laughing and shaking her head.

Joe, who is originally from Shiprock, just forty-five minutes away from Farmington, then shows up. Taken a bit by surprise, he hops out still in his ACU flight suit as he just got off work. He's a Blackhawk engineer for the National Guard and flies an air ambulance as a full-time gig. I have to say, not bad. How did that call go again?

He then tells me to start up my car so he can listen to the sound, but lo and behold, my car decides to work. He Fonz'd my car. Slapping the side of my poor Kia like a used juke box, he exclaimed, “Ow!” and stepped forward, just inches away from me and whispered, “So do I at least get a kiss?”

Shaking my head, I shoved him in the chest saying, “Calm down, Fonzarelli, it’s still early.”

After dropping off Charlotte, simultaneously belting out the Indian Love Call goodnight, I dropped off Major B, and met up with Joe. We headed to local diner and hung out while he caught up on some late-night breakfast. Afterward, we went walking around near the San Juan River, which appeared to be crawling with tweakers and other shady characters. We chatted away for hours and decided to go off-roading somewhere out in the outskirts of Farmington, or so it seemed. It was hard to tell where we were. We started telling each other ghost stories as we zipped through the desert dodging rock walls and other desert shrubbery.

As we headed back through downtown Farmington we spotted what looked like an unconscious woman lying face-down on the sidewalk under a streetlamp on one of the main roads. Joe immediately pulled over, hopped out and checked her pulse. She was barely breathing, but breathing. We called 911 and they arrived within a few minutes as my Iraq paranoia set in, scanning the area around as though the Muj were getting ready to start blasting. Joe standing at about 6'4", 200 lbs., pulled me in closer before the police arrived.

"Uh, this is a man," the police officer tells us.

An intense moment of fearing for this person’s life took a turn for the better as our full-bearded, smashed sidewalk friend regained composure, dusted their dress off and walked on. Joe and I looked at each other and both sighed with relief and surprise.

In the history of first dates, this unexpected, unplanned evening topped the charts. A completely unique date night with car trouble, tweakers, an almost-rescue, ghost stories, off-roading, and a romantic stroll around the desert. We ended up dating, officially, after this night. Joe set a different tone for me in terms of romantic encounters. We both felt so comfortable with each other and considering all the prior terrible suitors in the past few months, maybe Joe is an actual nice guy? Every time we meet up with each other, which had to be planned as he lived in Albuquerque and I in

Phoenix, it feels like an adventure. While I enjoyed our road trips to see one another and weekend escapes, the idea of loving someone again still felt so far away. Not wanting to overanalyze, I let go and allowed myself to live in this moment.

During a trip we planned to the Petrified Forest in Northern Arizona, we drove around the park in his Jeep and were having a great afternoon horsing around together. I found it endearing that my often lewd or suggestive jokes would make Joe blush, which only encouraged me to push the envelope further. As there was a pause between thunderstorms and intermittent lightning, we ran across the moonscape of a desert, chasing each other like children.

Before we knew it, there was another storm cloud about to open up on us and we bolted for his Jeep as the rain began to fall. I jumped onto a brick partition, only a few feet high, near the parking lot and yelled, "Look, now I'm your height, tall tree!"

"You're still bite-sized, no matter where you stand," he laughed, walking closer.

As he approached me, doing terrible plie's and jumps as I balanced myself, he grabbed my hips and spun me toward him. He looked me in the eyes and appeared to be somewhat nervous. Before he spoke, the rain began to fall upon both of us.

"I…, I wanted to tell you I love you," he said, looking deep into my eyes waiting for confirmation and reciprocation.

In that moment I felt that the words he uttered might as well have been Greek. I didn't understand what he was saying to me and why. We've been dating each other for a little over two months and it was the first time I heard those words directed at me since I was married to Tony. I froze.

"Doooooo you feel the same way, or am I looking totally stupid right now?"

"You don't look stupid," I said, trying to playfully shove him away.

"You can't keep running forever," he said jokingly with a tinge of disappointment.

"Wanna bet?"

Joe didn't look amused. Immediately, I grabbed his face and kissed him.

"I love you," I said, almost shocked at how it sounded escaping my lips. I haven't told someone I loved them in years. I was worried that the love I just spoke of might not be enough, that I was still too numb, too closed off to truly feel anything. I cared about him, had a great time with him, but there was still a lot of gray within me. Ramadi, which is Arabic for gray, was an appropriate combat and post-war homecoming metaphor. The gray Iraqi city turned my heart, my passion for life into ashes. No hot, no cold, no love, no hate, just neuropathy. Nothingness.

Weeks later as we attended a party in Albuquerque, one of Joe's friends who was also in the Army began to antagonize me. He was really condescending with Joe, particularly about being Native, and Joe would just take it. Seeing a Native guy getting shredded to pieces by a white "supposed" friend infuriated me. I didn't understand the friendship; it was more like Stockholm syndrome, and Joe was the tolerant hostage.

As Joe's friend came to realize that I didn't think his persistent bashing was hilarious, he toned it down and challenged me to try some of the hot sauces he collected in the house. Anything he tried, I was to try. Not knowing of my background, I was more than willing to accept a challenge from this brand of Death Star Anglo-American hubris. We got pretty far to the point where he appeared to be in pain. Good. He then tried a pin drop of a hot sauce called Black Mamba, then stopped immediately, telling me that there was no way I could do it. With a reddened face and sweat beading up on his skin upon ingestion, he was in trouble. Yes. He was obviously in agony, and called a time out.

It was then that I decided to show him what a weakling he was. I took a toothpick and stuck it inside the bottle as far as I could and pulled it out, covered with this lethal hot sauce that typically calls for a health waiver to consume. Instead of the drop that acted like a can of tear gas in Joe's domestic terrorist friend's mouth, I got a higher and more painful dose.

Without flinching, I ingested it with a straight face like a hot sauce boss. I looked at Joe's friend, still writhing and gagging into the sink from the hot sauce, and said, "Why are you crying? It's not that bad."

Everyone in the kitchen at this party gave me a high five, but deep inside I was dying. My mouth felt like lava as I kept salivating and couldn't feel one side of my face. It felt like someone took a canister of CS gas and pumped it right through my lungs. It was absolutely terrible, but I owned this stupid contest. FYI: This brand of sauce was not exactly designed for consumption; it was made for stupid dares by impulsive veterans and college kids.

This little stunt was more like walking into the prison of Joe's social life and punching the biggest inmate in the face. However, he kept berating Joe. I talked to Joe on the side, asking him why he didn't defend himself. He said he didn't know and that his friend was always like that. This friend was also quite a drinker, sounded borderline white supremacist while drunk, and indulged Joe on his apparent out-of-control habits. Joe was an Afghanistan veteran, but seemed to turn inward and quiet when his "friends" pressed him. While we had seen each other and gone out on typical dates for a few months, seeing racist rhetoric tolerated before my eyes, suggested to me that it was time to part ways. If anyone was going to be in my life, they had to be strong; I couldn't be the only one.

When you're part of a minority group that's greatly underrepresented, and you find yourself alone in many spheres racially, the usual risks manifest. No matter how empowered, efficacious, and resilient you are, when people see you are the only one around and seemingly without a community, you not only look vulnerable, but appear as a target for sociopaths, manipulators, abusers, and other shadowy figures looking to exploit you, take your power base, or conquer you to fill their own personal voids.

The situation with Joe and seeing how much he tolerated abusive people around him reminded me too much of what I went through as a kid and with Tony.

Words are like guns and racial slurs are the bullets. Many of the racial slurs used in the United States today were all white European settler-invented terms. Even if you don't think of yourself as a racist and desire to use the terms in what appears to you as 'harmless' via art, music, or prose, save yourself the trouble – just don't do it. And don't try to use a ridiculous excuse such as sanctifying your use of slurs by stating that you're related to Pocahontas or some obvious non-white historical figure; that shit will eventually get you punched in the face – hopefully. You don't have to live everyday life as the person in your fabricated story. Minorities don't need to be reminded of the power of privilege; we're aware of it every day.

If you want to find the solution to violence in the United States, follow the bread crumbs of slurs into the hidden corners of history books, the torn and discarded pages that were colored with blood and tears and conveniently tucked away. There, you will find a foundation in which this country was built: justifiable genocide rebranded as Manifest Destiny; a Biblically-sanctioned slave trade; the decimation of cultures, languages, and spirits and calling it "assimilation."

Go to the source of this insidious weed we've come to know today as gun violence and examine those roots carefully. Until, we as a nation start being honest and stop telling people to "get over" lifetimes of humiliation, struggle, and persecution, perhaps applicable solutions will surface. Until then, there's no point at a futile shaking of fists at the stars asking 'why' when more senseless deaths take place, as no response will ever come from the heavens so long as the privileged perpetuate hell for others here on earth.

The next time you envision belittling someone with slurs, staring down your nose like the barrel of a gun, realize that you're reopening a Pandora's box of history where actual firearms were used in conjunction with those slurs while demanding land, resources, non-consensual sex, or life all together. And when one is comfortable staring down their nose at another race like a gun, a real gun is validated as an instrument to enforce further privilege and the removal of rights of the person on the bullet-receiving end of your barrel. This is all just a piece of a present festering wound where unarmed children are shot point blank for their clothes, music, and color. It remains an echo of hearts and minds unevolved and successfully colonized. I let Joe go as I didn't want to fight that battle in a relationship again.

As days and weeks passed, I moved to a condo in Scottsdale and found myself in Las Vegas for a veterans education conference close to Halloween. Hafiza was picking me up in the evenings or spending the night with me in my huge room at Rio Hotel & Casino.

Hafiza, aside from her good news on her recent engagement and wedding plans to the son of a famous Afghan singer, wanted to take me to see a Persian tarot card reader named Nasrin. Hafiza is, let's just say, a tad naïve. As a friend, I was worried about her being duped, so I didn't protest against the idea to go along, but was secretly intrigued to see what this woman had to say. Would it be the generic advice on love and life? Kitschy, saccharine wishes coming true? Hafiza was ecstatic. She was insistent that Nasrin was the real deal.

We drove through a nice suburb of Las Vegas, somewhere in the heart of Summerlin, and parked in front of Nasrin's house. She greeted us at the door and offered us coffee, which would be part of our readings. Nasrin, asked us who wanted to be read first and Hafiza, eager to disprove that Nasrin was yet another fake, insisted that I go first.

As I sat down, Nasrin finished making the coffee, a traditional Iranian cup, and had me drink it through the beginning of the reading. It was espresso-sized and still had much of the fine loose grounds left in the coffee. It reminded me of coffee I had in Iraq, which I loved.

Nasrin began to shuffle, and as she laid down the cards one by one, she began telling my life story as though she were looking directly at the reel in my mind's eye. Having instructed Hafiza not to tell her anything about me, she kept true to her word. I even tried tricking her, in which she caught on, and kept discussing my past, present, and future without any need for fishing or extraction.

"You were in a relationship with someone who is a pilot or flies as part of his work, is that right?" Nasrin asked.

I paused for a second, and began shaking my head until Hafiza nudged me and said, "Dude, she's talking about Joe!"

That's how it was. If someone was out of my life, they were also out of my mind, I had pushed Joe, as quickly as possible, out of my psyche.

"He loves you very much, but he is a little lost. Expect a call from him in three hours or at 3am. He is calling you very soon to ask for something. Maybe to marry him," she said.

It was impressive that she picked up on Joe and his profession. If she's right about the call, I would be sold on her abilities. She went on to tell me that she saw that I had endured war and catastrophe, that my life had fallen apart as a result, and that there was so much pain inside, but I laugh to keep everyone from suspecting anything is wrong.

"You also had a dream of a relative, a tall man, very strong, but he's not wearing much clothing. His head is shaved with only some hair on top. Looks like he is part of a tribe here," she said seeming to not know what to call this person or how to categorize him ethnically.

"You're onto something," I said, still thinking she just might be one great guesser.

"This strong man, he came to help you through your bad dreams. Horrible dreams. He feels pity for you, but he's been through something similar. A war too, perhaps. Your nightmares disappeared because of him. He knows what you feel like and wants to protect you," Nasrin added.

Hafiza asked me what she was talking about, but I gestured not to say anything.

"He heard you say thank you. But he also wants you to use your talents in thanks. You're an artist, right?" Nasrin asked.

"Yes, indeed, and you're correct about the dream. He's called Taotaomo'na," I replied.

"It seems like he wants you to draw him. You should start working on this to thank him," she insisted.

Nasrin continued to give me insight over the course of the next few years, telling me that I was going to marry again in three years, that I'd have children even though I thought I never would, and numerous specific events to come true before the end of the year. After I finished my coffee, she read the loose grounds and told me more about my current state.

"You have to learn to love yourself, take care of your spirit. You made the first step by moving to the desert, but your story has just begun," Nasrin said.

I knew I had to continue to heal from years of putting my own needs aside, and in some odd way, this was probably the best talk I've had about my own problems in years. Hell, since the VA won't pay me any mind, all I had a Las Vegas oracle to break it down and validate that yes, my life has not been a bed of roses, and yes, there is a purpose to all the pain.

In the end, my reading was impressive. Hafiza received her incognito reading about her soon-to-be husband, her personal and professional life and was pleased as usual with Nasrin's advice.

"Don't think negative, think positive," Nasrin kept repeating to both of us as we made our way out.

Hafiza dropped me off at the hotel and I went to bed right

away, not wanting to meet with coworkers for gambling or buffets, but just wanting to catch up on sleep.

At 3am, my phone rang. Still fuzzy from dreamland, I'm wondering, who the hell is calling me at 3am? I looked at the number, a familiar one, but not a number I had saved. Perhaps a deleted number.

"Why don't you love me anymore?" said a weepy, deep voice over the phone. It was Joe.

"Have you been drinking?" I asked, rubbing my already rolling eyes.

He sighed, "A little."

I stayed quiet; waiting for the real answer.

"Okay, I've had a few drinks," he said. "But you didn't answer my question, young lady." Even though he was just a few months older, he spoke to me like an old man to a little girl, attempting to sound wise beyond his years.

"I can't love you. It's not because you're unlovable, but because you don't even love yourself. How can I trust you to love me back when you don't have a backbone to stand up for yourself? You can't love anyone, not right now at least. And it's not worth my time to give any more to someone who doesn't get that."

A long, labored sigh on the other end of the line followed.

"I'm sorry, okay. I'm an asshole. A stupid, stupid asshole. I should have been better," he said in what actually sounded like genuine remorse followed by a moment of silence. It was nice to hear a bit of validation and I wasn't going to counter that statement either.

"Just take care of yourself, okay?"

"Will you ever be able to love me again? I miss you so much," he said sounding sorry for himself as his voice cracked like an adolescent boy. "I want you to marry me. I'll do whatever it takes, I swear to you," he said.

"Worry about loving yourself first."

"I love you. You have no idea. You're perfect to me. Don't push me away and act all hard," Joe said, beginning to sound agitated.

"Really? You just asked me to marry you while drunk and over the phone. I'd hardly call this the proposal of my dreams," I said, just wanting to get him off of the phone so I could sleep.

"Why are you so mean to me?! Give me another chance," he said with what now sounded like childish frustration.

"Have a good night, Joe."

With even the slightest upset, detachment soon followed. I didn't lose sleep over anyone, and I was too restless to be tied down. The grass didn't even have time to grow around my feet before I was planning my next escape – whether it was to another state or out of someone's life.

Back in Scottsdale, I got word of a job opening in Tucson and raced down Interstate 10 for the interview. During the trip, I of course had to visit my love: Saguaro National Park West. The desert's beauty enthralled me.

There is beauty in life thriving in adverse circumstances. The desert does not accommodate all, but what does survive the harshness is a type beauty that manifests in dreams. In the harshest environment, the majestic Saguaro refuses to surrender. What little it has to survive nourishes it, and all tiny glimmers of life are miraculous and luminous as under the sun as they are under the moonlight. I have never felt so in love. Not like this.

Lust that we feel for others, or even things, means there's the desire to take. Love exists when we desire to give. In the desert, all I wanted was to give her my time, my love, and my attention. Through the wind, the rattles of the snake, the flapping of cactus wren wings, and in the rugged solace of the Sonoran Desert, I heard a song that my heart fully understood. I felt embraced in the presence of nature in the raw – and it was pure joy.

Mediocrity cannot exist in nature. Sacred Earth needs nothing in its way. When I stand in the middle of sand, mesquite, cacti, and the desert sun, I realize my smallness in the universe as well as the regrowth of the passion, the fire in my heart. I belong nowhere. I belong here.

We're all linked to so many stars, so many particles that make this vast universe around us; and the stardust of the universe lies within all of us. The question inside me has long been where I actually might belong, but the universe tells me to look within. The stars tell me we're all connected to one another no matter where we are. The desert tells me I am home wherever and whenever I feel comfortable to remove my "armor" from Iraq.

In this quiet moment, I see myself in full battle rattle, weighed down by body armor, ammunition, my weapon, Kevlar, switchblade, K-Bar, and supplies. As I look into the depths of the desert night, a veil of moonlight falls upon me as I put down every piece of Iraq weight that I carry. I feel an almost unbearable lightness; it's alarming, frightening. I'm used to rolling about life like a tank, covered with plates of psychological steel and ready to fire. Here, I stand vulnerable, emotionally naked. I’m ready to keep marching ahead into the unknown toward home. I walked out alone under the stars, spending midnight with the desert.

21 SCOTTSDALE, ARIZONA

Picture this, if you will: A combat veteran is getting publicly shamed. Their service is spat upon; various media outlets perpetuate misinformation about them; veterans' charities and nonprofits exploit them; and the general public doesn't seem to accept them either. They are criticized, scrutinized, and are often spoken about with disdain, question, and shame. The combat veteran faces constant antagonization and, as a result, experiences a failure to reintegrate after war and is vulnerable to homelessness, substance abuse, prison, and/or suicide.

No, this isn't 1968. This is the beginning of the 21st century. And that combat veteran is a woman.

One doesn't have to look very hard to see not just the war on women, but the war on women veterans. Men are writing books protesting integrating women not just into combat arms, but the military all together. Women are willfully defending misogyny and are utilized as puppets for publicly disgracing women's abilities, accomplishments, and honorable service. As a female combat veteran, I have spoken up quite a bit about this and have been pushed aside and silenced. I've been there, done that. Yet I get a clear view of a non-stop circus shredding my service apart quite vividly. After all, in an age where military rape is more palatable than hearing a story about a woman performing effectively in direct combat, it's convenient to leave out any possible accomplishments and highlight victims not as survivors, but victims alone.

Both men and women are being subjected to violent Military Sexual Assault (MST). However, I watch women get singled out not as survivors of a corrupt system that exploited and failed them, but as objects to pity or shame. The humanity from much of the coverage and the depth of the problem is missing, and I shudder at how these traumatic stories are handled.

If there's an article about women in combat or infantry-related roles, we're often portrayed in the worst light possible. The popular coverage of women veterans seems to cater to fragile male egos who can't stand a woman who refuses to submit, whether they're an MST survivor or a combat veteran.

As a female combat veteran, one struggles in finding any real reasons to continue living in such an environment with no apparent and attainable way out. Is it any surprise that women veterans are committing suicide at alarming rates?

The underdogs of before certainly have more compassion. There was a group that Gabe introduced me to recently, a veterans art group called "Los Veteranos de Arizona," predominantly male Vietnam combat veterans - and Native American and Hispanic.

At first I was apprehensive about joining any veterans group. After all, so many white-male dominated veterans' groups and nonprofits basically blew me off, spied on me, or slandered me to keep voices like mine away. Gabe intervened and talked with the group's organizer, Jim Covarrubias of Ariztlan Studios in downtown Phoenix.

Gabe suggested I give it another chance, and for this group in particular.

"What makes you so confident that they'd accept a female combat veteran whose heritage is from a remote Pacific Island? I'm not ready for more bullshit or political games," I sneered.

"I'm confident especially after their response. They said you are fully welcome, because while they don't know what it's like to walk in your boots as a woman, they know what it's like to come home and have your military service shamed or ignored, and how lonely it can be especially due to the color of your skin," she said.

That was probably the best response I've ever heard from a male group in regard to women veterans. They were original, sincere, and best of all, they were passionate artists too. Los Veteranos de Arizona were incredibly supportive to the point where they convinced me to show my work for a Veterans Day exhibit, and show art which I had held onto for years, in a public setting. No pissing contest of 'who did what and when' that you often see with the Iraq and Afghanistan veterans groups. While they snubbed me to maintain their boys' club status quo, Vietnam veterans groups, especially those of color, took me in. They just allowed me to be me and didn't judge me. And really, that's all I ever wanted.

Minority Vietnam veterans knew not only of being shunned upon return to the United States and being judged, but also the discrimination faced due to their race. Vietnam veterans of color have been one of the most supportive groups of me being a female combat veteran. They not only served in severely traumatic environments, but they were treated as outcasts - and dealt with everything female combat veterans have been experiencing outside of the gender-bashing.

While people nowadays are far more supportive of "the troops" in general, it still tends to be male-centric. Just take a look at your local community resources and what's really there for women. Give those resources a call and put them to the test if they offer anything for women. You're in for a real treat. Despite studies that show that women perform effectively in combat and that there is no real difference in handling PTSD when it comes to gender, we're still slammed quite openly even in this flag-waving, yellow ribbon-wearing environment. Vietnam veterans I've worked with seem to get that and see history repeating itself under a different banner.

Homelessness and suicide rates are climbing everyday not just for veterans in general, but more specifically women veterans of recent conflicts. There's a lot more work to do in properly reintegrating women veterans into civilian life, to include validating their service and allowing for opportunities for growth, self-worth, and self-actualization – you know, reasons not to commit suicide. It's not just about resources and emergency services, it's about addressing the problem with long-term solutions. Not just waving the flag and slapping on bumper stickers, but offering chances to improve, develop, and contribute to society with pride and dignity without dealing with the current judgment and public humiliation. However, in order to establish adequate resources for women, we must address everything in the root causes of our problems first.

The art shows hosted by Los Veteranos went very well also, and one Vietnam veteran approached me inquiring about my artwork. He had also heard that I had trouble with other veterans groups from my era.

"Do you think those people care about you? Those shiny Iraq veteran groups and the VA? People who pretend to be your allies and hate you as much as you now hate them?" he asked, seeming to have an idea of the answer already.

I smirked, and shook my head. No.

"Do you think they'd band together and give back all those medals that your Army officers stole from you? Would it be enough to remind you of your integrity and courage?"

I looked at him with a hardened gaze, with the bitterness in my heart pouring through my dry eyes.

"You don't need their validation to see your worth, soldier. Just take a good long look in the mirror, and that's all you'll ever need to know. No lip service or ignorant bullshit is going to erase what you did, even when no one was looking or appreciated you," he said.

Looking into his eyes, I smiled in confirmation, and nodded.

"Welcome back, dear. It's a long, gray road and we're all lost in this desert in search of home," he sighed, patted me on the shoulder and walked away.

The following morning, before waking in my bed in Scottsdale, I had a dream. My paternal grandmother appeared before me, smiling. It appeared as she had just found me and was overcome with joy. I met her smile with a hardened gaze and promptly told her to get the fuck away from me, and that she was not welcome in my home. She looked at me wide-eyed and confused, as though she had no idea as to the source of my anger. It were as though she was that oblivious to how much damage she had done. She faded away, like Tinkerbelle without applause. I woke to a phone call from my mother. My paternal grandmother was dead.

My mother groaned as I disclosed the recent dream and she responded, "You shouldn't speak ill of the dead."

What a cliché. If she lived as a horrible person and died as a horrible person, why should death change my opinion of her? She was a terrible human being while alive and she lived comfortably surrounded by like-minded bigots on my father's side of the family. That side of the family was the source for so much pain, and I wasn't above forgiveness or compassion; it's just that she never asked for either. She had the time, the means, and the open door to do so as I smiled painfully through a few events where she was present at the request of my parents who were, let's face it, desperate for her approval. I couldn't bring myself to care, to be upset, to be sad in any way. My mother might as well have told me that fertilizer was going on sale later in the day as it was met with just as much interest accompanied by an apathetic shrug.

However, my Irish-American grandmother taught me an important lesson, one in which I took straight on through my divorce from Tony. It was from her that I learned how to stop loving someone after discovering that they didn't love me back. It was quite the useful coping mechanism. I learned to love myself even when it was apparent that reciprocation was simply not happening. Someone who never could bring herself to fully accept me, even though I was the only blood grandchild to carry the family name, was so ashamed of me. She protected a child molester, the man who molested me, solely because no one wanted to hurt my aunt's feelings – after all, it was her husband. They chose to protect the feelings of a grown white relative instead of a mixed-race child who they deemed unimportant, un-American, a lesser being.

She did give me something useful; it just wasn't love. She gave me the bittersweet gift of trauma-induced apathy.

Healing with family never happened. Healing with Vietnam Veterans took their place. With the passing of my grandmother, I felt free. Now, I know no remorse would come, instead of waiting for years for a meaningful connection. Instead, I moved forward with a group of warrior artists who didn't judge me. They accepted me. Even though I know I will never get this from blood relatives, I have found far more depth and meaning in these new friendships in this wonderful desert.

22 NEW YORK, NEW YORK

While driving happily to Tucson after getting hired with a new company, I was making mental notes in my head for an upcoming trip to New York to shoot a pilot for a television show on veterans. After I had finished unpacking with Gabe, who dutifully volunteered to help a veteran sister, we went to dinner at a nearby Mexican restaurant. She gave me warm hugs and warm wishes, then she took off.

Living and working in Phoenix is a completely different animal from making a life in Tucson. Metro Phoenix is a behemoth of a desert city whereas Tucson is a fraction of the size, slightly to the left, and has a lot more character. I maintained regular contact with Rufus' organization – although they were far more motivated to use my name on grants geared toward women than actually paying or hiring me. I volunteered and helped when I could on top of my new gig at a Tucson-based nonprofit. Since moving to Tucson, it didn't take long to see Rufus' behavioral changes and how he often vacillated between what felt like resentment and admiration toward me – it was unnerving. Yet I attributed the traits to possible trauma and it was evident he was still looking for a way to make peace with his past, which he often ruminated over and over.

He asked me, "How can you just be like a...dude?" – which was in reference to my casual views on subjects (relationships, politics, trauma, religion, etc.) that he thought would make most women "emotional." In his eyes, I appeared callous, detached, and impervious to emotional pain and he constantly questioned why I didn't appear affected by things that seemed to traumatize him. This wasn't true, but that was his perception.

The next minute he was sending me drunk-texts in the middle of the night where he would wax poetic about my eyes, lips, and figure. I treated him like a lost, confused friend and forgave a lot of his short-comings, believing that he needed far more guidance – not by me, but the actual founder of the organization who was supposed to be training him. The founder knew Rufus was a mess, and hired him anyway.

He often touted his musician persona as well as his identity as a Pentecostal Christian, despite his flirtatious build-up. Please understand that I do not give a shit about whatever religious label one chooses to wear. Do not expend any energy worrying that I give a shit about how you live your life. Unless you're a heinous, exploitative sociopath or psychopath, chances are great that I couldn't care less. My life is interesting enough on its own and I have a long list of adventures yet to be had to concern myself with someone else's business. I genuinely do not care. However, Rufus kept pushing this carefully-crafted image of himself that often contradicted his actions.

However, this friendship and any remaining confidence I had in him soon took a nosedive. He had attempted to get a little beyond our friendship one night while we both traveled to film in New York and knowing him - let alone his wife and three children - I passed. We went to a sports bar outside of out Kimpton hotel near Times Square and commenced the drink-fest. I ordered my first drink, but he insisted on ordering for me, completely taking responsibility for my tab.

"You do know that I'm a big girl and can buy my own drinks, right?" I said as my Tom Collins arrived.

"I know, but I'll take care of you tonight. Let me have this. You can get the next one," he said winking as though we were a lot closer friends than we really were.

I knew what he was doing. The cynical part of me, no matter how kind I may appear at any given moment, kicked in as he appeared unusually confident with me this evening. He's thinking I'm unaware of what he's planned. My gut instinct spoke quite loudly at this point indicating that he was going to make a move, but he needed me drunk beyond all cognition before doing so.

The drinks kept coming, and we were keeping up with each other matching drink-to-drink in count. I recall by drink number eight, he was looking at me from across the table a bit disturbed that I wasn't curled up underneath in the fetal position. Nope. I was lucid, still. I could hold my liquor, even at my 5'3", 125lb frame like I've been training for the drinking Olympics since I was a teenager. Sorry, Rufus, I am no cheap date.

In my mind, this had immediately evolved into a competition, and his efforts to drink me under the table were visually under question as I was keeping up with his mixed drinks. He was 82nd Airborne infantry and he was apparently expecting to easily outdrink the "girl" in front of him.

The drinking competition soon took us from the sports bar to the lounge inside the hotel. By this time, things were starting to get foggy and he was getting sloppy, so I bowed out of this pathetic battle as soon as he started to get googly-eyed and began going on about how he thought I was beautiful, sexy, mysterious...

Not again.

As I boarded the elevator, Rufus was right behind me and on his way to his room, which was not so coincidentally right across from mine. I knew that the drinking match couldn't last any longer and all I wanted was to get to bed, but not his. He kept talking to me, and as I started to ignore him and wander into my room, he followed as well.

"Don't you have your own bed to sleep in tonight?" I barked at him, feeling almost irritated as my buzz was starting to wear off and reality had set in. He, a married man with three kids, was definitely not invited.

"I just enjoy talking to you, is that a crime?" he said, smiling, as he stumbled onto a chair and started drawing me a picture of Snoopy.

"What the fuck is wrong with you?" I said shaking my head, staring him down.

"Here," he said as he handed me multiple, terrible sketches of Snoopy.

"Dude, you've gotta go. You're not okay right now, and you have no business being in here," I said, almost sounding like a mother to him now.

"Why? Are you afraid of what's going on between us?" he said as he stood up and stepped closer to me as though he were initiating physical contact.

Immediately, I backhanded him across his right cheek. I hit him so hard, and even as drunk as I was, my hand was numb and tingling.

"Kiss me, then tell me you don't feel anything," he said.

I slapped him again. Then he stepped closer to me, smiling.

"Hit me again," he said, looking into my eyes with what looked like a masochistic sense of lust. He was enjoying it. I'm not going to lie, for a split-second, I was turned on and thought, "Hmmmm, interesting…," but that immediately followed with a big "fuck no" considering what a mess he is and that he is married with children.

Then I grabbed him by the shirt, which caused him to grin in delight, thinking I was going to rough him up in bed. Instead, I pushed him out of the room and into the hallway before his door.

"Get some sleep, ass-face. And don't fuck things up, tomorrow," I said before slamming the door.

Throughout the night, I felt the weight of his persistent faint knocks.

While I wasn't terribly surprised at Rufus' gall, I was disappointed in myself for even having had him in the confines of my hotel room. I felt disgusted with myself. I texted Genevieve, who then called as I broke down the details of that evening. She was proud of me for not giving in to what would have been a horrible deed, but also equally disgusted with Rufus. Someone who was a supposed veteran brother was clearly attempting to take advantage of me, and although his efforts were successfully thwarted, it didn't make what occurred feel any less terrible. To these men, I was mere territory to be conquered.

That night, as I disclosed the conversation and Rufus' attempts, I felt that perhaps dying wouldn't be so bad. I wasn't appreciated in this life, and really, what was there to live for in this plastic world that obviously wanted to repeatedly use me. Drinking so much certainly didn't help my decision-making at the time, nor did it shine a light on anything going well, but I didn't feel like I wanted to be here anymore. I told Genevieve that I wanted to leap out of my hotel window, and I was as serious as I've ever been.

Gazing into the darkness of the isle of iron and concrete, twinkling lights danced around and I felt life leaving my body. I was tired of people using me as an escape, a conduit to feel alive. To be used and discarded so often leaves one feeling exhausted. A terrible emptiness filled my soul and I'm sure the gin assisted in my growing rage. I wanted nothing more in that moment than to get off this planet. It wasn't the mere act of a thirsty, married man coming onto me, it was a sense of absolute disgust with everything awful I had experienced since Iraq. For some odd reason, alone in this posh hotel room after belting Rufus in the face, I just decided I had enough of life. Arizona had been good to me for the most part, but here in New York, I felt the desire to put everything to an end.

Ending my life seemed all too tempting, ending the pain. I was tired of marching on, and without rest or reprieve. My parents or family had no interest in helping me through the trauma, the veteran services organizations were only interested in helping their buddies and using a select few as grant and donation-generating show ponies, and the general public apparently had a problem in conceiving the idea that a woman, let alone one of color, could serve in combat successfully. My head was filled with demons as I sighed in drunken melancholy with my forehead pressed against the window overlooking Manhattan. I was born here, but I felt dead inside after all that had happened. My life felt like a pitiful, tragicomedy that had gone on too long. That night, Genevieve, with tears and sobbing together in unison over the phone, talked me out of killing myself.

My friends are the stars in my dark night sky, keeping my eyes open and focused in a place in my life where I longed to shut down; give in to a grave. My spirit was a reflection of the desert. The tears would emerge and tremble on the edge of my eyelashes, yet dry up and turn to dust before they could fall. Cried out and alone, this journey was no pitiful parade, but an introspective walk to right oneself after such a soul-sucking spiritual catastrophe in war. That it would be a disservice to those who died and didn't have a chance to come home, that I had to find a way to live, find a purpose to make the most of what chance I was given to not come home in a flag-draped box.

The next morning, Rufus immediately asked me to his table at breakfast in the main dining hall, and apologized for his behavior the night before. I accepted, but the conversation took an odd turn when he asked why I divorced Tony. Finally, I sat down, wondering if he was willing to continue to act like an adult now that we were both sober.

"I was a novelty to him. I'm a novelty to men. What can I say? They want to sleep with a Lioness, but then they wake up to Michelle."

Rufus looked down in what looked like embarrassment. I saw through the shame in his eyes as that's how he viewed me; not as a partner or a business associate, but as a carnal conquest. This happens so much that I'm beyond disgust over the topic. This morning, post suicidal ideations, I just feel indifferent, and perhaps I subconsciously anticipate disappointment that one can only experience on the road toward intimacy, running into superficial lust and physical exploitation.

In attempt to deal with the awkward situation as adults, I discussed it with him, letting him know it was because I care about him as a person that things should not traverse beyond a certain boundary and he appeared to agree. We had filming to do, after all. After breakfast, we made our way to finding Christina, a former NBC Nightly News reporter and Air Force veteran. She was warm and genuinely kind. She emanated a kind of passion for the greater good that was contagious.

We then began to stage different sessions where women veterans talked, male veterans talked, and the whole group spoke of their personal struggles and successes. However, the most memorable of all was the taping of a female veteran, an Iraq war veteran, with whom I shared much in common.

In a videotaping session about the positive effects of combat veteran peer support, I had the privilege of sitting with a kindred spirit. We were surrounded by cameras and production-crew members, while we took turns discussing the problems we had faced. We could have discussed anything in our 45-minute session, but we chose to go straight for the "relationship jugular." In a matter of a few minutes, we discovered that we had considerable and startling experiences in common.

Since returning from Iraq, we had both dealt with a significant number of situations where men seemed intimidated by our combat experiences—seemingly to the point where they felt emasculated or determined to devalue our experience as some sort of "defense mechanism." Both of us had met men who seemed to be fond of us until they found out about our combat tours of duty in Iraq. Some even sought to physically or emotionally abuse us as a result. Is it that women serving in the military are so threatening to because of the prescribed roles women are "expected" to serve in society? I've found that my duty in Iraq is intimidating, to men in particular, and leaves them believing that women veterans who have been in combat have no room for their instruction. This belief or attitude is quite problematic for women veterans who are seeking a partner, not a teacher or a master.

In short, our experiences seemed to demonstrate that most men, in one way or another, did not handle our résumés very well. Another point was that we ourselves were disinterested in their military experiences or lack thereof—all we wanted was to engage in happy, fulfilling relationships. From co-dependent types, to sociopaths, to abusers and users— we had seen them all and we were waiting patiently for someone who's secure and genuine.

Near the end of the interaction, and after a few zany and sometimes tragic stories of love gone wrong that left the crew giggling or shaking their heads, this fellow female veteran said something that has always remained with me as a personal truth: "I don't want a father in a partner. I've got a father. I don't want to look after my partner like a son. I'd like a son one day, but my own. I want an equal to walk beside me, not in front of me or behind me. And I won't accept anyone who I can't look in the eyes and not feel that way."

Sex sells in America but it's done so aggressively that it's devoid of sensuality. It's get off quick and get back to whatever. No seduction, no intrigue, no soul. In the process, women veterans, who appear to be less compliant with the objectification process, appear to see more of an aggressive response from men in seeking a romantic partner.

In prior relationships, the nature of adventure in sex has primarily been rough sex, simple aggression. It stops being sexy when it's viewed from an observer stance rather than a participant. Let me explain. Being with other men who feel they're sexually advanced tends to mean they feel comfortable roughing you up as though you're engaged in making porn. The talk is like porn, the moves are like porn, and while it may feel adventurous to them, it feels predictable to me. I desire much more than fast motion and tired old lines about my anatomy that are regurgitated online. I crave seduction, intimacy, and to be taken to another level -

something that simply hasn't happened yet. I don't long to be conquered, I crave a ripening.

There are many men who appear uncomfortable with women veterans who've been able to succeed in the male-dominated military system as well as being comfortable with themselves sexually. They seem to find this troubling or challenging to their own sense of self. I'm proud of what I have accomplished, both personally and professionally, and have no desire to pick someone apart for their achievements in life—or the absence of them. Like other women veterans, I simply wish to find a partner who I could consider an equal and who would reciprocate this sentiment.

Unfortunately, when we got back to Tucson, it was an entirely different story. Rufus had painted a picture of himself in an entirely different light, making himself out to be a helpless victim in a fabricated story that made me look like Glenn Close in Fatal Attraction. Needless to say, I called a time-out.

It was a whirlwind of a nightmare. In short, the founder of the organization stood behind Rufus and justified his behavior as a response to me being a "strong-willed, assertive woman" that he didn't know how to handle. I was mystified. The founder basically arrived at gaslighting me to protect Rufus. The other women in the organization, one a non-veteran and the other an Air Force veteran with histrionic features, once rallying to my side, stood silent and washed their hands of it. The Air Force veteran invited me to her house to talk about her failing marriage and my frustration in being treated like expendable, sexualized meat.

In between wine glasses she asked about what happened with Rufus in New York, in which I was candid, and explained why his behavior must've been a result from rejection. However, I felt far more pain of being exploited. She nodded her head and held my hand in solidarity.

She was merely spying on me, collecting information to see what way she could best get me ousted and to the benefit of this nonprofit who was using my name in order to acquire grant money to work with female combat veterans. This organization had used me, never paid me for my consultations, attempted to garner attention for funding through my affiliation with Team Lioness, attempted to victimize me, and turned on the gaslight when I protested their behavior.

After the Rufus incident, I had another typical late night. I went driving around Tucson, north to south, east to west, just driving, driving, and driving. Channeling my desert driving from Iraq was something I needed to do, be reminded that I survived way worse just a few years ago. Thinking about how Rufus tried to paint me as a "shark" as he supposedly stated, I thought back to a time when someone else had once called me the same.

Sharks are sacred to Micronesians. They are often viewed as merciless predators of the sea in the West, but without them, we can't survive. Taking the shark out of our oceans would disrupt the ecosystem, and barracudas and other lower-level powerful sea creatures would devour the food we eat to survive. My ex, the one who stole my Bordeaux dress and money post-Iraq to punish me, once told me that I had the look of a shark, that it must be an islander thing. In Iraq, after I broke off our engagement, he said I was a killer without a heart. People often assume those who survived combat can't see things as they are, like sharks, but we do see. Clearly. Differently. When it comes to those we love, we can be gentle and patient amid a destructive power within, to protect those we love the most from harm. We can gauge our response in a way that will push our loved ones to safety, and away from the dangers we know all too well. Perhaps my ex was right; I am that shark, but not the one he knows.

Finally, I came to a stop en route to another part of Saguaro National Park. I got out of my car, and all around me was the desert and the starry sky. Alone, I could breathe here and give myself time to reflect in this generous, empathetic desert that was always ready to listen.

No one is perfectly built for the desert, but the desert cares not. It will remain as it is forever and changes for no one. Sans judgment or care, the desert is not your place for exile, but rebirth. If you welcome the desert as she is, amid her grandeur and cruelty, she will welcome you and show you who you really are.

It was an awful feeling to have done the right thing and have people turn on you and hurt you even more so. It just felt like the hits kept coming and every horrible person I had encountered was adequately backed with 10-100 more horrible people just like them. I wanted to walk into the desert and become a hermit, to stay away from people and not be hurt. They say that the human heart grows hard when one is away from nature, and I couldn't let that happen. Being here made me want to live much, much more. I wasn't ready to give up, but I certainly needed a timeout from the insanity of others – other veterans of my own era no less. I looked into the sky filled with glimmering and shooting stars, closed my eyes, and inhaled the clean, calm desert air. Just breathe.

Blanketed by the night sky, I thought about the beautiful Desert Warrior from my dreams. She's been silent in the dream world since I moved to Tucson, yet I feel her so close on these solitary desert walks.

"Where are you?" I whispered. Staring at the moon, then all around me in the otherworldly beauty of the desert, I thought back to how that dream felt. To be loved. To love someone back. To feel fulfilled, to rid myself of this chronic emptiness. I wanted to weep in the desert, drown the pain of seemingly infinite loneliness. I inhaled the scent of desert flora, the green of cacti sleeping through the night under that perfectly starry indigo sky. I imagined a life where I was loved, and could love back without fear.

"I'm ready to meet you," I whispered, as though she could ascend from a saguaro and fly toward me like a Sonoran Desert angel. The hope within me was almost feeling like desperation, a deep inner longing to feel connected in a world I where I was losing my ground. Somehow, if this presence I had felt in my dreams, if this Desert Warrior would emerge, I believed the answers would manifest, a purpose to life would be reissued.

My phone vibrated in my pocket. I took it out and saw that Eugenio had sent me a message, asking what I was doing, as usual. I laughed. From Iraq to Arizona, from Baghdad to Tucson, here he was again, checking-in.

"Where are you, hermosa?" Eugenio texted.

I responded and we met up shortly before sunrise inside a local diner. We talked over coffee for hours.

23 TUCSON, ARIZONA

Here, I am free and see no borders ahead of me keeping me away from my home. Here, time stands still while I sprint over mountains and arid lands in search of my safe, sacred space, my inner altar that I'll call home. In the desert, my soul danced to a different rhythm and flowed freely high above the sand and into the cloudless skies. I'm close. So close I could feel it.

All the things that once held me down, I banished from my sacred space, as imperfect as it is. No more hurt is going to be tolerated or allowed in anymore. The home I envisioned was one of peace, calm, and a safe area where I didn't need to feel like a moving target evading gunfire.

Home was being built within first, and only those that I could trust, people I felt safe to be around, would be allowed to be part of this construct. No one from my past or present could overextend their stay if I wanted them out.

Nighttime was magic time in Tucson. When the whole city fell asleep, I took to the streets and back roads in my rickety sedan taking photos of old neon signs and shots of the moon light over the desert in the painted rocks area. I never felt alone, even though I was by myself during these nocturnal excursions. There was a persistent feeling that I was present, in the moment, rather than waiting for something to happen. I was right where I needed to be, and it was the first time I had felt this strongly, and united with my environment, the universe, since Iraq.

After having a few months to settle in Tucson, I contacted Eugenio and we commenced the first of many late-night rituals: breakfast at 3am in a shitty diner. Eugenio often reminded me of an old man. He is actually three years younger than I, but often referred to me, in spite of my typically prickly demeanor, with diminutive terms. He referred to me as “little miss” or “young lady,” as though he were going to take off a brimmed hat and hand me a freshly-picked flower. He appears to have been born in the wrong era, someone propelled out of the past and hopelessly lost in the present, stumbling blindly toward the future. His time capsule presence was confounding, but he was always lending an ear to my post-war woes.

I did appreciate that Eugenio was there for me in quite a few difficult situations ranging from Iraq to divorcing Tony to living in a new state and city. We had a string of these late-night talks at diners on spirituality, love, lust, passion, career, direction, goals, family, life, and anything else that crossed our minds.

“Have you ever felt like you were alone in the world, even with all these people around? Like you're just wading through an ocean of cold, vacant gazes?” I asked him.

He looked at me, smiled, and shook his head.

"I know it sounds silly. I know, but I've felt alone in life before, I'm sure everyone has to a degree, but I've never felt like this. In Tucson, oddly enough, as a place I've never lived in, I feel like I'm almost home. This is the most at home feeling I've felt since coming back from Iraq. Hell, Ramadi felt more like 'home' than much of the US. It's the last time anything made any sense in life. Iraq was where the new reality kicked in, the Matrix pill that's too far gone to spit out and reality sucks. But it’s lonely, isn’t it?"

"Tucson is your home now. Now you see why I like it here?"

I'm not sure if he really knew what I meant. Eugenio never saw a minute of combat from the confines of his compound in Baghdad's Green Zone. His palatial digs were worlds away from Ramadi, the bottom of the barrel of Iraq. The Green Zone was Beverly Hills, opulent, metropolitan, and still had an air of decadence. Ramadi was Appalachia, where its inhabitants held on tight to firearms, fundamentalist religious views, and inbreeding.

Eugenio hadn't the faintest clue of what I was going through, but he was there. Like he was just there when I was going through hell in Iraq and we met in passing. Doe-eyed, naïve Eugenio. Just listening and nodding, thinking we were on the same page, hearing the same music when we weren't. Sometimes I envied his naïveté. What I would give to have my mind clear of all these ghosts. So, we sat there. Two warm bodies present in a diner at 3am talking over old coffee and stale toast in the middle of a Sonoran Desert town.

That was the benefit of Tucson. Insomnia, unlike what I had experienced in Massachusetts, was relished. I adored being up at night and finding warmth in the dry desert air. It's pure and comforting. The feeling of the barren, unforgiving desert and the aging neon signs against the backdrop of a defiantly clear desert sky told me I was welcome in a world of contradictions; that the absurdity that I've seen since coming home from Iraq was just an illusion, and I was loved again. I felt that love. It wasn't from a person, but it was all around, in the air, in the stars.

Watching avant-garde films, talking about his relationship with his second soon-to-be ex wife falling apart, and staying out late was the norm for Eugenio and I. During a night out with friends, we were getting a bit more comfortable with one another. In front of a pizza place in downtown Tucson, an old friend of Eugenio's appeared and they began catching up.

Eugenio started to introduce everyone and then turned to me saying, "And this is my girlfriend."

I paused for a moment and looked at Eugenio sideways, thinking to myself, "Did I just hear what I think he said?"

Oddly enough, the idea didn't bother me at all. If anyone else would have said it, I'd run through a wall like a Warner Brothers cartoon leaving behind a silhouette carved out in brick. Yet Eugenio was always there somehow and the idea of even moving in that direction, all of a sudden, didn't seem so scary. We danced throughout the night with friends and toward the end of the night, Eugenio and I were hand-in-hand. Outside of Hotel Congress on the way out, we kissed. We both were tipsy, but I looked at him differently. I wasn't so scared of being in a relationship anymore.

After turning down Rufus in New York, I found myself with a stalker. After going out with Eugenio on another night, my neighbor mentioned two men had shown up at my apartment. His description sounded a hell of a lot like Rufus and quite possibly one of his brothers.

Immediately, Eugenio helped me move out and into the same

house his best friend Richard lived. The owner of the house, Nathan, lived there as well and everyone seemed to get along. Eugenio stayed over every night, only going back to his parents' house perhaps one day a week. One night during that first week in the new house, both Eugenio and I couldn't sleep. We began talking and rambling on about everything and anything, but then the subject of children came up. As Eugenio was going through a struggle with his ex over his son after his second marriage collapsed earlier this year, he asked me if I wanted children.

"Of course I do, I'm hoping that happens sometime in the near future, before I'm too old to have children. But if anything I want something stable, not like my first marriage where I was practically living with a stranger," she said.

"You should have at least one, or try to sometime soon," he said in response as we both stared out the window, lying in bed observing a sea of stars above.

Before any more of that conversation could continue, both Eugenio and I were locked up in an embrace that was different from any previous time. Aside from laughter, joking around, and jaded talks of not believing in love, something else was taking place that night.

One morning, I went out on a run the day before Father's Day and began to black out. I had run less than two miles away but was already feeling dizzy. While sitting down on the side of the road the fear set in. I raced to a drug store where I bought a pregnancy test. Rushing back to the house, I tried two test sticks. Both tests came out positive immediately.

You know, if you're anticipating pregnancy, the pregnancy test seems like it takes ages to show results. When you're actually pregnant, it really doesn't waste any time in displaying a positive reading. I didn't have a full five minutes to wait; it told me in two seconds. I stood in disbelief, and texted Genevieve, "HELP! Two pregnancy tests, both positive!"

Genevieve consoled me over the phone as I stepped outside to catch my breath. I realized I had contacted her just a few months ago where she talked me out of killing myself, and now it was a conversation about a potential new life – the latter inspiring panic.

I then decided to wake up Eugenio. I invited him out for breakfast and planned on telling him the news there, but once we were in the car, I broke down.

"I need to talk to you about something," I paused and took a deep breath. He sat there, silent, looking like I was going to surprise him.

"I'm pregnant."

"Nice," Eugenio said with a big smile.

"What the hell are you smiling about?! This is serious! What are we going to do?" I cried. I began talking about having a more solid foundation, working something out relationship-wise for the sake of keeping this new family together, but Eugenio protested.

Janessa, Nathan's girlfriend, started chatting with me the same evening and was there as soon as Eugenio decided to return home. He wasn't staying over after all, and even appeared slightly embarrassed. He didn't go into details of what might have happened, but I was losing a lot of respect for him. Looking at him was starting to make my stomach turn. What kind of friend he turned out to be. Instead of being there for me, he was obviously distancing himself from me while simultaneously keeping tabs on my whereabouts. I was getting that sneaking feeling that he viewed me in the same light as his former partners: an exotic pet. Some "thing" to own, but not to love.

Intrigued by our military backgrounds, Janessa began asking both Eugenio and I what we did in the Army.

"I was a nutrition specialist," Eugenio stated as he went on to mention how we crossed paths in Baghdad's Green Zone.

"What's that exactly?" Janessa asked.

"It's like being a food inspector," Eugenio said.

"You were a food-checker?!" Janessa asked, tilting her head to the side and squinting her eyes in what looked like a combination of confusion and insult.

Eugenio was clearly not amused.

Janessa looked to me and began laughing aloud, and asked Eugenio, "So, like, did you used to taste the General's food so he wouldn't die or something? What the fuck does that mean?!"

"I almost went artillery, but nutrition seemed like it would be a lot easier," Eugenio said appearing somewhat annoyed.

Janessa was still laughing, "Dude, you joined the Army for that?"

"What did you do, Michelle?" she asked, wiping tears away

and calming down her laughter.

"I was a medic and mental health sergeant, but I worked on something called Team Lioness while I was in Iraq," I replied.

"Holy fuck! Dying people and crazy people! That's pretty bad ass! But what the hell is Team Lioness?" she asked.

"It was an all-female team attached to Marine infantry units in dangerous cities in Iraq that conducted house raids, personnel searches, and checkpoint operations, and that's what I did in addition to my occupational duties," I said.

"Wow, you're my new hero!" Janessa beamed as Eugenio now appeared to look slighted. He was shamed by someone right in front of me, and his lofty experience in Baghdad's Green Zone paled in comparison to my grisly tenure in Ar Ramadi. Janessa had apparently stripped him of his man card in a matter of seconds as she turned all her attention to me, with the exception of teasing Eugenio about being a food-checker.

Eugenio got up and left the table and retreated to the room to play video games. Janessa and I continued to talk and she asked me a few more typical questions. What was war like? How did you keep from going crazy amid all the chaos? Were you scared? But then she asked a truly loaded question. She asked if she knew of a friend of hers who died in Iraq. Lo and behold, Janessa's high school buddy was someone I worked on in Iraq.

Someone whose life could've been saved if the medical transport had taken her to the emergency room instead of a mental health clinic by accident. She was bleeding for an hour before we got her and was slipping into shock as we tightened her poorly wrapped tourniquets and began CPR en route to the surgical hospital. It was a gruesome death, and I was now standing in front of her friend who was asking with concern and expecting honesty.

Janessa had heard a watered-down version of the story that the Army hospital used to cover up the MEDEVAC errors that allowed her to nearly bleed to death before finally dying on the operating table, but I told her the truth. Every gory detail.

"I knew it," she said, "something about the story just didn't sit right with me. It's so messed up that she died like that and she was such a sweet person!"

It didn't feel great to tell her the truth and see the sense of loss in her eyes, but I felt relief in knowing I didn't feed into the perpetuated lies that often come out of war.

"From now on, we're going to be good friends. You tried, and it's terrible that she didn't make it to you sooner, but you did what you could," Janessa said.

Janessa's words provided a small sense of assurance, but it was never enough. You can't change the past.

Eugenio and I continued to butt heads throughout the following days, possibly still reeling from Janessa's comments. I kept to my paintings in spite of growing tension, and reflected on the fact that moving to Arizona really helped bring out my artistic mojo once again. I wasn't going to let anyone, not even Eugenio, throw me off course. Hanging two large personal paintings, I looked beyond Eugenio and to the road ahead.

During the time that Eugenio was gone to a tennis tournament, one of my friends, Amira, was telling me that she felt uncomfortable with Eugenio contacting her via social media.

Eugenio had talked of Amira and a few other friends that he had seen via social media and had made comments about wanting to sleep with them, much to my dismay, which Amira brought up. Amira was right. Amira then blocked Eugenio, and then Eugenio blocked me. It wasn't just an argument or a lewd comment; it was all the issues finally coming to a head and Eugenio was clearly choosing sides. From his bizarre requests to live together in the same house but have an open relationship to making threats of burying anyone in the desert who remotely hurts him, all I knew was that I wanted a break from Eugenio.

"Why are you even staying with someone who doesn't even value you? He's worse than your ex-husband and you don't have any real commitment with him, get out of there!" Amira exclaimed.

She was right. Why was I sticking around?

"Look at how far he's willing to push you around to serve his interests, he's certainly proving that he is not you friend," Amira said. Right again.

What else was it going to take before I broke down and couldn't deal with him anymore?

I asked a favor of both Richard and Nathan. I asked them if they could not invite Eugenio for just one week so that I could think clearly and make a decision on what to do next. I was feeling overwhelmed, alone, and confused. Deep down, I cared about him, but I didn't want to continue to put up with the head games either. The request wasn't indefinite; if Eugenio could give me just one week alone, it would've been my saving grace. I wanted time to calm down and think things through before making any snap decisions. Both Richard and Nathan agreed.

The day after I stated my request, Eugenio was at the house again, laughing in Richard's room. I needed time and now felt this was a spiteful move on Eugenio's part. Nathan pulled me aside to the garage where he said that he asked Richard to agree but he went ahead and brought him over anyway. Nathan then went on to tell me that Eugenio said I needed to 'get on my knees and apologize' to him as this was all my fault. I was livid.

Not only was Eugenio not contributing anything while taking advantage of the situation, not helping out with rent, food, or any typical aspect of a person sleeping in a house almost every day, but now he was openly humiliating and mocking me. Both Richard and Nathan stated that Eugenio wasn't doing his part, but this was a demonstration of both tolerance and validation of his behavior aside from any words.

I knocked on Richard's door where Eugenio opened up, I began arguing with him. Eugenio smiled as though he were happy to see me upset. He enjoyed getting a rise out of me, hurting me. Eugenio attempted to swing the door shut on me while I was in the doorway. Yet, I blocked it and pushed back. It was like a flash of red blood overcame me and the feeling of my pregnancy invoked an animal-like anger that prompted me to snarl at him, "GET THE FUCK OUT OF THIS HOUSE!"

His eyes were wide, and it was the first time I saw genuine shock combined with fear in his eyes. It was evident that this was likely the first time any woman had stood up to him physically and verbally. I then called the police asking for him to leave, relaying the altercation. The first of the two officers appeared to be diplomatic, and advised me to get an order of protection against him until I was able to move. The other officer, before walking in to investigate, asked me quickly for my side of the story. I told him the argument escalated and I didn't feel safe with him in the house until I was able to relocate.

This officer began getting belligerent with me and stated

inches from my face, "Well, I can just go inside and hear his side of the story and you'd just end up being a lying bitch, wouldn't you?"

Needless to say, I wasn't expecting that response, especially from a police officer responding to a domestic violence incident. And I asked him to repeat what he just said to me. He rolled his eyes and as he began to turn away, his partner came outside and informed me that Eugenio was being hostile. When the officer called me a bitch, I took a mental pause. I was outnumbered by men who had no regard for my safety or well-being to include this Pima County Sheriff officer getting in my face despite my calm.

His partner, a far more even-keeled officer apologized for his partner's over-zealous verbal diarrhea. As the irritable officer went inside, I informed the diplomatic officer of what he said, who then looked down and shook his head, which said to me that he had witnessed this behavior before.

Witnessed this behavior before from his partner? It made me wonder just how poorly domestic violence was handled in Tucson.

He continued to tell me to make sure I get all of my valuables out of the house as soon as possible and to get the order of protection right away for the safety of my unborn child and myself.

"These sort of things happens more often than you think, but the best advice I can give you is to look out for the safety of you and your child, and ask yourself," while pointing toward the house, "is this the life that you want to give her?"

"I know what you mean, and this is not what I wanted for her, not in the slightest. I'm just going to rent a U-Haul Friday and leave," I responded.

"Do you have anywhere to go? Any relatives in town you could stay with in the meantime?" the kind officer asked.

That was the thing. I had nowhere to go in Tucson. I had no close ties here, no relatives. I was alone, and Eugenio knew this. Instead of being there for me, he had used my vulnerability to his own advantage.

After all, if I had no apparent place to run, he could treat me however he wanted, especially being pregnant. We heard yelling coming from inside the house. Apparently, the misogynist officer was on the brink of arresting Eugenio, who was apparently throwing a tantrum and defying the officer.

The rooster of an officer stomped through the front door and summoned his partner inside.

I could overhear some of the chatter, and both had ended up settling the argument going on inside. Eugenio would leave for the night, and I would execute the order of protection immediately. As I stood off to the side, the diplomatic officer stood next to me, appearing leery of Eugenio as the rooster cop ensured that he left the premises. Eugenio left with a bowed head as Richard and his younger brother followed with embarrassment.

As soon as the Eugenio was out of sight, I went back to my room and started to pack. Suddenly, I heard a knock at my door. It was the rooster cop.

"Yes?" I asked, not feeling safe being alone with this maniac either.

"Here's some information on domestic violence. Their number is right here on the card," he said with a flat affect, like he was just doing a routine part of his job that meant nothing to him.

"Thanks," I said, with an incredulous look on my face that meant to say, *"Are you fucking kidding me? After you witnessed all of that? That's all you have to say after calling me a bitch to my face just moments ago?"*

He turned and walked away.

In the morning, I called this domestic violence nonprofit and shared my story with a woman who then told me, "This sort of thing happens all the time. Some of these cops may be abusers themselves. You can try to file a report against the officer, but his department will do an internal investigation and nothing will happen."

"What about the restraining order? I don't think this is enough to stop Eugenio from coming after me. He's a malignant narcissist who's openly bragging about abusing and threatening to kill women!" I exclaimed.

"Well, if he comes near you, call the police," she said flatly. No strategy for women targeted by abusers, just hope for the best and hope you don't die. I was on the verge of being homeless or murdered, and had no one to turn to today. My heart started pounding in my head. But, hey, I'm sure their domestic violence prevention fundraiser galas are absolutely fabulous.

When you set boundaries, and rid yourself of toxic

relationships and behaviors, it is not a judgment against others but a declaration unto yourself. A declaration of self-respect and allowing yourself peace and a safe environment free of further harm. The right people will not force themselves into your life, or defiantly cross your lines, but allow you space to be yourself. In defining your boundaries, you liberate yourself from the entrapment of others.

Some people will only appear to "love" you to the extent that they can use you. When the resources have been exhausted, when you are of no superficial benefit to them, you're easily discarded, disregarded, forgotten. I saw that familiar look in his eyes. The look of someone unafraid to use me, unafraid to lose me. It reminded me of every other guy I have met since the divorce. Immediately, a light turned off inside of me, and I was numb again. If someone didn't care for me, nothing in my body or mind was going to make me care for them.

In his presence, I was just a punchline to jokes among his friends. Mocking me, in a similar chord that Tony and his friends mocked the women in their lives, and I knew that I wanted no part in this comedy routine. I left like it was funny.

The power to hurt me, to destroy my inner peace, needed to be repossessed. No one owns that right. Did he feel victorious in shutting the door on me like a dog in the street? Clinging to his video gaming buddies while shoving a pregnant woman aside, I wished he saw my fears, what being alone in this city, this world really felt like. Being without close friends or family in Tucson, he was all I had, and I was terrified - terrified to be this vulnerable. It wasn't combat that frightened me, it was motherhood.

Violence is not always a punch, a slap, or any direct physical contact. What was going on with Eugenio was a form of intimate terrorism. When one person in an intimate relationship systematically degrades, isolates, and punishes the other, this constitutes a form of violence that is not designed to bruise the skin, but to injure one enough to prevent them from having the courage to leave. Intimate terrorism is often a precursor to physical violence, but these were the red flags my mother had warned me about.

Such psychological abuse can lead to what feels like Stockholm syndrome, where the hostage experiences affection for their captor. This isn't what you would call a mature or rational relationship.

The following day, Nathan had invited me to his birthday dinner where Janessa, his family and friends would attend. It was then that Nathan proposed that I could move in with Janessa in order to steer clear of Eugenio and any attempts at harm. Both Nathan and Janessa were convinced that this would both keep me safe and provide at least some emotional support for what could be a frightening period alone. This was certainly not how I had planned things to be, but it was the smartest, quickest, option available. I agreed.

Unbeknownst to all of us, during Nathan's birthday party, Richard gave Eugenio the keys to the house to reportedly collect his belongings while everyone was gone. No one returned to the house, except for me that night when I discovered that two large paintings of mine were taken from the hallway outside of my room, which I had locked with a key before leaving to work. I asked Nathan if he knew what happened to the paintings and he mentioned that they were still in place at the house prior to his departure. Richard claimed that he didn't know what had happened either.

As soon as I saw this, I filed a report with the police who then advised me to go somewhere safer for the night and to not be alone in the house. The officer then asked about the paintings I had done, "Our Lady of Lucid Dreams" and "Desert Hallucinogens." I said it was to honor a dream of a figure that brought me to Arizona post-Iraq, that it was a thank you to her for getting me to Arizona. Both paintings were just requested by the VA after showing them when I went in for my first ultrasound. But now that request was now obsolete.

The police officer sighed, shook his head and said, "Bad karma always comes back. Those were sacred paintings, and for him to take them was not okay. Believe me, I've seen it happen and it may take a while, but it never fails."

I went to a hotel for the night and received a message from Eugenio taunting me via text: "Lol saying I took ur paintings!? Puh-leez…I wouldn't touch that garbage you call art with a ten foot clown pole. Please keep ur bullshit to yourself."

Clown pole or not, Eugenio made the mistake of confessing to destroying the paintings in the desert to Nathan who then told Janessa days later. He took the painting I first completed in Arizona, "Our Lady of Lucid Dreams" – yes, a painting of the dream that brought me to Arizona – and the first painting I completed in Tucson, "Desert Hallucinogens." He reportedly lugged the two paintings out to the desert, on Yaqui Indian Reservation land, and smashed and tore them to pieces. After filing a report on it, local law enforcement, again, dropped the ball.

Eugenio continued to not only brag about his glorious destruction to other people but to mock and threaten me from across town as well. Talks about setting me up, hurting me, getting even were occasionally relayed back to me, but all I started to see was who I saw in Iraq: a scared little boy.

I didn't hate him, but he was too cognizant of what he was doing to deserve my pity. Sometimes people feel the need to demonize you, threaten you, and fantasize about hurting you simply to feel better about themselves.

Accountability is truly what scares them most.

I told Louis, a Yaqui artist who worked with me about the paintings. He shook his head in disgust, and said, "He might laugh now for what he did, and I'm so sorry for what he's done to you and your hard work. But the Creator doesn't sleep, and the ugliness and damage he did, on our land, will not go unnoticed. He will get his, Michelle, believe me."

I wasn't so sure about that. Understanding what Louis said and looking back on my own past, it felt like Karma was fast asleep. Bad people don't always get their come-uppance and sociopaths constantly climb their way to the top. How was I any different in being yet another exploit? I didn't expect divine retribution, but simply accepted the loss and moved on.

"A man in his position has two simple choices: either step-up and be the man she needs you to be, or step aside so she can find a real man," Louis said.

A weak man wants a weak woman, one whom he can stare down his nose at her as a lesser being; a woman who is feeble, docile, unaware of her own power. Someone who relishes in trivial material things than her own education and rights. Someone who is asleep at the wheel of her own life.

That is where the weak man wants to be, taking control of her wheel to feel less adequate and he must make her feel the same. The day after Nathan's birthday party, I packed all my belongings in a van in one day and drove away.

24 NORTH BY NORTHWEST TUCSON

As I got settled in at Janessa's, using the spare bedroom and bathroom, we started going out together and were enjoying this awkwardly forged friendship.

"I'm glad that you left that fucking food-checker. I mean, what kind of loser do you have to be to treat the mother of your unborn child like trash and then steal and destroy her belongings?" Janessa said, shaking her head, after inquiring about my emotional state.

Janessa was going through a rough patch with Nathan, which I didn't know about until my arrival, so there were many a night spent ruminating over our lives during dinner and going on long walks under the moon or rain. Oddly enough, I felt happy. Walking through the Northwest part of Tucson off of Cortaro and I-10 at night was beautiful, especially when it rained. The smell of ocotillo enhanced this potent smell of rain that I had only experienced in the desert. Amid all the strange events that had transpired, I was finally beginning to feel a sense of calm. Sure, I was worried about what would happen after my daughter was born, but somehow I instinctively felt everything would be okay.

Tucson was a womb, an incubator of creativity and recovery, taking one through a rough-around-the-edges period through an era of much-anticipated catharsis. The sting of Eugenio was felt, but neither the pain nor tears lasted more than two days. Just like that, I was over it.

In the meantime, I was processing quite a stressful pregnancy. Eugenio had challenged the restraining order as I began my second trimester, which pulled me into court, to maintain it. He showed up with Richard. It's funny, they almost appeared to be a couple. As I entered the courtroom alone just a week before my birthday, I felt my blood pressure spike. I was furious and paranoid about what sneak attack he might have planned. While I was dressed in a black suit, he arrived in a t-shirt and jean shorts with disheveled hair. I could feel him staring at me from across the aisle, defeated and filled with contempt. He had friends and family on his side, enabling his behavior, and I was alone. The entitlement was stifling, and thankfully the judge upheld the order and dismissed Eugenio's pleas to have it lifted.

After a security official dismissed Eugenio from the courtroom, he then escorted me across the hall outside to the elevator. We pass Eugenio and Richard who are engaged in a heated discussion, shrieking at a clerk, demanding that a restraining order be put on me. Seeing this reminds me how much I don't miss Eugenio's wild moods, outbursts, and tantrums. Weeks later, another judge gave it to him. Eugenio claimed that since I was in Iraq and had dealt with killing, that I should have my right to carry a gun revoked. The court granted his request and stated in the order that I was not to carry or possess a firearm. That's Tucson's justice system.

He also called the same police department that kicked him out of the house on that last night saying that I threatened him with a knife and Richard helped corroborate the story. Thankfully, the police detective and I had a long talk and he closed the case of Eugenio's false allegations citing inconsistencies in their stories and as an attempt to seek vengeance upon me. Having to play law enforcement officer Russian roulette as a woman in Tucson was not only incredibly stressful, it spoke of deeper problems within the community.

Eugenio was still trying his best to hurt me without having to face me, to bring added stress and strain while pregnant. In some ways, I did pity his lack of a spine, his lack of courage and the cowardly attacks that were born of his own selfishness. The fact that I had the courage to respond, and to take care of myself and my unborn child was something no one else had done in his life. No other woman had the nerve to stand up to him, and he hated me for it. I felt nothing when I looked at him, and came to the realization that everything I felt for him was built on a misrepresentation, half-truths on who he was. Anything I had felt before was merely misattributed to the wrong person, someone I had merely imagined and never really existed.

Monica, a Navy veteran friend of mine, had given me a call to check in and see how I was doing. A voice of reason. We spoke once a month or so, often doing our updates on our personal life, coping mechanisms, and the like. She was also the widow of my late friend Jimmy who died while working as a Border Patrol agent in Yuma. While Monica was pregnant with their fourth child, he drowned after saving a migrant from drowning herself.

Monica's sadness was a realm of harsh reality, that justice sometimes does not prevail and how some are unfairly left to deal with the aftershocks of unmerited trauma. She didn't sugarcoat or mince words, making both her presence and advice unpalatable to some, but I loved her honesty. I told her about the sequence of events with Eugenio, to which she expressed a complete lack of surprise.

"You always have an escape plan. That's just who you are. War survivalist in every sense of the term," Monica said. I could almost feel her eyes rolling over the phone.

"But I didn't want this to happen. How do you figure this was part of some master plan of mine?" I replied.

"Are you serious? Where do I begin?!" she exclaimed emphatically. "You always find someone with something wrong, a notable red flag. You're not dumb; you just subconsciously prefer it that way. And why? Not because you're a masochist, but because it allows you to leave. You knew something was wrong with Tony, you knew something was wrong with every guy you've dated, and you definitely knew Eugenio was clearly not your equal. He was a gutless prick who was using you to make his ex jealous. But that's what you're afraid of: an equal. Someone who will turn your idea of love on its head and you will have no choice but to finally love someone without any chance of escape. Shall I go on?" Monica said.

No one else had the stones or insight to break it down this way, to tear open a bag of truths with a proverbial chainsaw. "Continue," I said smiling.

"Look how quickly you got over Tony, and everyone else up to now. A normal person would be beside themselves. Afraid. Panicked. Something deep down inside you knew this was going to happen. All of it," she concluded.

It finally struck me, and Monica was correct. While I don't feel like I consciously constructed the demise of my prior relationships, I certainly had a subconscious hand in constructing my exit strategy. Good ol' Monica.

You can't love anyone with one foot out the door. All of you must be all in, or not at all. I found it easy to leave people I tried to love, not because I was always dying to leave, but they didn't have the courage to embrace all of me, and ask me to stay. In these cases, I found partners who were never really there, but were preoccupied and never really got to know who I was, what I was about, what made my gears turn. I was property, a chick, a disposable thing, a warm body – but never a person.

Instinctively, perhaps I knew how they felt and was just going through the motions, thinking I was the eccentric oddity who wanted a human connection but thought none existed in real-life romantic relationships. Relationship purgatory no longer interested me. I wanted – no, I needed something more.

Eugenio thought I was settling by consciously choosing to be with him. But that wasn't true. Pregnancy shook me out of my self-loathing, and awoke me to growing the hell up. I was going to be a parent, and who better to build a home, a foundation, than with than a best friend.

I had the chance to make a decision, and I did. Eugenio had his doubts about me and himself, and he made his decision. Open relationship or nothing. A vague, confused lifestyle that lacked common vision or defined goals was not a life I felt I could thrive in, and his mindset scared me. This was the real pill to swallow, and I chose reality over a pointless delusion.

He sought to punish me while pregnant, and didn't care how the stress and isolation I felt hurt me and the baby. I did my best not to let the stress eat at me as I didn't want my little one to feel the angst or any toxic sentiment. I wanted nothing more than for her to be safe, happy, loved. Every night I told her as I stroked my belly, "Everyone is going to love you. You'll see."

It was never really the idea that I wanted to leave those people with whom I've been intimate; it was that I never felt that I would be missed if I left. Perhaps I was wrong in that assumption in some cases, but that lack of any real connection made it far too easy to make my departure in search of something else. Home never equated to fleeting emotion or feigned passion. Home, in my mind, meant a safe space where I could breathe, a place where I could be myself.

When it came to love, I still had that Army lesson in my mind: a moving target is harder to kill. Often men, all the men I had met thus far, looked at me not as a person, but a conquest. Perhaps deep down I knew I was just desired territory, and not seen as a person who wanted to be loved and love in return. So I kept on my feet and was either getting ready to high-tail it in the opposite direction or in the process of dodging romantic bullets as though being struck meant death – death of myself, death of my individuality, death of my voice.

All the while I was engaged in Monica-induced reality-checking, Genevieve messaged me, and asked me to fly back to California to be the Godmother of her son. Thus, I soon found myself ruminating over Monica's words and packing my bags for San Francisco.

The day before departing to San Francisco, Louis and I were engaged in our typical early morning banter about life, love, food, and everything else. He was asking me, in spite of being alone in Tucson without close ties, if I had ways to connect with my Chamorro roots and what I did to maintain balance. As we exchanged typical customs of both Yaqui and Chamorro peoples, he told me a story of how some of the Southwestern tribes came to be and a lost kinship with another group of people who were quite similar.

"You should read more about the Turtle People, you might find that we're more connected than you think," Louis said.

There were a lot of commonalities between Indigenous American and Oceanic cultures, and he offered a referral to his friend Paul, who sounded much like a Suruhanu, when I felt necessary. I kept the referral in mind, but didn't feel quite ready to delve into a much deeper realm just yet.

Another new friend I made since leaving Eugenio was a real estate agent named Janelle. She was very much into alternative medicine, natural living, and divination. Tucson was filled with unique characters. Janelle invited me over one night and did a card reading for me saying that while I was feeling alone, that a circle of women would soon surround me, showing love and sisterhood. She said that my daughter would be a shining star in my night sky, and that everything was going to be okay.

Aside from such prophecies and legends, I was feeling much better about my direction, although the destination ahead appeared unclear.

Getting an extra day off from work and getting the site director, Kelly, to approve might as well been like I was asking for a spare organ. She sucked her teeth and rolled her eyes. I hadn't taken any extra days off, even when the first trimester was particularly brutal, but she was never exactly grateful for the hours her direct clinical staff put in on a weekly basis. Her hours were 10am-2pm and when she was in, she was never really in, but on her phone taking personal calls and disappearing. Most of our patients didn't even know her name. After stressing that I got the clinic organized and there is no real reason for holding me back from one day off, I got the extra day to San Francisco. Part of me thinks she thoroughly enjoyed these little power trips, like a repressed Victorian lashing out on her savage servant. I definitely needed to leave before being tempted to incite an artist revolt.

Driving up to Phoenix to catch the flight went well at first as I left before sunrise to catch the flight. While sitting in Phoenix Sky Harbor, the gates changed last minute, and I found myself almost missing it, huffing and puffing my way to the new gate before they closed the door. I was coughing almost the whole flight from being barely able to breathe. It's crazy how pregnancy makes something that should have been a decent jog that much more difficult. I hadn't put on a lot of weight and still fit into my regular clothes at this point, but everything I did required ten times more effort and I would kill for a nap at any given point of the day.

Upon arriving to San Francisco, I exited the airport doors and waited for Genevieve curbside. The cool, crisp air of autumn brought on a sense of nostalgia that kept me warm. I remembered this air, when life was far simpler as a teenager in Alameda. How all those ridiculous teenage problems seemed to pale in comparison to the very adult issues at hand.

Genevieve and I shared a passion for food, and spent a greater part of the day sampling foods around San Francisco – old favorites for the most part. We had breakfast with her babies at Louis', snacks at Bella Trattoria where the owner and Genevieve exchanged friendly insults over the Dodgers verses the Giants, then traipsed about the city, grabbing early dessert near Height-Ashbury, and then the Stinkin' Rose in North Beach for an early dinner. It was wonderful to be back, see some old friends, and generally feel familiar surroundings after several years of being away. Friends asked me to move back, campaigning hard over quality of life and education. However, I wasn't sure if the frenetic and pricey Bay Area was going to be a suitable home for my little one. It didn't feel right just yet.

While in the Bay Area, my dreams engulfed me in the night and left me bewildered during the day. The first night I arrived, I dreamed that I was hiding behind trees with my daughter. A man who was covered in foliage wandered the woods and passed us by as we watched in what felt like fright and wonder. The Green Man presented a beautiful wood and glass cabin in the woods where we then sought refuge. Eugenio appeared before us and the Green Man then crushed him, leaving him as a pile of ash and leaves. I shielded my little one, and then everything else became tranquil. The sun shone and the cabin interior was filled with family, friends, food, and music.

The second night, I dreamed I was somewhere in the Balkans in the mid-1990s during the war. While I had never deployed there, the surroundings felt so familiar and probably due to the presence of heavy armor, artillery, and a war going on. It looked like footage I remember of Sarajevo at the height of urban warfare and ethnic cleansing. Eugenio appeared before me near a row of tank tracks in what looked like a wooded area in or near the smoke-filled outskirts of the city. He transformed into a deer and behaved erratically. He kicked into the air and swung his antlers menacingly as I stood across the road. Before he could cross the tracks, a dark-eyed grey wolf with wounds on the right and back side of its body surfaced from the shadows of the tanks and mauled Eugenio in deer form. The screaming was so intense that I covered my ears and looked away. When the grey wolf finished tearing him to pieces, he sauntered toward me. It put out its paw where I held him in gratitude. We walked together on a path between the trees as the sound of bullets and explosions echoed in the fog.

After returning from the baptismal in San Francisco, I ended up driving to Las Vegas to see Hafiza. She flew out to Tucson only briefly and invited me back for a weekend so I could consider Las

Vegas as a potential new home. The drive was not a comfortable one, as my little one was resting nicely on my bladder and putting pressure on my cervix. The seven-hour drive felt more like fourteen. Driving into Las Vegas while seven months pregnant was rough. However, out of all the times I've driven to Las Vegas from Arizona - this trip has been one of the most impressive in my memory. Aside from the baby kicking throughout the drive, I longed to see the lights. The luminescence hanging from the clouds above the city of Las Vegas turned the sky a faint orange, and it served as my finish line.

As soon as I started to notice that warm glow emanating from the Las Vegas Strip in the sky framed by craggy desert mountains, the more I could relax - I was close. Upon arriving in Las Vegas, I met with Hafiza, her mother, and sister, who were all eager to see my baby bump, which was still concealable under looser fitting clothes. As per usual, and prior to my arrival, we booked a session with Nasrin.

Since I wasn't showing much, and decided to wear a loose sweater to visit Nasrin and see if she could pick up on the past year of ups and downs. She did. Nasrin went onto explain in my reading that I had lost all desire to live, until I became pregnant. Nasrin explained my recklessness and solitude as a prelude to suicide, and while the approach of motherhood was near, I adapted to the new situation. I was going to succeed in the impending metamorphosis.

Iselda, my soon-to-arrive daughter, was saving my life, an angel put on this earth to rescue me. Nasrin also pointed out that Iselda appeared as a warrior in the desert, and how she had communicated with me before in my dreams, connecting me with my roots and future.

"You will see, everything will be okay. Iselda is special, and you will find that your daughter will bring about a new age of love and light. Soon after she's born, you'll meet the love of your life," Nasrin said.

She's been saying that for years, but I was more concerned about being prepared for Iselda's arrival. It took weeks for me to decide upon a name, and the name Iselda, a name that means "beautiful" in Celtic and "faithful" in old Germanic form, appeared to me in a dream. It was the only name I slept on that didn't make me nauseous.

"You don't need to worry. She will be so loved, and you keep talking to her in your womb, telling her everything will be fine," Nasrin added.

Finally, Nasrin concluded in telling me about not seeking revenge, that much of the pain I had experienced will take care of itself. After returning to Tucson, I had my mind made up and decided to start the process in moving to Las Vegas.

25 DESERT AWAKENINGS

Before Christmastime, I found myself taking more photos of my growing belly and soon moved into a five hundred square foot duplex in Tucson's Iron Horse Neighborhood. Iron Horse is one of Tucson's historic neighborhoods that is known for being the place where railroad workers lived in order to be at least within a mile of the train's whistle. That meant that my little duplex came with a soundtrack. It turned my forty-minute commute from the shared apartment in Northwest Tucson into a two-minute one, which was great for me in the beginning of my third trimester. Even thirty minutes spent in the car felt like an eternity, and I loved long drives, but any periods of sitting were very uncomfortable.

At work, I felt lucky to be in a position to practice in both mental health and fine arts. The combination of the two made sense to me. I watched as my clients painted, chiseled, and created; some to simply avoid crying or breaking down. Some of them in a Zen-like state. Just happy.

"You must feel great about not being one of us, and being an instructor," one of my clients stated with what appeared to be a smile covering shame.

"The line that seemingly separates you and I in this place is very thin. You could easily be wearing my badge, and I your client file. I am no better, and you are no worse. It's a matter of regaining control of one's life and if I didn't believe in any of you and your ability to move on well beyond my means, I wouldn't be here," I responded.

"Well, when you put it like that, I sound like less of a patient and quite possibly normal!" she laughed.

"You are normal. What happened to you wasn't and you responded accordingly and made mistakes. We all have to find ways to not let trauma or illness define us as people."

"Look at this, Michelle. Can you really call what I do fine art? I don't know all the rules of art," she replied.

"Fine art is the discipline of breaking rules. Pay no mind to those artists you've learned from in school. You have to find your own way through art as through trauma, and uncover your personal truth. That is where you uncover the beauty that has been within you all along," I said. She smiled, and returned to her project.

Many great artists experienced harsh life experiences ranging from deaths in the family, disability, or social ostracization. This sense of post-traumatic growth implied to me that while some of my fellow veterans were falling apart and, in turn, committing suicide, I was here creating. Creating in a group of other hurt people from all walks of life who were piecing their lives back together at various ages, recovering from abuse, sexual assault, drug use, or other forms of ailments and unfair cards dealt to them. Among them, I didn't feel as though I were above them, but walking with them side-by-side. In many ways, I was engaged in the act of support, a form of support that I had craved since returning from Iraq and didn't find. I didn't want anyone to feel the loneliness and isolation I felt. I was in the act of dealing the prescription I believed in most: art.

Innovative art and adversity seems to go hand-in-hand, and the trauma that was previously eating me alive was now continually transforming into my muse. Before moving to Arizona I had winced at taking hold of my past experiences for fear of them becoming overwhelming and owning me. Yet wielding a brush against a blank canvas, I was owning my trauma right back and taking ownership of everything that had transpired as moments in time that occurred but did not possess the best of me.

The events that occurred in my life, events in which I had no consent and others were not held accountable, were not my fault, yet I corralled all such horror and pushed them onto canvas like toxins leaving the body through activated charcoal. A purging via art was ongoing and the days where I cringed at Army mental health clinicians handing out psychotropic meds like candy with no regard for tardive dyskinesia, suicidal tendencies, or other harmful side effects on patients were no longer my reality.

While I had no doubt that DOD and VA mental health were

persistently peddling drugs, I was pushing creative healing. I finally had results within my grasp that what I do not only worked for me personally, but was working for the dozens in my care on a daily basis. Any naysayers suckling from the teat of pharmaceutical giants were instantly regarded with the same smug grin I received for questioning their practices.

Discussing mental illness, or even such treatments, often came with stigma. Stigma's power lies in silence. The silence that persists when discussion and action should be taking place. The silence one imposes on another for speaking up on a taboo subject, branding them with a label until they are rendered mute or preferably unheard. I encouraged my group of artists to find their voice, to speak in spite of stigma, so that others may be invited to do the same and in a safe space. Getting past the stigma was more often than not the first hurdle in overcoming artistic block. The pressure of judgment and the need for acceptance needed to be addressed.

In the presence of pressure, some people focus and some people fold. The perception of opportunity in the midst of chaos is a habit that was being instilled within my studio. Not every light at the end of the tunnel was a train, as some of my clients joked. Developing an open-mind to both trauma and creativity was key to ensuring that this habit of persistence remained. In order to love oneself again was to embrace all the oddities that made us unique individuals and to them, I wasn't merely the war veteran or the psychosocial rehab arts instructor; I was Michelle the sarcastic surrealist who played "Closing Time" when it was time to clean up art supplies and go home. I was a unique person telling them it was okay for them to be unique people too. I was more than the war, and they were more than their war within.

Uniqueness is a launch pad into other creative ventures and one no longer needs to search far for inspiration when you trust your intuition and instincts. There is plenty in the world that inspires awe, disgust, happiness, and melancholy. Trauma has a way of taking a hammer to your reality and smashing it to bits along with your sense of identity and the world as you knew it.

Everyone in here was well-acquainted with the hammer, but it was our job as behavioral health art instructors was not to drone on about the hammer or wax poetic about the shards of glass. Our job was to hand them the Modge Podge and glue sans judgment to piece themselves together and tell them it was okay to have been broken, to find oneself as a marvelous creation again.

Trauma doesn't always equal artistic inspiration, but the shaking of anyone's foundation plus the confident embrace of one's identity can surely lead to outstanding, innovative work that is both healing and gratifying. Trauma may often indicate mental illness symptoms or worse, but it can also indicate a form of cognitive flexibility taking place in the creation of art. The ability to see things differently and to solve problems that some take their own lives over was an amazing feat.

Art is a powerful instrument when it comes to communicating the aftermath of trauma, whether it's physical or psychological. For me, it was combat and imperial prejudice. As a female combat veteran, it was especially difficult to make the transition back into the US after spending a year in one of Iraq's most dangerous cities, Ar Ramadi. Upon returning from a year of deaths, injuries, seeing some of the most glorious and hideous aspects of humankind in an uncensored montage, many judged me for what I had done (in their minds) without even asking me as well as insulted my experience using gender-related or racial remarks.

I was fortunate that I was aware that art was my personal pressure valve.

Since I was a child, drawing, writing, painting, and even sculpting were my passions. Growing up hearing that artists never make enough money to live on, I attempted to pursue a degree in psychology. Unfortunately, I did not have the money to attend college, as it tends to be expensive here in the US, so I joined the Army, which promised me thousands to pay for school. They did not, of course, explain to me how I'd be working 60 hours a week while trying to accomplish my educational objectives. By the time I received orders for Iraq, I was halfway through college and upon my return, I changed my major from psychology to political science/international relations. After all, how can one make a difference in Middle Eastern policy when many of our elected officials – like most Americans – have never left the country? I have traveled to twenty-two countries and counting. I was a force to be reckoned with in foreign policy debates throughout my upper-level courses, but inside, I was empty.

After some thorough introspection, I decided to paint again. After such a gruesome experience, I had lost my interest in art, as I did all other passions and dreams. I felt numb, but I knew art always had a way of unlocking a door into new ideas and plans. Even if I didn't want to, I painted, wrote, sketched, and even took part in Middle Eastern dance as a hobby and side gig.

In Arizona, I felt warmth return to my veins via creativity. Art was giving me a transfusion.

Eventually, since following my dream of moving to the Southwest, my artistic talents truly blossomed. Before I knew it, I was creating depictions of the most painful memories, which reignited a state of insomnia but launched into a new level of artistic fervor. Then my art turned from wartime trauma to politics, which have been laced with both humorous satire as well as sharp criticism.

With military veteran friends and former colleagues suffering from mental illness and turning to over-medicating practices provided by the Department of Veterans Affairs and Department of Defense, doling out a litany psychotropic medications and narcotic painkillers to anyone who asked. I was incensed. It wasn't natural. While I have stared into combat's abyss, I can proudly say that I took the road less traveled. I followed my heart back to art where I could both express myself and ease my pain, venting my troubles through pens, paintbrushes, and clay and validating my experiences on my own terms with a finished masterpiece in the end that pushed me to be better. Art truly saved my life.

After working with other veterans as well as severely mentally ill clients and encouraging them to express themselves through artistic, literary, culinary, musical, and other creative means, I've seen the most dramatic, positive changes in well-being. Such transformations could not be accomplished through prescriptions drugs or any other poisonous substances, which are designed to further numb the senses and keep one from embracing personal truths and ultimately discovering one's own path to healing. I have, as a result, continued on this creative path, reclaiming my life one artistic step a time and finding my way out of a personal abyss by refusing to be a victim of trauma. Instead, I am an artist – who happens to be a survivor.

While you might not want to invite trauma into your life for the sake of artistic inspiration, and anyone can lose their groove, try doing something out of the ordinary in your daily routine. Walk somewhere instead of driving. Eat dessert instead of dinner at a restaurant. Pick up the phone and call someone you haven't talked with in years.

Regarding recent trauma, I wasn't sure if I was ready to trust and love again, but I wanted to be someday. That kind of love was the furthest thing from my mind as I was focused on having my daughter and staying as healthy as possibly throughout the rest of the pregnancy.

Living in Tucson had natural beauty and warm, arid weather drew me in instantly during a visit in January 2010 and I was hooked ever since. Yet I had seen my tolerance go out the window for people I once loved and respected, who more or less proved that they were deserving of neither all along. With this somewhat dissociative combination, it has caused me to reconsider my view on this landscape and re-evaluate what living here really meant thus far.

The time came closer to deliver and my mother arrived, accompanied by my sister, Jan, whom I hadn't talked with in two years. My mother spent the first few hours of her arrival whining and rolling her eyes at my small duplex space. Jan thought everything was okay, but the air was so dry it was chapping her skin. After my mother and sister argued in a deli in which we were having lunch, I called a time out. I explained to them both that this was the reason I left home as soon as I did, why I always looked to run away, and if they didn't stop arguing, I could arrange for an early flight for them. But I wanted them there, and told them I needed them. I had a hard time verbalizing to anyone, even my family, that I needed them.

My mother calmed down, and Jan wiped away her tears. My mother then spoke of something odd happening prior to arriving in Arizona. Tony had called my parents' house asking about me. Ironically, Tony and I had tried to conceive before and when we couldn't, Tony blamed me, which hurt tremendously. My mother knew this and delightfully informed the now-remorseful Tony that I was expecting a baby girl and was so happy to become a mother.

Tony was in shock, expressed his congratulations for me and ended the conversation after stating how miserable his life was. I could hardly believe it, but it didn't surprise me that Tony was still pandering to anyone he could for pity and that, in fact, he will probably remain indefinitely miserable underneath his superficial veneer of contentment. All those years of mental anguish with Tony were behind me and a new chapter in my life was beginning.

Days had passed and the due date arrived, so my doctor decided to induce labor. Walking, lying down, and sitting had all become so uncomfortable at this point that I welcomed the induction. As I endured otherworldly pain, my sister and Janessa held my hands as I screamed and wailed through each piercing contraction. Outside of my cries were the other screams of delivering mothers in rooms down the hall. It sounded like an asylum. My body felt like every bone was breaking simultaneously, and the nausea with near-fainting was overwhelming. The roller coaster of electric pain, as I had come to know it, was the most excruciating experience I have ever endured in my life. It felt as though my belly was a globe filled with lightning.

Hours had gone by and finally in the sixteenth hour of labor, I delivered my daughter.

As the doctor held up this beautiful little girl, I felt a wave of ocean water wash over me completely. I was immersed, drenched in a feeling that I hadn't felt in years, if ever. I felt love in its purest form soak through my bones and every fiber of my being. I cried like a baby, almost in unison with my daughter. Tears of joy, relief, and rebirth ran down my face as I was handed a beautiful little angel with her eyes wide open. She's now the center of my world.

Holding Iselda in my arms, I looked into her eyes, caressed and kissed her. A familiar feeling returned as I observed this angelic beauty bundled in a blanket of pearl and sea foam. The dream of the woman warrior in the desert. As everyone went home and allowed time for me to breastfeed Iselda, I held her in front of me. She was the vision, the lucid dream that came to me in Massachusetts in the middle of my personal winter. Iselda, my Desert Warrior, had saved me from the worst of myself, and ultimately saved my life. I embraced her, and started to cry tears of joy after years of frustration as a barrage of memories from Iraq until now flickered in my mind like a film reel in fast forward. After seven years of living as an amputated spirit, Iselda made my heart whole again. I kissed her cheeks and inhaled her scent, the scent of warm sugar cookies and love. Her presence pushed me to become a better, and more authentic, version of myself. My inner longing to love and feel life again manifested.

"It's so wonderful to finally meet you," I said as I cried with joy and held her to my heart. Iselda sighed, a sigh that sounded like the most beautiful note my ears have ever heard, and looked at me in wonder. How lucky I felt to be alive in this moment.

Her arrival was a wave that hit me with all the strength of the Pacific, it washed down through my body. I was reborn as a mother. With Iselda, a love so pure, so beautiful radiated as I had never experienced. In loving her, heart, mind, and spirit, I felt the love not only return for myself, but it was 100-fold. I had to love myself to be able to take care of her, to be a better person, the best person possible to provide a safe life and home for her. Along with this newfound love, I also took note of the protective, Mother Nature forces within me. That animal spirit within me, I now knew how to channel that energy. The Lioness I became in Iraq was reborn into a Lioness mother, protecting her young, designed to defend my sweet Iselda at all costs. The animal shadow within, now, was becoming quite the useful companion to my newfound wild-eyed romantic, in-love-with-life self. My heart, reserved for those I love. My teeth, my strength, my shadow – for those I don't.

After an odyssey from war to reintegration to moments before her birth, I felt numb as a result of all that I had endured in Iraq and in childhood. As I stared lovingly at Iselda, that pain had dissipated and now I was ready to love.

Once I delivered this ethereal girl, the darkness in my heart lifted and I could breathe again. She arrived with black hair, olive skin and multicolored eyes that lit every obscured corner of my heart in an instant; through a smile, a yawn, squeezing my fingers. I wasn't angry, I couldn't be angry with this smile on my face.

I didn't know what love felt like after Iraq but it took the birth of my daughter to feel love again. It took holding this little angel in my arms for me to realize that love was in me all along and that home was right here in my arms. It wasn't merely having children that solved my problems, but it took something drastic to shock me to my core, to make me actually feel alive again. It took love to overpower all else that haunted me for years. To love again, to be able to love anyone in such a capacity, is the greatest gift I could have asked for from this universe.

The time came soon after to decide upon another path. I received a job offer with a company in Las Vegas, Nevada. It was a well-paid position, and it was a lot more income than I was making in Tucson. It would require uprooting the life I had created in Tucson, which started from nothing to a strong network of support with amazing friends who were now like family to starting all over again with a clean slate for my daughter and I. It offered a lot more stability for Iselda and she could grow up around close family who lived there as well. I didn't want abusive Eugenio in our lives, but I did consider his family might want to see her. After talking with a mutual friend between Eugenio and I, it was clear how he felt about Iselda.

"I have my son, she has her daughter," he relayed from Eugenio.

Even though he still proved to be unreliable and still extremely immature, I hoped that he would somehow grow up for Iselda. It was a devastating thought that she would learn what kind of person Eugenio is and, in many ways, I feared how that may hurt her. I wanted to protect her from that. And if anyone was going to be a father to her, Eugenio definitely wasn't that person. At best, he was like an anonymous donor, and his added denial of paternity said far worse.

Before leaving Tucson, I flew with Iselda and my mother back to Florida where she would stay until I had a home for both of us. This was a time of risk, and I felt Iselda would be safer with my parents throughout this move from the Sonoran Desert to the largest city in the Mojave Desert.

As I packed up my belongings in storage and took what I could in my sedan, I was hit with what felt like panic. I talked to a few friends before leaving, Magdalena, another veteran who was part of Calpolli Teoxicalli, an indigenous rights group that mobilized Tucson youth and protested racist legislation in the state, whom I regularly ate sushi with and chatted for hours. And Rachel, an Army veteran of Desert Storm and middle school teacher who helped me adjust in the latter part of my pregnancy, checking in on me knowing I was wanting to do everything on my own and too proud to ask for help. Both of these amazing women were because of Gabe Forsberg in Phoenix, who also sent love and gift cards, telling me it was okay to be vulnerable and that while I was being strong, to know that I was very much loved. In that instance, I realized that prior to my leaving, I was indeed surrounded by wonderful women, many of which were veterans like me, who helped me, cared for me, and made sure I wasn't left behind.

On a hot, sunny afternoon in May 2012, I drove away from Tucson toward Las Vegas, feeling the anxiety leave, the gratitude set it, and a feeling of freedom and optimism as I raced toward the future.

26 VIVA LAS VEGAS

Las Vegas is a city of extremes, where human behavior is observed and experienced either at an apex or an abyss. A place where people shake themselves of their mores and just let go.

Visitors to Sin City are encouraged to do their worst, to forget their woes by reaching the bottom of multiple over-priced alcoholic beverages or the indulgence of any other vices, to let their alter ego take over. A place for winners and losers, and I have seen the majority of my life through the lens of the latter.

Las Vegas residents are well-aware of this range of extremes, and often are subjected to the mortifying behavior of out-of-town guests who unleash their inner demons onto Las Vegas Boulevard, intoxicated and in search of flesh to devour. I love this place. For all its honesty about this country, it acts as the Id, the primal instinct of humankind at its most depraved, sensual, and gluttonous. After years of being deceived and hurt by those I loved, I yearned for this brand of honesty, no matter how vile. Las Vegas makes no exceptions and knows that deep down inside, we're all animals.

With all its quirks and madness, I've quickly come to know the personification of Las Vegas. Its bright lights and glitter often accompany the scent of cigarette smoke and strippers' perfume, that weird watermelon bubblegum smell you find in the specialized lube section of adult stores, morphing into somewhat of a high-end exotic dancer with a colorful past. Sure, she turns out to be much smarter than she appears, yet she’s still wildly unstable and untrustworthy.

When you live in Vegas, you’re not a citizen, but a co-conspirator in the many sins that occur in the shadows of the glitz and narcotics. Las Vegas is a service industry town bent on robbing visitors of dignity and dollars all while smiling and taking drink orders.

It's a place that responds to the hidden desires of America. After seeing the side of the US that lets its veterans commit suicide by the platoon and squander funds that could feed and house the poor nationwide, I was ready to go to the core of America's Caligulan empire and stick my fist back through the other side of the plastic flag I was handed. There was a deep-seated desire within me to see the full spectrum of the depravity and beauty of humanity for what it was in this country. No sugary euphemisms; just bile and brilliance.

In my first few weeks in Las Vegas, Genevieve flew down for a quick visit, and I took her to meet with Nasrin. I had told Genevieve over the years what Nasrin had predicted and what manifested, so she was eager to meet this oracle of Las Vegas for herself. Genevieve recorded the reading which included many of the things that had come to pass as I write this years later, and events that were predicted for me. Nasrin was intent on telling me that I was going to meet someone who would change my life for the better, happily ever after, and all that jazz. Let's just say I was still feeling a bit doubtful about that. She's been saying this for years, in spite of all else that's occurred, this was one area left wide open for my skepticism.

After two months passed, and staying with Hafiza, I was still in the middle of real estate paperwork, waiting back on bank approval, and just hoping for the best. I had found a house that was less than two miles from Hafiza that was never lived in, had energy efficient upgrades, and was being sold at a reasonable price. Much of my earnings from doing nonprofit consulting was going straight to home inspection costs, earnest money, and every additional fee that kept popping up in the process. I was thankful to Hafiza for being there for me in this time, and we often went on nightly strolls throughout Las Vegas talking about our futures. Her husband was due to arrive from India upon approval of his visa, and I couldn't extend my stay.

While I had relatives in Las Vegas, I wasn't close with them, and didn't feel comfortable asking anyone for help. Yet I did reach out to veterans shelters who could help. Most temporary solutions in Las Vegas were either crack house motels or taking out a year-long lease at an apartment. There wasn't much for a middle ground. But veterans' organizations, and the few shelters for women veterans, required that I have a VA disability check coming in, which I didn't have due to that pesky female combat veteran title.

Much of my time spent afterward was staying in seedy, inexpensive hotels, sleeping in my car, or on someone's couch. It didn't matter, I was doing everything I could to save money to get a home for my daughter and I; there was no time for distractions that would take my attention away from my objective.

I still had to make two more trips to Tucson to pick up my last boxes from storage. Louis, my artist friend in Tucson, suggested that my last trip was probably a good time to see his curandero (healer) friend, Paul. I took him up on his offer, and much like my sessions with Nasrin, we talked about past traumas, from childhood to war, and now being a single mother.

As I met with Paul, in what looked like a low-income hospice, an image came to mind of a time Eugenio and I encountered a rattlesnake as we walked through the desert. Observing the snake, respectfully, and continuing on our walk separately to explore on our own, I thought of how we parted ways. How he later destroyed my paintings in that same patch of desert, which happened to be on Yaqui reservation land. I informed Paul of what happened in Eugenio destroying my art. How painfully predictable.

"I don't want to carry anymore bad energy that took place here," I told Paul.

"Don't look at it that way. You came to the desert to find your home, your heart. You found it. As a gift back to the desert a piece of your heart remains with her, visions that she inspired in you have been given back. Consider it a gift and a reminder of impermanence. We all come from the earth, and after death, we return to her," he said before starting the cleansing.

While I didn't intend for my paintings to end up there, I realized that I got the actual manifestations in the end. Those paintings were the wishes of my heart, to feel serenity through the desert and to find home. Just before I reached both, the paintings found their way back to the heart of the desert that lured me through dreams in the first place. In someone else attempting to destroy my dreams, the desert immediately granted me both wishes in full. In the Sonoran Desert of Arizona, my art awakened; in the Mojave Desert of Nevada it ripened. I left Tucson when I needed to, and to build a solid foundation. Yet I was worried about my own ability to hold onto a healthy relationship.

"It's not that relationships don't work for you, it's that you gave your time and spirit to those who didn't deserve to be in your life. You didn't deserve what they did to you," Paul said.

I looked at him, and shrugged. What could I say? I know? I didn't know? What does it matter anymore?

"You can be loved, you can - you just didn't believe it. You were always waiting, anticipating the hurt. But you are not an island, Michelle," he said.

His words soaked through my skin and went right to the bone. Sitting quietly, I listened.

"There are many around you who love you, so don't believe for a second that you are out in the ocean alone. Your heart is not as hard as you would like to think, how you would like those around you to think, and you push people away. No. You run before they can hurt you."

Paul paused. A brief silence set in and preceded his "a-ha" moment that lit up his eyes.

"You, Michelle, are running for safety, like you did in war, like you did away from your ex-husband and his damaged family, like you did from a painful childhood, like you do in driving constantly on any lonely road you can find, searching for a way to safety, to home. You've been searching for years, so deep down you instinctively know home exists."

He stepped closer, Paul grabbed my shoulders.

"You will find a place to take off those combat boots, those invisible desert boots you wear that no one else can see but you. Where you can feel safe to hold and house your daughter. You don't need to worry; things will unfold in a positive way sooner than you think. Go home, meditate, visualize, and think about what we've talked about here."

Looking at Paul, I smiled in agreement. He didn't ask for any money, as is typical for a traditional healer with an ounce of integrity. Yet, as in Chamorro custom for showing gratitude for time and energy, I left him with what I could spare without breaking myself.

In this session, mental feng shui, or compartmentalizing my memories, became easier.

Like a Saipan suruhanu, Paul helped me in clearing the negative energy, spirits in an overgrown yet inhabited area. In Chamorro culture, clutter and overgrowth of plants meant were not just a reflection of the care of the property, but that of the land and the mind of the owner.

When you have a cluttered, unkempt environment, your mind mimics the disorder. Forgetfulness, negativity, confusion, frustration – the list goes on. Messy environment, messy thoughts. A messy head meant an unlucky, chaotic life. No matter where I was, my things were in order, neatly kept in both Chamorro and military style, but my mind was another story.

As he walked me outside his house filled with the forgotten, I thanked him for everything. It felt almost insufficient, as being understood still such a new feeling. Looking around the desert road, observing my surroundings as though they were made anew, I got into my car, and drove away as I saw him waving to me in my rear-view mirror.

Paul helped me focus, clear my head of worries, anxiety, and much of the remnant pain I was hiding deep within. I left Tucson on that last moving trip in late summer 2012 feeling brand new. Much like Magdalena in the Calpolli, getting back to ancient, mindful tradition aided me in my journey to feeling whole.

Soon after my meeting with Paul, everything settled with closing on my house. Soon after moving in, Pat, a friend I met through one of the Las Vegas nonprofits I worked with, and I went out to see Nasrin on Halloween. She was curious about her abilities and found a similar feel for great advice and support. After Pat's reading, we were all still sitting around the table when Nasrin asked to read me as well. I accepted. She then told me that I was going to meet the love of my life in nine days. I laughed at the notion. She had been telling me for years, and now she was giving me an exact date and describing this person's personality, looks, and how he was to be the man of my dreams. I laughed harder.

Falling in love at this point felt like such a foreign concept.

Regardless of how many times we trust or love someone, it's always a new, scary situation. Who we choose to let into our weird little worlds can often determine if our daily life will be heaven, hell, or maybe even a tolerable purgatory; painful yet routine and passively accepted. Being single sounded more appealing if I wasn't going to improve my surroundings, and I wanted no part of a relationship underworld. However, if we are to love, we have to surrender pride, overcome our fear of being hurt and take the risk. If we find the right person, we can reach a new level of intimacy. I knew I had to make a serious decision as to whether or not I really wanted that, to go beyond casual dates with people that usually ended in casual friendship, and if was I ready to be with anyone after such a crushing experience in Tucson. I took a risk.

After Nasrin's reading, I started an account on Match.com. There was no way I was expecting to meet someone I could respect out at a club or elsewhere in Las Vegas proper, and I didn't have time for small talk. This was a way of getting the important issues on the table and saying, "This is who I am, take it or leave it."

Having scared people before with my occupational choices, particularly service in Iraq, I made that apparent right away, and I was getting mature responses. I grabbed coffee with one someone who was an engineer for one of the major casinos, but we didn't click, and that was fine. It made me a bit more optimistic about interacting with someone else with a similar maturity level.

The second date I had was with a real estate agent who was still successful in spite of the housing bubble bursting in Vegas, but they couldn't handle the fact that I had a child. That was fine. We spoke like mature adults and wished each other well. So far so good, and not so scary.

The third date was set at a little over a week later from Nasrin's reading. From what I could tell on his profile and what he told me via message and text, he was tall, dark and handsome, four years older than me, in the hospitality industry, had a daughter, served in the Italian Army, knew what he wanted in life, and was very easy to talk with – a great start. We planned on meeting at Kona Grill in Summerlin, a somewhat upscale part of Las Vegas just south of where I lived. He was coming from Las Vegas Boulevard, so it was somewhat of a halfway point.

As I pulled into the plaza where Kona Grill stood on November 8, 2012, it appeared a bit busy and parking was scarce, so I circled the lot a few times. As I was coming around a dark corner, a guy came out of the corner of my line of sight and I nearly hit him – but I didn't. He was walking beneath the streetlights but I could hardly see his face. I stopped and motioned him to pass, and he waved in thanks. I think that was him, I almost ran over my date. But don't I run over most of my dates in some form anyway?

Instead of continuing to plow through, I allowed an evening for the chance to meet a wonderful, warm, kind, and amazing man named Alessandro; Alex for short. We spoke for hours, all the way to closing.

Looking back on anyone else I've ever met, I don't think I've gone this far in-depth and intrigue during a conversation on a first date. From talking about our daughters to travel shows, we finished off sushi rolls and planned for our next date.

Alex, wanting to share an Italian secret of authentic pizza hiding in plain sight in Las Vegas, recommended Settebello for our second date. He arrived at my door, I was that comfortable with him already from the first date – and took me to a place that served Vera Pizza Napoletana, real Neapolitan pizza. It was a bit of a drive from my house in the Lone Mountain area of Las Vegas to Henderson, which is south of the city of Las Vegas. But it was worth it. I was enjoying Alex's company and we talked the whole way, of course. Going on and on about food, where we've eaten and where we want to eat next; what we like to cook or what we're looking to try. Finally, someone who understands food as an experience and appreciates it in all its forms. Since he had experienced various forms of military food as well, he could appreciate food as I did: as a unique gift to always experience gratitude.

Settebello was packed that night and it wasn't an uncommon sight. We ended up waiting at the bar for a table close to forty minutes, where we drank red wine and talked about food, life, things we adore and things that piss us off, and everything else in between. This was only my second time with him and it felt like I had known him for years, like I was out to dinner with my best friend shooting the breeze and hunting for great eats.

Finally, we got our table and continued on with the friendly, flirty banter then ordered our pizze. He was right. The quality, the taste, every little ingredient made this pizza as a whole, probably the best pizza I've ever had. Mind you, this is not New York style, but Neapolitan, and it was amazing. Bonus points for Alex on a great recommendation. Over pizza, we shared photos of our little ones and talked about how they are as their little personalities grow and become more vibrant and colorful. The look, the twinkle, in his eyes when he spoke about his daughter was one of a proud father who genuinely loves his children and is an active parent in ensuring they knew they were loved. We went on about each other's babies and how adorable and wonderful they are, continued talking about how they might be when they grow up, and how we were going to handle that. The more we spoke, the more we were on the same page, and I was beginning to see him not just as a great date, but someone I could see as part of my family.

We stayed at Settebello through dinner and dessert, but Alex insisted that we could continue the conversation elsewhere as we were almost about to shut down another restaurant. I suggested the next place: The Lady Sylvia.

The Lady Sylvia appears as a speakeasy-era bar and lounge with no exterior signage and an unmarked door. Its interior was inspired by Prague's Strahov Monastery Library, with black and white checkered floors, bookshelves with various textbooks and novels lined the lounge wall-to-wall. Mounted televisions in some areas playing black and white films ranging from Shakespeare adaptations to German drama-thrillers. It was a great place to go, without the burden of cigarette smoke and annoying tourists.

Alex looked impressed. It's the least I could do after he introduced me to the only Vera Pizza Napoletana place I have ever seen in North America. When we arrived, the tempo of the lounge was already at a dynamic level, but as the hours passed, it became a bit more difficult to have a conversation. We both ordered a drink called "The Surrealist," a chartreuse-based cocktail, a rarity to acquire at any establishment in Las Vegas. The great drinks kept coming and we were still talking, laughing, and having a wonderful time. In between taking a breath and taking a drink, I looked up toward one of the TV's playing the 1935 adaptation of A

Midsummer Night's Dream and Alex kissed me.

Decolonize love. Imperial thought that I've witnessed for years completely ruins love and sex. The moment we stop treating people like conquests, territory, and expendable objects, we can finally open the door to experience true intimacy, otherworldly sensuality, and peacefulness. The first kiss from Alex was the beginning of a new era and the end of the old chapter on love in misguided imperial form, being treated as a target or conquest instead of a person who was simply looking to love and be loved back.

All this time since my return, I felt love to be this sensation of standing in the middle of a firing range. If I stood up, I could die. I had to keep moving, avoiding any means of detection, and if I stopped, I could get hurt again. This time, it was different. It wasn't a firing range I was standing on, but something that felt like an airstrip where I could take off at light speed into the sky. Above all harm, I could fly and nothing or no one could hurt me. As he held my hand, I sensed that I was not only going to take flight, but I had a parachute of reasons to give this whirlwind of a moment a chance.

Someone who looked me in the eye as an equal, who didn't scoff at my confidence or self-worth, who empowered me to be a better, stronger version of myself – it was all new. The chastisement, the belittling of who I was, or the minimizing of previous accomplishments I have seen in others remained absent.

We closed the doors of Lady Sylvia, went back to his place to walk his dog, who nearly knocked me to the ground with kisses, and spent the rest of the night and early morning at the Seahorse Lounge in Caesar's Palace. We talked, kissed, and shared what felt like a day in paradise in each other's presence.

Alex was an officer in the Italian Army's Special Forces. A Sarajevo war veteran, he suffered from traumatic brain injury from a vehicle roll-over during the war that damaged the right side of his body as well as persistent pains also stemming from his time as a paratrooper. Alex is humble, affectionate, and appears intrigued by my past – not threatened by it. He held my hand and instead of judging me, he held me, kissed me, and looked me in the eyes. Not down at me or up at me on a pedestal, but right in my eyes as an equal. He held my hand as I passed my fingers over the old injuries, where I could feel where he fractured his ocular cavity and where the bones have not healed quite right. While tall and strong, he was tender, passionate, and present. I kissed his scars on the right of his head, then he immediately pulled me in for quite the long, passionate kiss in the middle of this bright, loud Las Vegas casino. At around 7am, he dropped me off at my house, where we kissed each other goodbye for the day. This was a 12-hour date.

Days and nights from there on were spent together and it became very clear, very early on, that having found each other also meant we could start planning a future together. When I met Alex, I found his sense of open vulnerability to be both a relief as well as overwhelming at first. I wasn't used to hearing "I love you", "I need you", and "I miss you" said in so many ways and so often that I didn't know how to process such open display of affection. Yet something primal, internal, indicated home entailed that uninhibited love was a must. In turn, I learned that it was, in fact, okay to return such sentiment and not fear of being shamed for expressing who I was, how I felt.

Weeks later, I flew back to Florida to pick up Iselda. After a difficult flight, Iselda and I entered the baggage claim area where Alex awaited us with balloons and a stuffed animal for Iselda. She looked up into his eyes with awe, and from there, a father-daughter bond was formed. Alex and I looked at each other with love, and looked in the same direction.

In addition to meeting the love of my life in exactly nine days as Nasrin predicted, I had also found quite a few new friends around Las Vegas in the process. One who ended up being a journalist who asked about my experience in coming home from Iraq.

"How did you get through Iraq, and how do you deal with it now? You hear about so many veterans coming back, on tons of medication, and so many suicides. It's terrifying. What have you done different?" she asked.

"I didn't turn to psychotropic medication and painkillers. I didn't have a VA doctor or the like. So I stuck with what I knew: Art, journaling, road trips, and a Persian clairvoyant, which served as my medication pairing and my counselor - way more cost effective than pharmaceuticals and psychotherapy in the end. And hell, at least with Nasrin I was getting advice that made any sense along with a cup of coffee," I replied.

She laughed, and I realized how much of what I had been through had brought me to this precise location where love, life, and happiness finally made sense. By this time, I had met Alex's beautiful daughter, Aurora, and his parents. The fears I had of being mistreated again by in-laws were dismissed by a rising tide of love that was inescapable. In spite of what life had hurled at me, I was still standing, and had succeeded.

Romantic love can deceive us all. It's based on flawed self-talk and idealizing the object of our affections as just that, an object. Our infatuation thrives on conflict, perhaps a sense of the forbidden or taboo, and requires much more effort than any of us should have to bear. While romantic love can be intense, it is temporary, fleeting, and eventually it fizzles out like a forest fire. At the end of the all-consuming blaze, one is either left with ashes or love.

With Alex, the sensuality felt like a reenactment of an eternal love story. The waxes and wanes of pleasure and adventure kept me stimulated, intrigued, seduced. Not once with him have I felt used or guilty. I had never communicated about love, sex, and sensuality so interchangeably with anyone like I have with Alex. My appearance, sexuality, sensuality, and anything else about me was no problem with him, and I didn't feel like a novelty - something which I felt with other men. Alex, indeed, made me feel like an equal.

Rational, intimate love is what happens what is left when the wildfire is over. In this form of love, we're comfortable, but not complacent. Our identity and development thrives and we are called to not change, but ripen into our highest selves. Desires, life goals, and values are shared, perhaps not entirely, but both people share a common vision of happiness. Open and clear communication conducted with integrity honors each person as a constant kindness and consideration is present in daily life. I wasn't sure if this type of love was real, or if it was possible for me to experience, but in having the home life I have now, the giving and receiving was done freely. No guilt, no pressure. Just love, the yearning to be near one another whether in words, touch, or silence.

27 MOJAVE DESERT

Peering over the top floor balcony of my house toward the twinkling lights of the Las Vegas Strip in the distance to the south, then at Hayford Peak and the fuchsia-colored desert mountains in the north as the sun began to set, a sense of peace came over me as I purged what I needed to in the manuscript for "Quixote in Ramadi." It was my experience in Iraq transcribed from my travel journals from start to end. No matter how raw and flawed, my story was there, and more importantly, it didn't own me anymore. It didn't own me anymore.

A few weeks before I released it to the public, I still had Quixote in Ramadi set as a non-fiction, autobiographical piece – until I got a phone call. It was an independent publisher, a Vietnam veteran who mostly published romance novels, sci-fi, and a few military non-fiction books. After a two-hour conversation, it had been concluded that he was highly interested in my story, but he was nervous about backlash in publishing it.

While he agreed with my sentiments on war, from orchestrated chaos to war-profiteering, he confessed that he had no idea what to do with it, and for me to think about releasing it as fiction and moving a few components in the story around. He seemed particularly worried that I was speaking out with little support, and would receive little to no attention for releasing some ugly truths on the realities of contemporary imperialism. I appreciated his feedback, his positive review of my work, but once again, I was still being denied a chance to speak.

I decided to independently publish, with no ghost writer, no editor, nadie, nada. What had happened in Quixote, from childhood and on through Iraq, had set the tone for much of my life and truly tainted my outlook on the future. My story was a recipe for either suicide or homicide – and in this case both were considered in a different order.

While I received positive reviews and private messages from readers who had experienced similar trauma, I did have quite a few critics – none who criticized any white veterans who had publishers, agents, editors, and ghost writers.

After releasing my novel, "Quixote in Ramadi," I felt a great deal of relief. Finally, I was able to communicate my experiences with racism as a child from real life encounters with my father's side of the family. Needless to say, being mixed race on that side of the family meant one thing: you were not welcome. They made no hesitation in letting you know that you were not wanted.

My paternal grandfather then wrote a scathing letter to my parents telling me to rot in hell. My parents were devastated, embarrassed that he had written so many hurtful things to them about me, and supposedly about my daughter. I didn't want to know the details of the letter, lest I write something back of equal or greater damage.

My parents had put up with so much on that side of the family, and ol' racist gramps knew he could best hurt my parents as he had no effect on me as an adult. They yearned for his approval and that of the rest of the family because, in reality, they were never really accepted. An interracial marriage and a granddaughter who was the only one left with the family name? The family name dies with me, and it's quite possibly a great way to end a long line of hateful, spiteful people that fill pews at church and spout foul, hateful garbage every chance they get.

My parents hadn't read the book, but knew the gist of the contents. Apparently, one of my cousins from my father's side read Quixote, drove to Alabama and had a family meeting about it, briefing them on what I had written like a clandestine operative during the McCarthy era in the 1950s. It was really such a small part of the book, but it was a vital component in explaining my attitude toward racists and bigots in general. I didn't name any names, and the culprits in the story know who they are. Quixote was about what happens when people have unchecked power and how it is used on a macro and micro level, how sociopathic power-plays affect nations and individuals respectively. They were angry that I spoke of the sexual abuse and the way they mistreated my family. Of course, they were enraged and how dare I hold them accountable? Who am I to question them?

Well, I'm sorry to break the news, man. Perhaps if you were a better person, maybe the family wouldn't have been in the book. You're no villain in my nightmares. Oh, no. Such spiteful bigots are now material in my writing. Sad, pitiful, comedic material to make others laugh when years ago it made me cry, made me feel that no one was capable of understanding or loving me the way I felt I deserved. Those painful memories and trauma no longer have a stranglehold on me. It's all art now.

Children don't naturally hate and are not born with ingrained racism or bigotry. Even as a child and seeing children spout racist terms, I knew that someone much older had quite possibly instructed them on their rants. Through their children, racist adults could tell me how they truly felt about certain minority groups - and that they were assuming that I belonged to whichever group du jour that was in the crosshairs.

I can't return the favor to bigots, no matter how much any grown bigot in question deserves it. It's like being bit by a bigot vampire, it seems like it only makes sense to hate back with a vengeance or die, but there is another way to drive a wooden stake into the problem itself. To be free of past paralysis involving fear, sadness, or anger, we must constantly regroup in the present. People project onto you - when you're ethnically ambiguous, a woman, something they fear or desire - their own phobias, lusts, wrath, and the deepest inner hurts and longings as though you are the canvas in which they try to paint you, but end up painting the emptiness of their inner selves.

Energy of a painful past doesn't ever disappear, but it can be converted. We can all do better to work smarter to expose the people that hide in the shadows and inflict trauma. We can all do well to not be reactive, but to be proactive, to plan, and remain vigilant in the present. In turn, we can remove the chains that keep us down and utilize them to pull us out of despair while shining the light on those who've done us harm. You never have to be silent about your trauma, but it pays to be smart about it and converting your energy to end suffering.

Outcry from even more perpetrators whom are depicted in the

novel continued – mostly blood relatives. Such individuals have resorted to telling me that speaking about abuse in a book is "wrong" and that I should be "respectful" and maintain my silence, so as not to offend the people I'm portraying. It didn't matter what people, whether racist relatives or emotional terrorist exes, thought. Writing my pain was a chance at reclaiming my voice, my power, and my sense of inner peace. So, I didn't give a damn what anyone else thought.

This demonstration in a lack of self-awareness is part of what contributes to abusive behavior. Abusers who cry foul when confronted while continually victimizing others is not something in which I can remain silent. There comes a point where one can either choose to succumb to the abuse or draw the line by addressing the root causes. I choose the latter.

Whether one is enduring or has experienced physical, psychological, or sexual abuse, here are some factors that abusers often resort to in order to keep someone in a victim mindset:

1. Disempowerment - The goal of the abuser to take away any power base from the victim, leaving the individual to question their self-worth and disabling any thoughts on self-defense, physical or emotional. This is done in anticipation that the victim will either become dependent on the abuser or will have little to no resources to turn to in the event of any rejection of the abuse. Sources of support to include friends, family, colleagues, and other avenues of assistance to remove the abuse are, in turn, attacked by the abuser to further disempower the victim. The goal is for the victim to acknowledge the abuser as an unquestionable authority figure regardless of legal or ethical conflicts.

2. Exhaustion - An abuser intends to not only take away one's ability to thrive, but also resorts to tactics which are intended to exhaust the victim on a physiological and/or psychological level. The intent is to overwhelm the victim, cause confusion, and ultimately halt any rebuttal or conscious efforts to maintain personal security. When one is confused, one loses their situational awareness and any efforts in effective decision making and communication become impaired. The goal is to diminish motivation and ability in the victim to fight back. People like Yves, Tony, and Eugenio certainly didn't want me fighting back. Instead of folding in exhaustion, I channeled a second wind and

left.

3. Humiliation - Efforts to exhaust and degrade the victim are often accompanied by behaviors and speech involving humiliation. From hate speech based on gender, ethnicity, background, beliefs, or anything belonging to the victim's identity to physically embarrassing the victim, humiliation takes on various forms. Humiliation involves violence on some level and most of such violence involves some knowledge, familiarity, or intimacy between victim and the abuser. Institutional violence (discrimination, racial persecution, etc.) or direct violence (hate crimes, sexual assault, etc.) are forms of humiliation. Victim-shaming after a traumatic event also falls into this category. The goal is to cause intense anguish and pain in order to prevent the victim from believing that there is any hope and for the victim to perceive that they are "beneath" the abuser.

4. Manipulation - An abuser, in effort to maintain power, may resort to manipulating previous positive memories or prior intimacy to convince the victim that they are cared for in spite of abuse. When one is busy questioning the presence of love in the realm of abuse, one is also too busy to confront the abuser effectively. Efforts to make the victim feel isolated, invisible, or insignificant can be committed through manipulation involving indifference, apathy, or denying the victim's experience. The goal is to confuse the victim and convince them that the abusive behavior is acceptable instead of addressing it.

5. Distortion - In effort of self-preservation, an abuser will often turn to distorting events to refrain from any accountability or responsibility toward the victim. Distortion is an egregious effort to silence the victim through insidious speech or behavior that involves a gross lack of integrity, accountability, and respect. The goal is to convince the victim that the abuse simply "didn't happen" or to forget about pursuing justice related to the trauma all together.

While these are only a few aspects of abusive behavior, these manifestations of abuse can exist in families, relationships, workplaces, and everywhere else involving human interaction. Abuse can only be stopped through confronting and halting the behavior, in addition to acknowledging any enabling factors or parties and addressing them accordingly. In the end, if we are victimized, we can choose to survive, to end abuse and, ultimately, lead the way into a healthier future.

Love changed me, but it was loving myself that had to happen first. When I looked in to my daughter's eyes for the first time, my world mended. It was because of her that I finally stopped making concessions for the wrong people. In loving her, I learned to put myself first in order to be at my best for those who need me most. I had a moment of clarity in being able to think outside of myself, outside of my armor for once and embrace a love like no other. Then, I met Alex and everything changed even more so. I was ready for a meaningful relationship, and I'm glad that he arrived in my life when he did. When I looked into Alex's eyes, I wasn't scared anymore.

"No one is going to hurt you ever again," Alex said to me while holding me close to his chest. He was worried what my grandfather had done and how little my parents did to defend me yet again was affecting me. But I felt numb. I had been through this so many times that I didn't feel I had any more room for horrible relatives who harass, condescend and aim to wound. It felt so commonplace and predictable that by the time Iselda and Alex came around, life seemed so surreal and filled with a love that abuse seemed foreign to me. A new feeling that I want in my life forever.

After discussing the reactions to the book and assuring him that I was fine, Alex held my hand and walked down a dark path with me to an open road with orange streetlights. The moon added extra light to this path, enveloping us, illuminating us. His voice was very comforting. He told me everything would be okay, even though what I was feeling was a vast emptiness and pain I could hardly verbalize. I thanked him, and he told me that we were meant to meet when everything was right. We had both been through so much and the timing in which we met was at a critical point in both our lives.

From the dreams of the Desert Warrior that brought me to Arizona, and manifested as Iselda in the Sonoran Desert to meeting Alex in the Mojave, I was eternally grateful. Then I remembered that dream from Savannah. I looked at him for a moment and thought back to the tall dark figure I kept seeing in those dreams.

"You're the man of my dreams," I told him.

"You're the woman of my dreams," he said smiling, looking into my eyes, unflinching.

"Really, I dreamt about this years ago. What we're doing, what you're saying."

He smiled at me, and kissed my hands as we continued to walk together.

At long last, I was walking down this long dark road hand-in-hand with someone who wasn't giving up, someone who not only spoke love in words but sang it through my entire being with a wonderfully mindful love. I used to roll my eyes when people talked about true love and soul mates, and think to myself that it was nothing more than saccharine romance novel palaver that looked spectacular on parchment paper but was entirely unrealistic in real life. I discovered home; not in the form of a house or anything else one could buy. My home was discovered in this journey down a desert road in my own spirit, in the people that I love, in a passion reignited, and the will to live.

Home was never a place on a map. Rather, it's a sense of peace and security we find within ourselves. A place that is found after a long, personal road trip filled with people you meet along the way who show you those vital signposts or exits that lead you to your true self. You define the perimeter of your home by the boundaries and expectations you set. We all decide who we allow into our circle, our sacred space. Even though I've had the walls of my heart and spirit shaken, shattered, and fortified for war accompanied by a difficult journey home, I've maintained the desire for a place I could feel safe, unjudged, understood. Now, I could share my sacred space with someone who accepts me as I accept them.

We walked, not ahead of or behind one another, but side-by-side and holding hands as we continued to merge into one. Equally. Love is not about losing oneself, but a higher calling to ripen, to be a better version of yourself. In this magical Mojave night, we heeded that call.

We walked together into eternity through a quiet, moonlit road in the desert.

ACKNOWLEDGEMENTS

This book was written during the course of my graduate school program at USC, which required a ton of family support, espresso, and weekend road trips. With that said, a special thanks to Alex, Iselda, Aurora, and Allie for preserving my sanity and joining me in the journey. Many thanks to my editor, Shaun Leonard, who provided the necessary feedback, guidance, and moral support to help craft this piece into something that didn't induce projectile vomiting – for me at least. Thank you to Sonya Padgett for the brainstorming sessions and conversations of a future literary Las Vegas over coffee at Sambalatte. A mountain of gratitude to the "characters" in this book who helped keep me together, including, but not limited to: Genevieve Perez, Monica Epling, Sue, Maya, Louis, Janelle, Janessa, Zdeněk, Pavla, Colonel Katherine Platoni, Gabe Forsberg, Riga, Lori, Patty, Marcia, Daria, Meg, and many more inspiring individuals who motivate me to be a better person.

ABOUT THE AUTHOR

M.B. Dallocchio is a former member of Team Lioness, an all-female team attached to Marine infantry and Special Forces units to conduct house raids and searches for weapons and explosives. She served as a U.S. Army medic and mental health sergeant, and was deployed to Ramadi, Iraq from 2004 to 2005. She is also a National Security Education Program (NSEP) scholar. M.B. Dallocchio authored the "Women Warriors" chapter in *War Trauma and Its Wake*, *Quixote in Ramadi*, and *Everyday Chamorro*. She has been featured in the San Francisco Chronicle, New York Times, NPR, Las Vegas Review-Journal, MIT Press, and the Huffington Post. She's been featured in the documentaries Lioness and The Long Road Home.

M.B. Dallocchio received her Master of Social Work degree from the University of Southern California in May 2016, and continues to work in behavioral health and artistic psychosocial rehabilitation. She currently resides in Las Vegas, Nevada with her two children, spouse, and a rambunctious Golden Retriever.

www.thedesertwarrior.com

CPSIA information can be obtained
at www.ICGtesting.com
Printed in the USA
FSHW011953090921
84682FS

9 780692 945797